# BROKERS OF DECEIT

ALSO BY RASHID KHALIDI

*British Policy towards Syria and Palestine, 1906–1914*

*Palestine and the Gulf* (coeditor)

*Under Siege: P.L.O. Decisionmaking During the 1982 War*

*The Origins of Arab Nationalism* (coeditor)

*Palestinian Identity: The Construction of Modern National Consciousness*

*Resurrecting Empire: Western Footprints and*
*America's Perilous Path in the Middle East*

*The Iron Cage: The Story of Palestinian Struggle for Statehood*

*Sowing Crisis: The Cold War and American Dominance in the Middle East*

# BROKERS OF DECEIT

How the US Has Undermined
Peace in the Middle East

## RASHID KHALIDI

Beacon Press
Boston

BEACON PRESS
25 Beacon Street
Boston, Massachusetts 02108-2892
www.beacon.org

Beacon Press books
are published under the auspices of
the Unitarian Universalist Association of Congregations.

16  15  14  13        8  7  6  5  4  3  2  1

This book is printed on acid-free paper that meets the uncoated paper
ANSI/NISO specifications for permanence as revised in 1992.

Text design and composition by Kim Arney

*Library of Congress Cataloging-in-Publication Data*
Khalidi, Rashid.
Brokers of deceit : how the US has undermined peace
in the Middle East / Rashid Khalidi.
    pages  cm
Includes bibliographical references and index.
ISBN 978-0-8070-4475-9 (alk. paper)
1. Arab-Israeli conflict—Peace. 2. United States—Foreign
relations—Middle East. 3. Middle East—Foreign relations—United States.
4. United States—Foreign relations—1981-1989. 5. United States—
Foreign relations—1989– 6. Palestine—Politics and government. I. Title.
DS119.7.K4278 2013
956.05'3—dc23            2012044821

TO DR. HAYDAR, FAYSAL, IQBAL,

EDWARD, AND IBRAHIM,

ALL OF WHOM FORESAW THE PITFALLS AHEAD.

# CONTENTS

# DISHONEST BROKERS

*The slovenliness of our language makes it easier for us to have foolish thoughts. . . . If thought corrupts language, language can also corrupt thought. A bad usage can spread by tradition and imitation, even among people who should and do know better.*

—GEORGE ORWELL, "POLITICS AND THE ENGLISH LANGUAGE," 1946

In politics and in diplomacy, as in much else, language matters greatly. However debased political discourse may become, however disingenuous diplomacy often is, the words employed by politicians and diplomats define situations and determine outcomes. In recent history, few semantic battles over terminology have been as intensely fought out as those concerning Palestine/Israel.

The importance of the precise use of language can be illustrated by the powerful valence in the Middle East context of terms such as "terrorism," "security," "self-determination," "autonomy," "honest broker," and "peace process." Each of these terms has set conditions not only for perceptions, but also for possibilities. Moreover, these terms have come to take on a specific meaning, frequently one that is heavily loaded in favor of one side, and is far removed from what logic or balance would seem to dictate. Thus in the American/Israeli official lexicon, "terrorism" in the Middle East context has come to apply *exclusively* to the actions of Arab militants, whether those of the Palestine Liberation Organization (PLO), Hamas, Hizballah, or others. Under these peculiar terminological rules, the actions of the militaries of Israel and the United States cannot be described as "terrorism," irrespective of how many Palestinians, Lebanese, Iraqi, or Afghan civilians may have died at their hands.

Similarly, in this lexicon, "security" is an absolute priority of Israel's, the need for which is invariably described as rooted in genuine, deep-seated existential fears. "Israeli security" therefore takes precedence over virtually everything else, including international law and the human rights of others. It is an endlessly expansive concept that includes a remarkable multitude of things, such as whether pasta or generator parts can be brought into the Gaza Strip, or whether miserably poor Palestinian villagers can be allowed water cisterns.[1] By contrast, in spite of the precarious nature of their situation, Palestinians are presumed not to have any significant concerns about their security. This is the case even though nearly half the Palestinian population have lived for more than two generations under a grinding military occupation without the most basic human, civil, or political rights, and the rest have for many decades been dispersed from their ancestral homeland, many of them living under harsh, authoritarian Arab governments.

This book is concerned primarily, however, not with the misuse of language, important though that is, but with an American-brokered political process that for more than thirty-five years has reinforced the subjugation of the Palestinian people, provided Israel and the United States with a variety of advantages, and made considerably more unlikely the prospects of a just and lasting settlement of the conflict between Israel and the Arabs. This is the true nature of this process. Were this glaring reality apparent to all, there might have been pressure for change. But the distortion of language has made a crucially important contribution to these outcomes, by "corrupting thought," and thereby cloaking their real nature. As we shall see in the pages that follow, language employed in the Middle East political context—terms like "terrorism" and "security" and the others mentioned above—has often been distorted and then successfully employed to conceal what was actually happening.

Where the Palestinians are concerned, time and again during their modern history, corrupted phraseology has profoundly obscured reality. The Zionist movement decisively established a discursive hegemony early on in the conflict with the Palestinians, thereby significantly reinforcing the existing power balance in its favor, and later in favor of the state of Israel. This has placed the Palestinians at a lasting disadvantage, as they have consistently been forced to compete within a field whose terms are largely defined by their opponents. Consider such potent canards as "making the desert bloom"—implying that the six hundred thousand industrious Palestinian peasants and townspeople who inhabited their homeland in the centuries before the relatively recent arrival of modern political Zionism were desert nomads and wastrels—and "a land without a people for a people without a land," which presumes the nonexistence of an entire people.[2] As the Palestinian literary and cultural critic Edward Said aptly put it in 1988: "It is by no means an exaggeration to say that the establishment of Israel as a state in 1948 occurred partly because the Zionists acquired control of most of the territory of Palestine, and partly because they had already won the political battle for Palestine in the international world in which ideas, representation, rhetoric and images were at issue."[3]

In this book I attempt to pierce one aspect of a carefully constructed realm of obscurity, a realm in which the misuse of language has thoroughly corrupted both political thought and action. I will do so by focusing primarily on three sets of events, each to be treated in a subsequent chapter, which constituted moments of relative clarity in the fog of obfuscation that has surrounded US policy on Palestine for more than three decades. These are crucial junctures when unusual circumstances worked to draw back a veil masking underlying realities, underlying structures. The eminent French historian Fernand Braudel noted that even a minor event "could be the indication of a long reality, and sometimes, marvelously, of a structure."[4] I am arguing that these three moments likewise signify beyond themselves, however relatively minor they may have been in and of themselves.

The veil I am most concerned with in this book, however, does not primarily conceal basic verities about the situation in Palestine per se— although it is certainly true that the unpleasant realities of this situation are carefully hidden from the American public.[5] Having dealt with historical dimensions of the situation in Palestine in earlier works, I want to examine here instead the veil that conceals how the policy of the United States toward the Palestine question has actually functioned to exacerbate rather than resolve this problem.[6] My primary objective is to reveal how closely entwined have been the respective policies of the United States and Israel toward the Palestinian people over recent decades. Logically, this should have disqualified America from playing the role of intermediary between the two antagonists: needless to say, it did not. This aim is thus quite limited: my purpose in what follows is *not* to chronicle or analyze the entirety of American diplomacy in the Middle Eastern arena, or to provide a comprehensive history of efforts to resolve the Arab-Israeli conflict in all its aspects. A number of books attempt to do this: this is not one of them.[7] Although I will necessarily touch on the larger American role in the Middle East, and will consider the issue of Palestine against the context of the broader dispute between Israel and the Arabs, my focus throughout will be on how the United States has dealt with the Palestine question.

A second objective of this book is to examine how constant have been certain key elements in US policy on Palestine over many decades. Much has changed in this policy over time. However, there are underlying continuities that have allowed the United States and Israel—whose overwhelming might enables them to dominate the entire Middle East—to control and shape outcomes in Palestine. The three revealing sets of events I focus on in this book show how central the support of the United States was for the enduring system of control of the millions of Palestinians living under military occupation, a system that was conceived, constructed, and maintained by Israel. In June 2013, this complex but largely invisible structure, consistently upheld and defended by the United States, will enter its forty-seventh year. The Israeli occupation has been made so (politically) invisible in the United States that then presumptive Republican presidential candidate Mitt Romney apparently could not, or would not, see it while in Jerusalem on a campaign visit in July 2012.[8] The existence of this structure explains in large part why the Palestinians have not been able to achieve their national objectives of liberating themselves from occupation, unifying the scattered segments of their people, and exercising self-determination.[9] It also helps to explain why the continued survival of the Palestinians as a people has been in question since at least 1948, and remains so today.

The assertion that the continued existence of the Palestinians as a people is endangered requires some explanation, in light of the ubiquitous invocation of the precarious existence of Israel in American and Israeli public discourse. Since memory of the most somber chapter in all of Jewish history, the Nazis' genocidal destruction of much of European Jewry, is still vivid, it is understandable that existential fears are often evoked where Israel is concerned. This tragic past notwithstanding, the state of Israel has in fact been a resounding success story throughout its sixty-four-year history. But the fears provoked by this grim recent history obscure the fact that as Israel has gone from success to success, victory to victory, the Palestinian people have been repeatedly shattered and dispersed as a social and political entity. This sequence of tragedies for the Palestinians was most often a result of these very Israeli successes and victories. Thus it is understandable that the Palestinians confront profound existential anxieties as a people, for very real reasons rooted in their experiences over more than three quarters of a century.[10] Nonetheless, in American public discourse it is the existential angst of the Israelis that is continually emphasized, and their anxiety-driven quest for security that is consequently paramount, never that of the Palestinians. This is a matter of political realities, of course, which allow one people to be highly visible and another to be virtually invisible, but it is another instance where flawed political ideas are powerfully reinforced by the employment of subtly distorted language.

Examining how American objectives were achieved in the three instances I will focus on provides insight into some of the reasons why a just, lasting, and comprehensive peace, which would satisfactorily and finally resolve the problem of Palestine, has never emerged. Although other crucial aspects of the Arab-Israeli conflict were settled, via peace treaties between Egypt and Israel in 1979 and between Jordan and Israel in 1994, peace has not been achieved between Israelis and Palestinians. There is no peace in spite of decades of futile initiatives that were ostensibly directed at achieving this aim, under the Orwellian rubric of a "peace process." I place this ubiquitous term in quotation marks in my text because whatever concrete effects this process may have had—whether it marginally ameliorated a colonial status quo in the occupied Palestinian territories or exacerbated it, and whether it has improved the strategic position of the United States and Israel in the region or harmed it—it is manifestly clear that it has not brought peace to the Palestinian and Israeli peoples, nor has it resolved the conflict between them.

Looked at objectively, it can be argued that American diplomatic efforts in the Middle East have, if anything, made achieving peace between Palestinians and Israelis even more difficult. These endeavors go back to the US-brokered 1978 Camp David Accords between Egypt and Israel, which constituted the first American attempt following the 1967 war—indeed the only serious effort since soon after the 1948 war—to address the Palestinian-Israeli component of the larger conflict. They encompass initiatives of the Carter, Reagan, George H. W. Bush, Clinton, George W. Bush, and Obama administrations. These initiatives were necessarily affected by the prior policies of the Johnson, Nixon, and Ford administrations, which, like most of their predecessors, never attempted to deal in a fundamental manner with the Palestine problem.

The first of the three moments of clarity I propose to focus on came in the late summer of 1982 when it briefly appeared as if there might be an opportunity to put into effect the unimplemented provisions of the 1978 Camp David Accords relating to Palestinian autonomy. As mentioned, those accords, which had been incorporated into the 1979 peace treaty between Israel and Egypt, amounted to the only serious American effort since the Truman administration to address the question of Palestine and the Palestinians, and constituted the first effort to address certain of its political dimensions. However, in a series of follow-up negotiations that took place between the 1978 Camp David Summit and 1982, the three parties to the accords, Israel, Egypt, and the United States, had been unable to agree on the interpretation of their provisions relating to the Palestinians.

In the latter year, Reagan administration policymakers perceived an opportunity to address this impasse in the wake of the Israeli invasion of Lebanon. After two months of bombardment of besieged West Beirut,

an American-brokered cease-fire on August 12 finally halted the car-
nage, which had produced nearly fifty thousand casualties.[11] This cease-
fire was linked to the evacuation of the leadership, civilian cadres, and
military forces of the PLO from the Lebanese capital, which took place
at the end of August.[12] Washington viewed this dramatic change as reinforcing the American position regionally and globally. It was thus considered the appropriate occasion for the release of a US proposal later
known as the Reagan Plan, which was publicly announced by President
Ronald Reagan on September 1, 1982.

Particularly revealing in this context is a recently declassified confidential memo, most likely written by a senior officer of the Central Intelligence Agency, which predicted that Israeli prime minister Menachem
Begin would react with extreme inflexibility to the Reagan Plan.[13] This
US intelligence analyst predicted that in response to President Reagan's
effort to resolve the conflict via reframing the Camp David autonomy
accords more objectively and more favorably to the Palestinians, Begin
would adamantly refuse to budge from his own narrow, reductive interpretation of these accords. This assessment proved to be highly accurate. Equally revealing was the eventual unwillingness or inability of the
US administration in the subsequent weeks to hold firm to the positions
publicly enunciated by the president, or to overcome Begin's strongly
worded objections to any change in the American posture supportive of
Israel on the issues in contention with the Palestinians. As we shall see,
this was not the first time that American policymakers were to acquiesce
unwillingly in the Israeli position on Palestine, nor was it to be the last.

The second set of events to be examined occurred during the nearly
two years of bilateral negotiations between Israeli and Palestinian delegations in Washington that followed the October 1991 Madrid Peace
Conference. These talks were ultimately rendered moot by the secretly
negotiated Oslo Accords, which were signed on the White House lawn
in September 1993 by Israeli prime minister Yitzhak Rabin, PLO chairman Yasser 'Arafat, and US president Bill Clinton. Nevertheless, the
confidential documents and public statements produced by the Palestinian delegation to the pre-Oslo Madrid and Washington negotiations—to which I had access as an advisor to this delegation—expose

much about the fundamental positions of the United States and Israel. These documents, especially minutes of meetings with the American and Israeli sides, are revealing in showing the high degree of coordination between the positions of the two countries. Most striking here was the unmistakable continuity of the restrictive Israeli position on Palestinian autonomy—which in its essence remained unchanged from the time of Begin though the governments of Yitzhak Shamir, Yitzhak Rabin, Shimon Peres, and all of their successors. Equally importantly, these documents reveal the acquiescence of American policymakers in this position. Just as little noticed in the euphoria over the signing of the Oslo Accords was the utter unreliability of what appeared to be unequivocal American commitments made to the Palestinians at the outset of the Madrid talks. One can contrast this with the faithfulness of Washington to its pledges to Israel regarding the question of Palestine, and its unremitting responsiveness to Israeli demands in this regard.

The third moment is much more recent. It emerged during the latter part of the Obama administration's first four years in office. Over this period President Barack Obama faced relentless pressure from Israeli prime minister Benyamin Netanyahu, acting in concert both with the Republican leadership in Congress (newly energized after its Tea Party–fueled victories in the 2010 midterm elections) and with the potent congressional lobby for Israel. The latter is composed of an archipelago of organizations rooted in the older, more affluent, and more conservative sectors of the Jewish community and headed by the American Israel Public Affairs Committee (AIPAC), allied with a range of right-wing Christian evangelical groups passionately supportive of Israel.[14] The tripartite pressure of Netanyahu, the Republicans, and the Israel lobby forced Obama into humiliating retreats from the positions he had staked out during his first two years in office. Notable among these positions, all of which had been standard fare for most of the preceding administrations, were his stress on halting the expansion of Israeli settlements in the occupied West Bank as a precondition for Palestinian-Israeli negotiations; his assertion of the necessity for the rapid achievement of full statehood by the Palestinians; and his insistence that a return to the 1967 frontiers with minor modifications, as per Security Council Resolution 242, was the only suitable basis for negotiations between the Palestinians and Israel.[15]

In the fall of 2011, the embarrassing abandonment of all these positions culminated in a major campaign led by the United States to obstruct a Palestinian bid for recognition of a Palestinian state as a full member of the United Nations. In this context, Barack Obama in October 2011 delivered perhaps the most pro-Israeli speech any US president has ever made to the UN General Assembly, adopting an unprecedented range of standard tropes in Israeli discourse on the conflict. Thereafter, Obama received Israeli prime minister Netanyahu at the White House in early March 2012, for a discussion of several hours that was mainly focused on Iran.[16] So little attention was devoted to the Palestine issue, Israeli settlements, the "peace process," or related matters which had been the central topic of all their previous meetings, that there was barely a mention of them in the official White House statement on the meeting.[17] An Israeli analyst wrote in amazement: "When [Netanyahu] came back his adviser was asked what was new about this meeting. And his adviser said, 'This is the first time in memory that an Israeli Prime Minister met with a US president and that the Palestinian issue was not even mentioned, it never came out.'"[18] Indeed, matters related to Palestine had been central to virtually every previous meeting between a US president and an Israeli prime minister for many decades. It was not these issues, on which the president had focused almost entirely during his first two years in office, but the question of Iran's nuclear program, Netanyahu's preferred topic of discussion, that predominated.[19] Obama's climb-down was complete, and was only confirmed in the succeeding months of 2012, as the presidential election campaign gathered steam and both candidates pandered shamelessly to win the approval of fervent supporters of Israel.

My approach to the sets of events that provided these three moments of clarity will be based on an examination of declassified US government records and of confidential documents produced before, during, and after the 1991–93 Madrid and Washington negotiations that are in my possession. It will include as well a survey of public statements and actions taken by the American and Israeli governments with respect to these three instances over a period of nearly thirty-five years. Such an examination provides a clear sense of the long-term core policies of both sides. These policies are thoroughly, and in some cases intentionally, obfuscated in much of the superficial writing on the subject. Here again, language has played a crucial role. Since the Camp David Accords in 1978, and especially since the Madrid Peace Conference in 1991, the incessantly repeated American mantra, whether in official statements or writing that is policy-oriented, academic, or journalistic, about a "peace process" has served to disguise an ugly reality: whatever process the United States was championing, it was not in fact actually directed at achieving a just and lasting peace between Palestinians and Israelis.

A real, just peace that would bring the conflict between the two peoples to a final conclusion on a fair basis would have had very different requirements from those the United States has pursued for most of this period. It would necessarily involve the following: a complete reversal of the Israeli military occupation and colonization of Palestinian land in the West Bank and East Jerusalem that was seized in 1967; national self-determination for the Palestinian people; and a just resolution for the majority of Palestinians who are refugees or descendants of refugees made homeless by the establishment and expansion of Israel in 1948–49 and its further expansion in 1967. If seriously undertaken at any stage over the past four and a half decades, an effort to achieve these ends would by now long since have resulted in Palestinian sovereignty and statehood on the 22 percent of the territory of former Mandatory Palestine that comprises East Jerusalem, the West Bank, and the Gaza Strip.

Instead of trying to achieve these goals, the process actually undertaken by the United States was aimed primarily at pressuring the weaker Palestinians into conforming to the desiderata of their much stronger oppressor. Israel's main objectives were to maintain permanent effective control of Jerusalem and the West Bank and to prevent the Palestinians from achieving any of their own national objectives. The Palestinian leadership was eventually forced to acquiesce unwillingly in much of this as a result of its own feebleness and the impact of American-supported Israeli pressure. A subsidiary objective of US policy often seems to have been the avoidance of lasting differences with its potent and inflexible Israeli ally on the hot-button Palestine issue. Such differences were seen as highly undesirable by one administration after another since well before the thirty-five-year period I will focus on. This reluctance to engage in disputes with Israel over the Palestine issue occurred for reasons ranging from crass domestic politics to serious strategic considerations. They included the fact that the Palestine issue was not considered very important by most policymakers and politicians, and was certainly not as important as avoiding antagonizing the Israeli government and its influential and prickly supporters in Washington.

William Quandt, who dealt with this issue on the National Security Council staff during the 1970s, puts it thus: "One must frankly admit, the American political system makes it difficult for a president to tackle a problem like that of the Palestinians. Presidential authority in foreign affairs is theoretically extensive, but in practice it is circumscribed by political realities. And the Palestinian question has proved to be so controversial that most presidents have been reluctant to get deeply involved in it." He adds that "the Palestinians had no domestic constituency."[20] A deep and carefully cultivated American cultural and religious affinity for Israel and the growing closeness of the two countries in various fields were also crucially important factors in the background. What the United States therefore ended up doing over several decades was actually most often conflict management, and thus amounted to conflict perpetuation. It was emphatically not conflict resolution or an effort to bring about a real, lasting, sustainable Palestinian-Israeli peace.

Although I will focus most closely on episodes from the "peace process" over the past thirty-five years, the core dynamics at work in American policymaking toward Palestine have been remarkably stable for much longer. In these dynamics, domestic political calculations have generally taken precedence, while occasionally being balanced or overridden by strategic considerations. It is striking how rarely the United States was forced by such considerations to modify its policy on Palestine over many decades. This left the growing closeness between the United States and Israel in a variety of spheres a chance to play an increasing role. We can see the basic outlines of this procedure from a brief examination of the earliest phases of American involvement in the question of Palestine, under President Harry Truman from 1945 until 1948. Three basic patterns were laid down during this period.

From the time of President Woodrow Wilson onward, many American politicians had shown strong sympathy for the Zionist movement.[21] This was based on deep cultural and religious affinities rooted in the Bible and in a shared "frontier ethos."[22] Except in the financial realm, however, the United States had little or no impact on events in Palestine before World War II because of its relatively low profile in the Middle East until that point.[23] The political influence of the United States in the region began to grow measurably, however, as a result of the massive World War II American military presence stretching from North Africa to Iran, starting in 1942. Meanwhile, Washington's recognition of the vast strategic importance of Saudi Arabia ensured that President Franklin Roosevelt took pains to meet with that country's monarch, 'Abd al-'Aziz ibn Sa'ud Al Sa'ud (hereafter Ibn Sa'ud), while the American leader was passing through Egypt on his way back to Washington from Yalta in March 1945.

By the time of this meeting, Saudi Arabia, which in 1933 had negotiated an exclusive deal with American companies for oil exploration and exploitation, had been found to contain what were believed to be the world's largest oil reserves, was producing considerable quantities of oil in support of the Allied war effort, and was the site of an important US air base, at Dhahran. It is today the world's largest oil producer and largest exporter, and continues to hold the world's largest proven reserves of oil.[24] Meanwhile, developments during World War II had decisively proven the role of oil in facilitating attempts to achieve global mastery. Indeed, a State Department report in 1945 noted that Saudi "oil resources constitute a stupendous source of strategic power, and one of the greatest material prizes in world history."[25]

During their March 1945 meeting on the deck of a US cruiser, the USS *Quincy,* only a few weeks before Roosevelt's death, the Saudi ruler stressed to the president the great importance of the issue of Palestine to him and to the Arab peoples. He received a promise from Roosevelt, set down in a subsequent letter, to the effect that the United States would not act in Palestine in any way that was "hostile" to the Arabs of that country, or without first consulting with the Arabs, as well as the Jews.[26] These were clearly far-reaching commitments and were never kept by Roosevelt's successors. It cannot be stressed enough that had these pledges been scrupulously respected by subsequent US presidents, events in Palestine might have transpired very differently.

If the war had suddenly revealed the United States as the greatest global power in human history, Roosevelt's death brought to the presidency a man whose experience of the world was relatively limited. Harry Truman had served in combat in France during World War I as an artillery officer, but his career thereafter as a farmer, as a clothing salesman, and in Missouri and national politics had poorly prepared him for some of the international duties he would face. He had little sense of the strategic importance of oil, unlike Roosevelt, who had served as assistant secretary of the Navy during World War I, and who had approved the 1943 order to the United States Army Air Forces to focus its strategic bombing effort on German oil resources.[27] However, Truman was a man with a strong personality and a mind of his own, and he was an experienced and canny politician. He had a clear understanding of what it would take to help his party's chances in the hotly contested 1946 midterm elections, and then to get elected as president in 1948, which he succeeded in doing against all odds.

Where Palestine was concerned, Truman demonstrated his acute political instincts from the outset of his presidency. He strongly supported the pressure that the Zionist movement was placing on Britain over Jewish immigration to Palestine and other issues that were of deep concern to American Zionists and to a broad section of the president's liberal political base. Truman had in October 1945 denied publicly that Roosevelt had made any wartime promises at all to Ibn Sa'ud, and only grudgingly later acknowledged them when the State Department eventually produced the relevant correspondence.[28] But in his policy on Palestine thereafter he resolutely ignored Roosevelt's pledges, as well as the advice of the State Department, the Pentagon, and the US intelligence services. He did instead mainly what his instincts and his closest advisors told him was politic in American domestic terms.[29]

Thus, while meeting with four American diplomats serving in Arab capitals on November 10, 1945, Truman received them cordially, but responded to the concerns they expressed over American policy on Palestine by saying bluntly: "I'm sorry, gentlemen, but I have to answer to hundreds of thousands who are anxious for the success of Zionism; I do not have hundreds of thousands of Arabs among my constituents."[30] The president told the four envoys that the question of political Zionism "was a burning issue in the domestic politics of the United States," and added frankly that it had caused him and his secretary of state "more trouble than almost any other question which is facing the United States."[31]

On the advice of his counselors, Truman had kept these senior diplomats—who had been called back from the Middle East by their superiors at the State Department specifically to meet with the president—waiting for weeks. One of Truman's confidants, Secretary of State James F. Byrnes, noted that "if the President should see them it is certain that the newspapers would suspect that the conversations were being held here as a result of the promise [to Ibn Sa'ud] as to consultation. Certainly the President is not going to see them before November 6 [which was Election Day], and I think it would be equally unwise for me to do so."[32] Byrnes and the president's other advisors clearly felt that any perception of contact, however indirect, with representatives identified with the Arab position, even in this case with *American* diplomatic envoys to Arab countries, might leave the administration politically vulnerable. They were particularly concerned that such a meeting might harm the Democratic Party's chances in what was expected to be a hotly contested 1945 mayoral election in New York City,[33] and later in key districts in the 1946 midterm elections. The president apparently concurred, and the meeting with the envoys was postponed for weeks, until after the election. In the event, although the Democrats won the 1945 New York mayoral election, they were trounced nationwide in the 1946 midterm elections, losing one of New York's two Senate seats, as well as control of the House, in their biggest congressional defeat since 1928. Presciently, Truman concluded his meeting with the four diplomats by saying that "Palestine would probably be an issue during the election campaigns of 1946 and 1948 and in future campaigns."[34] He could not have known just how far-sighted he was in making this statement.

The 1946 midterm congressional electoral defeat only reinforced Truman's favoring of domestic political calculations over those of strategy and diplomacy where Palestine was concerned. Truman was the last American president without a college education, a plainspoken, self-made man who resented the way the State Department's well-bred Ivy League–educated personnel looked down on him. Unlike many diplomats, some of whom he suspected shared the casual anti-Semitism of their moneyed peers, Truman had a number of close Jewish friends.[35] He felt keenly the moral imperative of saving European Jews who had survived the Holocaust.[36] Nevertheless, in earlier years neither Truman nor most other American politicians, from Franklin Roosevelt on down, had done anything to save those Jews who could have been saved before they were murdered by the Nazis. This apparent callousness can be explained in large part by the pervasive anti-Semitism that afflicted many sectors of American society in the 1930s and early 1940s. At that time, it was simply not politic to favor massive Jewish immigration to the United States.[37]

However, after World War II, and particularly after the horrors of the Nazi death camps had been revealed, there was no political cost and much benefit to calling for the surviving Jews to be liberated from the displaced persons camps where they languished and sent elsewhere, specifically to Palestine, to obtain a state of their own there.[38] Truman was strongly influenced by a coterie of advisors and friends like Eleanor Roosevelt, Clark Clifford, Max Lowenthal, and David Niles, all of whom were deeply committed Zionists.[39] In addition, he tended to listen most carefully to those like himself whose political lives had been primarily spent making domestic and electoral calculations rather than decisions about strategy or foreign policy or the national interest. Truman thus felt comfortable appointing as secretary of state James Byrnes, a South Carolinian who had spent fourteen years in the House, eleven in the

Senate, a year as an associate justice of the Supreme Court, and four more mainly in wartime domestic policy positions under Roosevelt.[40]

The final outcome regarding Palestine was thus overdetermined. Truman, supported by the strong pro-Zionist sentiments of those closest to him and of a set of core Democratic constituencies, and driven by fears that showing insufficient zeal for the Zionist cause might contribute to electoral defeat for the Democrats, in essence imposed support for Jewish statehood in Palestine from 1946 until 1948 on a reluctant Washington bureaucracy. Over the opposition of most of his permanent officials, the president thus pushed through a 1946 proposal for an Anglo-American Committee of Inquiry in Palestine, mandated support of the 1947 partition resolution, and immediately recognized the new state of Israel in May 1948. These officials opposed this policy essentially out of fear of the possible damage to American strategic interests in the Middle East that would result.[41] Truman took positions supportive of Zionism notwithstanding the entirely accurate warnings of senior figures in the State Department, the Pentagon, and the new Central Intelligence Agency that this would provoke decades of strife, create profound anti-American sentiments among Arabs, and involve the United States in lasting support of an isolated Israel. A 1945 State Department memo noted presciently regarding the Palestine question: "Unless our attitude in regard to it be clarified in a manner which will command the respect and as far as possible the approval of the peoples of the Middle East, our Middle East policy will be beset with the greatest difficulties."[42]

In the end, however, although every one of these dire predictions by the experts eventually came true, Truman proved more far-sighted about one crucial matter than his diplomatic and military advisors. He and his successors in the White House could afford to ignore completely Roosevelt's promises to Ibn Sa'ud to consult with the Arabs before taking any decision on Palestine and to take no action there that was "hostile" to them. They could do this, moreover, without fear of losing the considerable strategic and economic advantages provided by the American-Saudi relationship. For although the Saudi king occasionally protested privately against the growing anti-Arab and pro-Zionist trend of American policy in Palestine from 1945–48, and regarding Truman's betrayal of Roosevelt's pledges to him, he was manifestly too dependent on the United States for support against regional rivals and the British to do anything about it. Ibn Sa'ud's dissatisfaction was so muted, in spite of the Truman administration's overtly "hostile" policy over Palestine, that Secretary of State George Marshall in 1948 wrote to thank him for the "conciliatory manner in which [he] has consistently approached Palestine question."[43]

The explanation for this Saudi passivity was simple. Saudi Arabia needed the external backing of the United States and its expertise in oil exploration and exploitation too much to break or even significantly modify their relationship, even at this early stage of a connection between the two countries that went back to 1933. In subsequent decades, Saudi Arabia was exceedingly careful to maintain its close ties with the United States, irrespective of the nature of American policy on Palestine. In the last analysis, over time it has become clear that these ties were far more important to that country's ruling family than was their proclaimed attachment to the Palestinian cause. Truman was proven right, at least insofar as ignoring Roosevelt's pledges to Ibn Sa'ud over Palestine was concerned.

Thus was established what became a solid Middle Eastern pattern that has endured virtually unaltered for more than three quarters of a century. In light of this pattern, the close relationship with Saudi Arabia can be seen as the first and most central pillar not only of the entire US position in the Middle East, but of American policy on Palestine, and indeed the sine qua non of all that followed in this regard. For this relationship precedes that with Israel by over a dozen years, and is even more fundamental than that with Israel to global US interests because of this Arab state's extraordinary economic and strategic importance.[44] However, it must be understood that appearances notwithstanding, these two relationships, and the alliances that have emerged from them, are not contradictory in any essential way, thanks mainly to the extraordinary complaisance of Saudi Arabia's rulers toward the United States' unflagging support of Israel, combined with its unconcern in practice for the rights of the Palestinians. The United States has in consequence been able to align itself firmly with the basic Israeli desiderata where the Palestine question is concerned without seriously jeopardizing its far-ranging vital interests in Saudi Arabia and the other oil-producing Arab monarchies of the Gulf. The ability of the United States to have it both ways was thus an essential precondition, and indeed the groundwork, of a policy that has not changed significantly since the days of Harry Truman. This policy has consisted of providing strong support for Israel, while paying no more than lip service to the publicly expressed concerns regarding Palestine of oil-rich Arab Gulf rulers, and generally ignoring the rights of the Palestinians.

What sustains this unequal equation, which on the face of it may seem strange? In the first place, for many decades vital American strategic and economic interests in the oil-producing Arab states of the Gulf have determined Washington's continued support for their ruling families. These monarchs in turn were in pressing need of American support, given their countries' military weakness and inability to defend themselves against external enemies. Even more important was the fact that most of them lacked any form of democratic or constitutional legitimacy (the conspicuous exception was and is Kuwait, which for over fifty years has had a constitution, a parliament, regular elections, and a free press). The United States thus helped to protect these rulers not only against external enemies, but also against the significant range of discontented elements among their own peoples. In consequence, even anomalous episodes like the economic upheaval caused by the Saudi-engineered Arab oil embargo in the wake of the 1973 October War did not change this basic equation. Thus, writing of the embargo, Henry Kissinger stated: "The rhetoric of Saudi diplomats on behalf of the Arab cause was impeccable and occasionally intransigent but, behind the scenes, Saudi policy was almost always helpful to American diplomacy."[45]

It should therefore not be surprising that at the end of the day, the massive support extended by the Nixon administration to Israel during and after the 1973 war in the form of weapons, aid, and diplomacy did not in any way affect the close American bond with the Saudi ruling family. This and many other similar episodes have proven that the United

States could do as it pleased regarding Israel and the Palestinians, and still retain its privileged relations with the governments of Saudi Arabia and other Arab Gulf oil producers. This pattern, which flowed directly from the internal weakness and lack of democratic legitimacy of these regimes and their resulting heavy dependence on the United States, was the first and most crucial one involving Palestine to be established as early as the Truman administration. It obtains down to this day.

The complaisance of the Arab Gulf states with respect to the Palestine issue constitutes further evidence that for all its influence, it is not primarily the Israel lobby that drives US Middle Eastern policy. Rather, since there is no contradiction between the vital American strategic interests involved in an alignment with Arab oil-producing despotisms and American bias in favor of Israel, the cost of the latter is relatively small to policymakers. Public opinion in the Arab world naturally abhors that bias. However, since most states in the region are not democracies, and their rulers are heavily dependent on American favor, Washington can safely ignore the peoples of these countries. It follows, however, that when—and if—fundamental and lasting democratization takes place in the key Arab states, there will necessarily ensue a day of reckoning for US policy on Israel and Palestine. This is another major reason for the long-standing US policy of upholding the fiercely antidemocratic Saudi monarchy.

The period between 1945 and 1948 reveals at least two more patterns in American policy over Palestine that also proved to be enduring, and which were grounded firmly in the fact that the United States could easily afford to ignore the feeble protests of its key Arab Gulf allies over the question of Palestine. The first was the pattern already mentioned of presidential solicitude for domestic constituencies generally taking precedence over other considerations, including ordinary foreign policy concerns, and sometimes even long-term American strategic interests. This was especially the case during presidential and midterm election years (and with monotonous regularity, these seem to coincide every two years with a crucial American decision on Palestine). We have seen the first instance of it with Truman's handling of the Palestine issue in 1946 and 1948. This pattern operated with more or less force in different administrations and under different circumstances, but it has obtained consistently in repeated cases from the time of Truman down to the present.[46]

For all of its importance, however, the basic pattern of presidential solicitude for domestic political considerations was often disrupted by the intrusion of Cold War issues during Arab-Israeli crises, when larger strategic interests momentarily came into play. One of the first examples constituting an exception to this pattern is the well-known episode of President Eisenhower firmly opposing Israel and its British and French allies during the Suez War in 1956. He did so in spite of the fact that 1956 was a presidential election year. However, this tripartite adventure was launched in secrecy without any consultation with Washington, took place simultaneously with the Soviet invasion of Hungary, and drew attention away from Soviet misbehavior and toward Western neocolonialism. For all these reasons, it infuriated the president. Thus Eisenhower showed absolutely no patience for Israel's foot-dragging in the aftermath of the war, when it tried to delay the evacuation of the occupied Sinai Peninsula and Gaza Strip.[47] Although his administration was by no means as close to Israel as later ones were to become, Eisenhower took this firm position almost entirely because of Cold War considerations, which in 1956–57 militated strongly against Israel.

By comparison with 1956, the situation was very different before, during, and after the June 1967 War, by which time circumstances had changed considerably. Starting with events around the Yemen Civil War of 1962–67, President Lyndon Johnson and his successors had come to see the leading "radical" Arab states, notably Egypt under President Gamal 'Abdel Nasser, in increasingly adversarial terms.[48] This occurred as what Malcolm Kerr described as the "Arab Cold War" between radical nationalist Arab regimes on the one hand and US allies like Saudi Arabia, the other Arab Gulf states, and Jordan on the other, coincided more and more with the larger American-Soviet Cold War.[49] In consequence, Middle Eastern polarization between Arab nationalist and pro-American regimes tracked more and more with Cold War polarities. With Israel's resounding victory over the Soviet-armed Egyptian and Syrian militaries in 1967, Israel could increasingly be seen in

Washington as a major Cold War strategic asset, and its Arab rivals as Soviet proxies. Partly in consequence, after 1967, the United States did not even attempt to force Israel to evacuate the territories it had occupied during the June 1967 War, as it had done in 1957. It has never tried to do so since.[50] This fact is an indication of how crucial the Cold War was in shaping American views of Israel as a strategic asset.[51]

Pursuit of Cold War advantage over the Soviet Union in the Middle East was so important, moreover, that at times it took precedence over all else, including even peacemaking. This was the case notably in 1971 when President Richard Nixon and his then national security advisor, Henry Kissinger, reacted indifferently to Egyptian President Anwar Sadat's explicit offer of a peace deal with Israel.[52] Sadat had told Secretary of State William Rogers that he was seeking a "peace agreement" with Israel, and made it clear that this was meant to be a separate peace, independent of what happened on Israel's other fronts with the Arab states. This marked a notable change from the position of Sadat's predecessor, Gamal 'Abdel Nasser, who had accepted Security Council Resolution 242—which entailed a "land for peace" bargain. However, 'Abdel Nasser had never explicitly referred to a peace treaty with Israel, and he had always linked any settlement involving the return of Egypt's occupied Sinai Peninsula to similar Israeli withdrawals from the occupied territories of Israel's other neighbors. Although Sadat's far-reaching offer failed primarily because of rejection by the Israeli government of Golda Meir, Nixon and Kissinger were uninterested essentially because such an initiative would not also have entailed the complete expulsion of the Soviets from Egypt, which was their primary objective in the Middle East.[53]

Kissinger had noted in his memoirs that an off-the-cuff remark he made to journalists in 1969 that the "administration would seek to 'expel' the Soviet Union from the Middle East . . . accurately described the strategy of the Nixon White House." The zero-sum, Cold War–derived logic behind the icy White House reception of Sadat's 1971 peace offer was implicit in Kissinger's further comment: "We blocked every Arab move based on Soviet military support."[54] This clearly included Sadat's offer of a separate peace with Israel, which Rogers and his advisors at the

State Department had considered highly promising, and which they had believed would lead to a diminution of Soviet influence in the Middle East. Nixon and Kissinger, however, were unenthusiastic, both because there was no explicit linkage to the expulsion of the Soviets from Egypt, and because Soviet military support for Egypt might be perceived as the reason Egypt was able to obtain Israeli withdrawal. The two inveterate Cold Warriors could not allow the USSR to obtain credit for an Egyptian success, even one brokered by the United States.[55]

Another example of how the Cold War intruded on the tendency of domestic politics to determine American Middle Eastern policy was President Nixon finally reining in the rapidly advancing Israeli forces on the West Bank of the Suez Canal at the end of the 1973 war.[56] This advance was in blatant violation of a cease-fire that Secretary of State Kissinger had just negotiated in Moscow. In response, the Soviet Union had threatened to intervene unilaterally if the Israeli advance was not halted immediately. It had backed up this threat by taking menacing military actions that included preparing to ship nuclear-armed missiles to the Middle East and mobilizing paratroop divisions for deployment to the region. This in turn provoked the United States to announce a nuclear alert, DefCon 3, and thereby produced "possibly the most serious international crisis of Nixon's presidency."[57] Incidentally, all of this happened after Kissinger had surreptitiously given Israeli leaders a green light for their tanks to keep rolling deeper into Egypt in spite of solemn assurances to the Soviets a few hours earlier in Moscow that the Israeli advance would be stopped.[58] Kissinger told Golda Meir and her colleagues during a meeting in Tel Aviv after his Moscow visit and just before returning to the United States: "You won't get violent protests from Washington if something happens during the night, while I'm flying." That very night, Israeli forces surrounded the Egyptian Third Army on the West Bank of the Canal, precipitating the crisis. However, while the United States has always strongly favored Israel,[59] major Cold War considerations, and grave issues of war and peace, invariably took precedence over the American-Israel relationship and domestic politics, albeit almost always in a way that further abetted the Israeli cause.

In a similar exception, over a six-year period, Nixon and Kissinger, and later Carter and his secretary of state, Cyrus Vance, pushed through a series of three disengagement agreements with Egypt and Syria from 1974 until 1975, and a peace treaty with Egypt from 1977 until 1979. In so doing, they repeatedly overrode the passionate objections of deeply reluctant Israeli governments to make what they saw as "concessions." They were willing to put up with the vociferous protests of Israeli leaders, and the outrage of the Israel lobby in Washington, who saw the United States as acting in a way that was inimical to Israel, for one reason: the immense strategic advantage that was afforded to the United States in the Cold War equation by "winning" Egypt away from the Soviet Union.[60] In consequence of the bold initiatives of these two American administrations, the United States for all intents and purposes achieved victory in the Middle East theater of the Cold War, thereafter reducing the Soviet Union to a subsidiary regional role. It goes without saying that in spite of the intense objections of Israeli leaders and their American supporters at the time, all of these actions, from the eventual outcome of the 1973 war and the 1974–75 disengagement agreements to the 1979 peace treaty, proved highly advantageous to Israel strategically. They were also very beneficial to it in terms of unprecedented new commitments for several billion dollars annually in American military and economic assistance.

These were the most important exceptions to the pattern of domestic factors predominating in policymaking regarding Israel and Palestine, exceptions that generally arose in moments of high crisis with the Soviet Union, where vital American interests necessarily took precedence over all else, including domestic politics. Much more frequently, however, during the three decades from the early 1960s onward, Cold War considerations militated unequivocally in favor of strong American support for Israel against the "radical" Arab states, which were increasingly seen in Washington as proxies of the USSR.[61] For this entire period, Israel benefited greatly from the perception in Washington that it constituted a major Cold War strategic asset. This factor was at least as important as domestic politics, and the significant impact of Israel's increasingly formidable lobby in Washington, in explaining the extent of Washington's military, intelligence, economic, and diplomatic support for Israel, and the high degree of cooperation between the two countries in all these spheres.

Finally, there were a few other illuminating cases, such as the deals to sell Saudi Arabia F-15s during the Carter administration and AWACS aircraft during the Reagan administration, where a coalition of formidably powerful American domestic economic interests like the oil lobby or the aerospace industry, combined with the overwhelming strategic importance to the United States of Saudi Arabia, overrode the strong opposition of Israel and its American supporters. It should be noted that the shrill warnings of the Israel lobby notwithstanding, these deals had a minimal impact on the military capabilities of Saudi Arabia, which have always been, and remain, extremely limited. Moreover, these arms transactions, which had no effect whatsoever on the situation in Palestine, in no way impinged on Israel's insurmountable military superiority over the Arab "confrontation" states. Barring exceptional situations like those just enumerated involving major American strategic or economic interests, US policy on Palestine and Israel has been made almost exclusively with an eye to those who, in Truman's words, "are anxious for the success of Zionism." Certainly this was the case wherever the Palestinians were concerned.

A third and final pattern, since the time of President Truman, has been an almost complete unconcern about the fate of the Palestinians, by contrast with a consistent and solicitous devotion to the welfare of Israelis. Unlike his predecessor, Truman does not seem to have been concerned about what might happen to the Palestinians as a result of his support for partition of their country and for the establishment of Israel. He never attempted to secure for them the political and national rights, like the right of self-determination, that had been denied them under the British Mandate and then again as a result of the 1948 war. He could have done so, for example, by insisting on the establishment of the Palestinian state envisioned by the 1947 UN Partition Plan, which called for a smaller Arab state alongside a Jewish state. Instead, the United States and the Soviet Union, the main sponsors of the 1947 partition resolution, stood by impassively while Israel and Jordan (with British approval and acquiescence) strangled the infant Palestinian state even before it could be born, and together with Egypt occupied the entirety of the territory allotted to it.[62]

This result should not be a surprise. For while the 1947 UN partition resolution ostensibly provided for self-determination for two peoples, that is not what happened, nor indeed was it what was intended to happen by its two main sponsors. Instead, only one people, the Israelis, obtained self-determination, or was meant by them to do so. Had the United States and the Soviet Union truly desired the universal application of this principle, they could have at least tried to see to it that that did take place. However, in the wake of the Holocaust, in view of the budding Cold War competition between the superpowers, and given the realities of American domestic politics about which Truman was so frank, the partition resolution was actually primarily intended by both of its main sponsors—the United States and the Soviet Union—to do precisely what it did. It was meant by both superpowers to result in the establishment of a Jewish state. Palestinian national rights did not seriously concern policymakers in Washington (or in Moscow, London, or Paris for that matter) in 1947 and 1948, or for long afterwards.

As far as other rights are concerned, in December 1948 the United States voted at the United Nations together with a large majority of states in favor of General Assembly Resolution 194, which promised the approximately 750,000 Palestinian refugees who had been driven from or fled their homes the right to return to them and to be compensated for their losses. Thereafter, however, in the face of Israeli obduracy regarding return or compensation for the refugees, whose land and property were confiscated and whose homes were demolished or handed over to Jewish immigrants to Israel, the United States never made a serious effort to see to the implementation of this important resolution.[63] There was also no serious American effort then or afterwards, only empty gestures, to ensure Israel's withdrawal from the largest part of the territories allotted to the Palestinian Arab state under the partition plan. This was land that Israel's armies had occupied in 1948–49, expanding its territory from the 55 percent of former Mandatory Palestine granted it under the partition plan to 78 percent. In this matter as in so much else, Truman established a precedent followed by his successors of occasional declaratory positions ostensibly favorable to the Palestinians, combined with active policies strongly supportive of Israel.

Typical of such supportive policies was the Tripartite (American-British-French) Declaration of 1950, which ostensibly blocked arms transfers to any of the countries of the region. Consecrating the military superiority Israel had established on the battlefield during the 1948–49 war, this declaration did not prevent subsequent secret French and British arms shipments to Israel, which it employed to great effect during the 1956 Sinai campaign. The clandestine transfer of French nuclear technology also enabled Israel surreptitiously to develop nuclear weapons. Through this declaration, therefore, the United States and its Western allies ensured Israel's considerable long-term military advantage over the Arab states. It thereby effectively consolidated in Israel's favor both its considerable territorial expansion during the 1948–49 war, and its concomitant forced removal of 750,000 Palestinians from its newly enlarged territory.

The policy of guaranteeing Israel's regional military supremacy is one that the United States has pursued with unstinting generosity down to the present day, with similar effects. It consolidated a status quo on the ground in Palestine that is massively favorable to Israel and disadvantageous to the Palestinians. In the words of one of the most incisive observers of the Middle East, the late Malcolm Kerr:

> The pre-1973 record of American initiatives . . . indicates a pattern of too little too late, of grossly inadequate political support from the White House, and of a curiously persistent misconception that America must bring together Arab and Israeli governments that really want peace and successful negotiations, rather than that America should crack their heads together. Intended or not, the consistent effect has been to buy time in behalf of the status quo, which is to say, in behalf of the Israeli accumulation of *faits accomplis* and the Arab accumulation of resentment.[64]

As we have seen, a distorted set of American priorities—largely directed at catering to the demands of Israel and of its vocal American supporters rather than doing anything substantial to resolve the struggle over Palestine, which is the core and the origin of the Arab-Israeli conflict—has contributed significantly to producing a broad range of intractable outcomes. One of the weightiest of these outcomes has been the increase since 1990 of the Israeli settler population in the West Bank and Arab East Jerusalem from under two hundred thousand to nearly six hundred thousand. These and other "facts on the ground" were largely created by Israel in the years following the 1978 Camp David Accords and have been considerably reinforced since the 1993 Oslo Accords. They constitute daunting obstacles to the prospect of a two-state solution, obstacles that, in the view of most objective observers, are now well nigh insuperable. The establishment of the settlements was intended by Israeli planners to produce precisely this result. The stunning success of their approach, which by now seems to be a virtual certainty, continues to be blithely ignored by most proponents of a two-state solution. This is the case although perceptive analysts like Meron Benvenisti have been arguing for nearly three decades that the option of a two-state solution has been systematically closed off by Israeli settlement activity and the consolidation of the occupation.[65] Indeed this activity has for decades undermined the possibility of any equitable peace between the dominant Israelis and the colonized, occupied, and dispersed Palestinians, whether this peace takes the form of a one-state, a two-state, or any other solution.

These and other hard, cold realities of how US policy affects the Palestinians (not to speak of the actual situation inside Palestine) are largely screened from the American public.[66] It is bombarded instead with dishonest and debased rhetoric about what is described as "progress" in a "peace process." This process ostensibly consists of negotiations between near-equals under the impartial gaze of a disinterested American intermediary, and is supposedly intended to create an independent Palestinian state, which is far from what is actually happening. Such corrupt language in fact successfully disguises the continuation and intensification of the dispersal, occupation, and colonization of the Palestinians. We shall see how this specific form of terminological dishonesty originally developed in Chapter I, which relates the first of the three episodes to be dealt with, that which took place in the wake of the Camp David Accords of 1978 and in the lead-up to the Reagan Plan of 1982.

Thereafter, I discuss the 1991–93 Israeli-Palestinian negotiations in Madrid and Washington in which I participated. During this period the deceitful description as "progress" of what was in fact significant movement *away* from a just, equitable solution reached its fullest and most complete form, and this was when the term "peace process" took on its most distorting effect. The subsequent chapter covers the dispiriting experience of the Barack Obama presidency between 2009 and 2012, when the so-called "peace process" was used to screen further the consecration of a status quo that is deeply harmful to the Palestinians and that renders the possibility of peace ever more distant.

What I intend to convey in this book is a sense of how the United States has never really operated as an honest broker between the Palestinians and Israel. Instead, it has ended up acting as "Israel's lawyer." These are the apt words of Aaron David Miller, who as one of the lead US negotiators with the Palestinians for many years was a key participant in this charade.[67] Together with senior colleagues like Dennis Ross and Daniel Kurtzer, he features repeatedly in the pages that follow. From Camp David in 1978 onward, the United States posed as an unbiased intermediary between Israel and the Palestinians, but in fact it operated increasingly in defense of Israel's interests, and to the systematic detriment of those of the Palestinians. All of this dissembling was cloaked in high-sounding but dishonest language.

Again and again, the three patterns previously identified prevailed: there was no real pressure on the United States from the oil-rich Arab Gulf states, far from it; there was an exaggerated attention to domestically driven political concerns as these were ably articulated by the Israel lobby; and in spite of occasional sympathetic noises from policymakers, at the end of the day there was little or no concern for the rights of the Palestinians. This meant that while Israel usually got what it wanted, a peaceful and just resolution of the conflict between the two peoples was certainly not the result. In consequence, American policy under a succession of presidential administrations has served neither the long-term US national interest—insofar as that would be well served by a lasting resolution of this conflict—nor the interest of international peace and stability, nor the true interests of the peoples of the Middle East, including both Palestinians and Israelis. It took a great deal of corrupt language to conceal these manifest realities, especially, in Orwell's words, "among people who should and do know better."

I

# THE FIRST MOMENT: BEGIN AND
# PALESTINIAN AUTONOMY IN 1982

*The right of the Jewish people to the Land of Israel is eternal and indisput-
able and is linked with the right to security and peace. Therefore, Judea and
Samaria will not be handed over to any foreign administration. Between
the sea and the Jordan River there will be only Israeli sovereignty. Relin-
quishing parts of the Western Land of Israel undermines our right to the
country, unavoidably leads to the establishment of a "Palestinian state,"
jeopardizes the security of the Jewish population, endangers the security of
the State of Israel and frustrates any prospect of peace.*

—LIKUD PARTY PLATFORM, MARCH 1977

Where the issue of Palestine is concerned, American Middle East policy
from Truman down to Obama has consistently hewn to the three patterns described in the introduction: an almost total lack of pressure from
the Arab Gulf monarchies; the impact of US domestic politics, driven
by the Israel lobby, and an unconcern about Palestinian rights. The preferred approach of US presidents has therefore generally involved de-
ferring to Israel and its American supporters, and refusing to advocate
forcefully for inalienable Palestinian national and political rights. They
acted thus notwithstanding sporadic tepid and cautious expressions of
support for the Palestinians, beginning with the Carter administration.[1]
There were a few rare occasions when the US government offered an
official endorsement of such rights. However, even if such an endorsement was not quickly withdrawn or qualified, as usually happened, it
was never offered without debilitating conditions, or in the context of
parity and complete equality with the rights that the United States ro-
bustly upheld for Israel.

1

For decades, however, the United States did support annual reiterations by the UN General Assembly of the important principles of refugee return and compensation embodied in its Resolution 194 of 1948, although this US support ended in 1992.[2] Return and compensation undoubtedly represented significant Palestinian human rights. But Palestinian political and national rights were not even mentioned by American policymakers between 1948 and 1967. These rights were ignored entirely in what became the foundation for future Middle East peacemaking, UN Security Council Resolution 242 of November 22, 1967. The carefully negotiated text of this resolution was shaped largely by the concerns of American policymakers, with substantial input from Israel.[3] Although Resolution 242 referred to "the inadmissibility of the acquisition of territory by war," thereby referencing in part the occupied Palestinian territories of the West Bank, East Jerusalem, and the Gaza Strip, it otherwise simply spoke of a "just settlement of the refugee problem," without even specifying the Palestinians by name.

Thereafter, mention of Palestinian national rights in the context of American policy or of UN resolutions was actively opposed by the Johnson, Nixon, and Ford administrations. The United States had long had a policy of not dealing with the PLO (which in 1974 the Arab states, and soon thereafter the UN General Assembly, had declared the "sole legitimate representative of the Palestinian people"), but under President Ford, American policy went significantly further in its rejection of the PLO. In September 1975, Henry Kissinger negotiated a secret Memorandum of Understanding with Israel, whereby the United States committed itself not to "recognize or negotiate" with the PLO until the latter met two conditions: recognizing "Israel's right to exist" (without any parallel demand on Israel to recognize Palestine's "right to exist") and accepting Security Council Resolutions 242 and 338.[4] The latter called for implementation of 242 in all of its parts, and for immediate negotiations "between the parties concerned under appropriate auspices aimed at establishing a just and durable peace in the Middle East." Again, Resolution 242 had made no mention whatsoever of the Palestinians, whether as a party or in any other way, referring only to a "just settlement of the refugee problem."[5] The PLO's renunciation of

terrorism was later added to this list of conditions, which were maintained in place until the PLO was formally considered to have met them
in 1988. The negative attitude of the United States toward the national
rights of the Palestinians and the organization that represented them
did not change until the administration of Jimmy Carter.

It briefly appeared as if President Carter would fundamentally
transform this approach. A few months after his inauguration, he was
the first US president to speak of the need for a "Palestinian homeland." His administration also alluded to political and national rights
for the Palestinians by suggesting that it might be possible to "permit
self-determination by the Palestinians in deciding their future status."[6]
The slippery nature of the language employed here deserves attention.
Self-determination is generally understood as a unilateral process: the
term is "*self*-determination," after all. However, what is apparently envisioned by this phrase is that the Palestinians would be permitted (by
others) to be involved in "deciding their future status." They would be
only one of several parties involved, and all of the other parties, as it
happened, were far more powerful than they. This phraseology, in that
it indicates almost the exact opposite of actual self-determination, could
have come out of George Orwell's *1984*. While this convoluted wording
was thus far from being a call for full Palestinian self-determination or
statehood, it nevertheless represented an advance on American formulations since the 1947 partition resolution, which was voted for by the
United States, had called for creation of a Palestinian Arab state alongside a Jewish one. Since it introduced the term "self-determination,"
albeit in this backhanded way, the Carter administration's new language
understandably incensed all partisans of the status quo in the Middle
East, first among them the new government of Israel.

It was the misfortune of Jimmy Carter to come into office with this
new approach only months before the Israeli elections of May 1977 saw
the defeat of the Labor Party, which had governed Israel since 1948, and
its replacement by a right-wing and ideologically driven Likud government headed by Menachem Begin. The government transition in Israel
opened a new page of almost constant contention between the two governments over Palestine that contrasted sharply with the far less strained

state of affairs that had existed between Israel and the United States on this issue during the decade following 1967.

After several months of tense relations between the Begin government and the Carter administration, on October 1, 1977, the latter further infuriated the newly elected Israeli prime minister by agreeing to a joint communiqué with the Soviet Union that called for an international peace conference on the Middle East. This move provoked a parallel firestorm of outrage among hard-line US supporters of Israel, who were newly emboldened by Likud's victory. That the United States should consider bringing the Soviet Union, patron of the Arabs and supporter of the PLO, into Middle East peacemaking was bad enough in the eyes of Israel's American supporters, and of the potent body of anti-Soviet opinion all over the United States. As it happened, the Israel lobby and the considerable cadre of right-wing Cold Warriors were gradually converging at this time, a phenomenon marked by the rise of neoconservatism.[7] Worse, in the eyes of both groups, the US-Soviet joint communiqué spoke not just of "legitimate Palestinian interests," the standard feeble American formulation, but rather of "the legitimate rights of the Palestinian people"—a clear acknowledgement of the Palestinians as a people with national rights, including self-determination and statehood. The communiqué referred as well to participation by representatives "of the Palestinian people" in a reconstituted and reconvened Geneva peace conference under joint American-Soviet auspices.[8] In its substance the communiqué was very much along the lines of the conclusions of the 1975 Brookings Institution Middle East Study Group, which had provided a blueprint for much of the Carter administration's subsequent policy.[9] The group's conclusions had brought fierce criticism from hard-line pro-Israel quarters, and were anathema to the Begin government.

The howls of rage and betrayal that greeted the American-Soviet joint communiqué in Israel, among its American supporters, and from anti-Soviet right-wingers, caught the Carter administration by surprise. It was rapidly forced to back down in clear disarray, disowning much of what it had just painstakingly agreed upon with the Soviet Union. Only a few days after the issuance of the joint communiqué, Secretary of State Cyrus Vance was obliged to issue a joint US-Israeli "working paper" together with Israeli Foreign Minister Moshe Dayan, who had rushed to Washington for the purpose of bringing the American position back in line with that of Israel. This joint document repudiated all the administration's new positions regarding the Palestinians, and much else, that had been set out in the US-Soviet joint communiqué. As a result of what amounted to an embarrassing U-turn, along with the ongoing uproar among both American opponents of détente with the Soviets and extreme supporters of Israel, the idea of a comprehensive resolution of the conflict, linked to an international conference at which the Soviet Union would serve as a cochair, went quickly and quietly into occultation.[10] It was not to be revived until George H. W. Bush was in the White House in the 1990s. For over a decade and a half after this debacle, senior American policymakers also carefully avoided using such forthright terms as "legitimate Palestinian rights" and "the Palestinian people." In the meantime, Egyptian president Anwar Sadat, impatient with the dilatory policy-making process of the Carter administration and disapproving of its approach to resolution of the conflict, had flown to Jerusalem in November 1977 and spoken to the Israeli Knesset. He thereby upended the entire Middle Eastern scene and set in motion the events that led to the 1978 Camp David Accords and the 1979 Israeli-Egyptian peace treaty.

It was during the negotiation of these important agreements in 1978 and 1979 that the moment of truth regarding the Carter administration's policy over Palestine came about. In spite of his initial willingness to challenge the dominant American paradigm where Palestinian national rights were concerned, at the Camp David summit with the Israeli and Egyptian leaders in September 1978 President Carter in the end meekly accepted the exceedingly restrictive terms regarding Palestine that were presented and ultimately imposed by Israeli prime minister Menachem Begin. Far from self-determination, at Camp David the Palestinians were promised no more than a five-year period of Israeli-regulated and -controlled "autonomy." While at the insistence of Egypt and the United States,[11] the accords mentioned "the legitimate rights of the Palestinian people and their just requirements," the agreement applied only to the minority of Palestinians who lived in the West Bank and Gaza Strip. They thereby left out not only the much larger number of Palestinians who had been driven out of the country in 1948 and 1967 (those living outside historic Palestine in fact constituted then, and still constitute, an absolute majority of Palestinians), but also those who were residents of Jerusalem or citizens of Israel.

Insultingly, according to the text of the Camp David Accords, the "refugee problem" was to be dealt with by Israel and Egypt and "other interested parties." There was no mention of the Palestinians themselves. They presumably could have petitioned to be considered an "interested party" in negotiations over an issue that loomed large in their national imaginary, and that had profound existential implications for them. Moreover, the accords allowed for the continuation of Israel's military occupation (some of its forces were to be withdrawn, others subject to "redeployment") and for the expansion of Israeli colonization of Palestinian lands. Carter and his colleagues believed they had secured a pledge by Begin to freeze settlement expansion while negotiations continued, but Begin later insisted he had only agreed to a three-month halt. To add insult to injury, Carter was obliged to acknowledge in a January 22, 1978, side letter to Begin five days after the signature of the Camp David Accords that wherever the expressions "Palestinians" or "Palestinian people" occurred in the text, they "are being and will be construed and understood by you as 'Palestinian Arabs.'" This was a term of art among those Israelis who denied that the Palestinians were a people.[12] Such purposeful exclusions, combined with a terminological sleight of hand, constituted a reprise of the systematic omission of the indigenous Arab people of Palestine from consideration of their own future. The omission went back to the Balfour Declaration of 1917, the foundational document for the British Mandate that followed, which never mentioned the Palestinians by name.[13]

Carter's retreat from the forthright positions he had staked out at the beginning of his administration was a result of the by now well-established American reluctance, going back to the time of Truman, to impose anything on Israel where Palestine and the Palestinians were concerned. The unwillingness to confront Israel was largely the result of domestic political considerations, but it was also caused by the absence of concerted, continuous, and effective pressure from the Arab states to do otherwise. This reluctance had been considerably reinforced by the Carter administration's humiliating repudiation of the US-Soviet joint communiqué, which served as a bitter object lesson to it and to later administrations. As a result, we shall see that Menachem Begin's narrow, legalistic formulations produced at Camp David—precisely as restrictively as his and subsequent Israeli governments chose to interpret them—in effect have become the practical working basis of US policy, or rather the low ceiling imposed on it, starting with the Camp David Summit in 1978, continuing through the 1993 Oslo Accords, and right on through the present day.

In addition to their central provision, for a peace treaty between the two countries, the Camp David Accords, agreed upon by Israel and Egypt under the aegis of the United States in 1978, called for negotiations for the establishment of a "Self-Governing Authority" (SGA) for the Arab population of the West Bank and the Gaza Strip. Jerusalem was to be excluded from its provisions. The accords stipulated "full autonomy for the inhabitants," but crucially, this did not apply to the land, which was to remain under full Israeli control. A bilateral peace treaty based on these accords was signed between Israel and Egypt in 1979, and Israel thereafter began a withdrawal of its forces from the occupied Egyptian Sinai Peninsula, which was completed in the spring of 1982. However, the modalities of the Palestinian-autonomy accords were a continuing source of dispute between the three signatories to the Camp David Accords, as well as with the Palestinians and other Arabs, and in the end they were never implemented.

Despite the fact that a major section of these accords related directly to Palestine and the Palestinians, the negotiation process had entirely excluded the PLO, the representative authority recognized by the Palestinians themselves and by most of the world. This was in keeping with the strong preferences of all three parties to Camp David: the United States, Israel, and Egypt. Each of the three had its own specific reasons for the exclusion of the chosen representative of the Palestinian people, which was unquestionably the party most concerned by Israel's occupation of their territory. It is worth examining the reasoning of each constituency separately.

For its part, the United States officially considered the PLO a terrorist organization, although it had maintained clandestine security and political contacts with PLO representatives in Beirut for several years, dating back to the era when Henry Kissinger was secretary of state.[14] These actions were in patent violation of the explicit commitments to Israel originally made by Kissinger in 1975 not to have anything to do with the PLO unless it met the Israeli-American desiderata previously mentioned. Kissinger's sensitivity on this topic is apparent in his memoirs.[15]

An equally significant commitment to Israel was embodied in a secret 1975 letter from President Gerald Ford to Prime Minister Rabin, which in effect made American diplomatic initiatives in future Middle East peace negotiations conditional on prior approval by Israel (it goes unmentioned in Kissinger's voluminous three-volume memoirs). The relevant wording about possible future proposals for a comprehensive peace settlement is explicit, and was to have far-reaching effects: "Should the US desire in the future to put forward proposals of its own, it will make every effort to coordinate with Israel its proposals with a view to refraining from putting forth proposals that Israel would consider unsatisfactory."[16] If strictly construed, this secret commitment gave Israel effective veto power over American diplomacy for peace in the Middle East, and it has been used in this way ever since. Legalistic Israeli leaders were always naturally quick to remind their American counterparts whenever they felt that this explicit pledge was not being honored in its strictest possible interpretation. This tremendously important commitment has ever since served to tie the hands of American diplomats, who to all intents and purposes are prohibited from putting forward any peace proposals without prior Israeli approval, reversing the relationship one might expect between superpower and client. In practice, it has also meant that the United States could no longer honestly play the role of good faith mediator between Israel and its Arab interlocutors, if ever it had done so in the past. We shall see the pervasive impact of this pledge in virtually every subsequent episode to be discussed below.

While the rhetoric of American policy as enunciated by both Presidents Carter and Reagan came to include recognition that the Palestinians had some "legitimate" rights, these rights only went so far. Moreover, in practice the United States would not allow those who were nearly universally recognized to speak for the Palestinians to take part freely in enunciating these rights or in the determination of their future as a people. In spite of the beginning of a formal US-PLO dialogue in the final year of the Reagan administration in 1988, when the PLO finally met the conditions laid down by Kissinger in 1975, the US policy of not allowing the Palestinians to choose their own representatives for international negotiations on their fate did not change for another decade and a half after Camp David. This was in large part because of the "self-denying ordinance" relating to the PLO secretly agreed to by Kissinger and Ford in 1975. It was only finally abandoned after an Israeli government headed by Yitzhak Rabin began to negotiate directly with the PLO in 1993. Thereafter this self-imposed constraint on American policy disappeared, although the other one, which allowed Israel to veto any American peace proposal it disapproved of, is still in place. The spectacle of a superpower near the apogee of its global dominance being inhibited from taking actions that might be in its self-interest, and being obliged to tiptoe around because of fear of offending its much smaller ally, is a demeaning one.

As far as Israel is concerned, it goes without saying that the PLO was anathema to the right-wing Begin cabinet, which had come to power in 1977. Like its Labor Party predecessors, the Likud government denied vehemently the very existence of the Palestinians as a people with national rights, or that there was any longer such a place as "Palestine." While the specific religious-chauvinistic Likud version of this denial can be seen in the party's 1977 electoral platform, cited in the epigraph to this chapter, the conventional cross-party consensus in Israel on this subject was expressed by Golda Meir, Labor Party prime minister until 1974. She stated in 1969:

> There was no such thing as Palestinians. When was there an independent Palestinian people with a Palestinian state? It was either southern Syria before the First World War, and then it was a Palestine including

Jordan. It was not as though there was a Palestinian people in Palestine considering itself as a Palestinian people and we came and threw them out and took their country away from them. They did not exist.[17]

In addition to this rejection of Palestinian national rights, and indeed of the very existence of the Palestinian people, by the consensus of virtually the entire Israeli establishment, Menachem Begin and his Likud colleagues were intensely disdainful of Palestinian claims to any part of the country, notably the West Bank, considered the core of the "Land of Israel"—"Eretz Israel." For them, this entity encompassed the entirety of former British Mandate Palestine, specifically the territory "between the sea and the Jordan River."[18] Moreover, they insisted on calling the West Bank by its long-disused antique name of Judea and Samaria. Carter's January 22, 1978, side letter to Begin after the Camp David Summit acknowledged the Israeli government's characteristic stress on just this terminological point. These examples once more underline the vital importance of language, in this case of how the establishment of discursive hegemony is central to the process of achieving complete control over a territory. Indeed, a central maxim of colonialism, "If you name it, you own it," has been followed by the Zionist movement since its beginnings. After the foundation of the state of Israel and the conquest of over four hundred Palestinian villages, towns, and cities in 1948, Arabic place names all over the country were effaced and replaced by Hebrew ones, most of them concocted for the occasion, in keeping with this principle and its obverse: "If you own it, you name it."[19]

Beyond this blanket rejection of Palestinian claims based on ideological principle, treating the PLO as nothing more than a "terrorist" organization representing no legitimate cause or interest because of its acts of violence against Israelis and others was an immensely useful tactical device. For many years, thanks largely to the acquiescence of the United States in this ruse, it neatly enabled Israel to avoid having to deal with the uncomfortable reality of the Palestinians and their national claims. The same tactic is currently employed by both the United States and Israel in regard to Hamas because of its espousal of violence, notwithstanding their own massive use of violence. As they use the term, the rubric of "terrorism" makes no distinction between violence directed against innocent civilians, which is banned under international law, and resistance against the armed forces of an illegal occupation, which is allowed.[20] The demonization of the entire Palestinian people because of accusations that Palestinian groups engaged in terrorism was a particular irony in the case of Menachem Begin and his successor as prime minister, Yitzhak Shamir. Both of them had been widely considered as notorious terrorist masterminds for their bloody assaults against Palestinians (when their targets were mainly civilians)[21] and against the British during the Mandate period in Palestine. They of course regarded themselves as freedom fighters, as did their followers.

Finally, where Egypt was concerned, in spite of his unfailing protestations of support for the Palestinian cause, Egyptian president Anwar Sadat himself had long preferred to deal with Israel directly and without the encumbrance of having to represent any of his Arab brethren, most of all the Palestinians themselves. As mentioned in my introduction, in the spring of 1971, barely six months after he assumed power, Sadat had been rebuffed by Israel when, via the intermediacy of Secretary of State William Rogers, he offered Israel much the same separate peace deal that he was to negotiate seven years later at Camp David. This would have involved a comprehensive "peace agreement" based on full Israeli withdrawal from all occupied Egyptian territory with international guarantees. There was to be no linkage to other fronts, no demands for ending the occupation of the Syrian Golan Heights, and no provisions regarding the Palestinians, or Jerusalem, or refugees.[22] We have seen that Rogers's efforts were undermined by the opposition to such an accord of President Nixon and Henry Kissinger because this deal did not explicitly include the expulsion of the Soviet Union from Egypt.[23] As already noted, the government of Israeli prime minister Golda Meir in any event spurned Sadat's proposal. Meir's deep skepticism about Sadat's offer, and her toughness and obduracy, come through in every one of her unyielding responses to Rogers, which fill nearly half of a fifty-six-page transcript of the meeting wherein the proposal was presented to her.[24]

Having failed to convince the Israeli or American governments in 1971 to accept his explicit offer of a separate peace with Israel, and after several further futile efforts in this direction, Sadat eventually saw that he had no alternative but to go to war in 1973.[25] Even then, Sadat showed his disdain for his fellow Arabs. In the opening weeks of the conflict, Sadat betrayed his Syrian allies, having previously assured them that his troops would push much farther east into Sinai than they actually did. He thereby left the exposed Syrian forces on the Golan Heights to bear alone the brunt of a massive Israeli counterattack. In his memoirs, the Egyptian chief of staff, General Saad El-Shazli, stated explicitly that Sadat deceived the Syrians, admitting, "I was sickened by the duplicity."[26] The Israeli offensive on the Golan Heights was backed by the full weight of Israeli airpower, transferred from the Egyptian front, which contributed to a near rout of the Syrian forces.[27] Sadat had thus manifested in practice the intention he had first revealed to Rogers in 1971, to act alone and with utter unconcern for his Arab allies. He did this long before his 1977 solo flight to Jerusalem in the face of Arab incredulity and opposition.

As soon as possible after the October War of 1973, Sadat began separate negotiations with Israel, via the intermediacy of Secretary of State Kissinger's shuttle diplomacy, for the first of two Sinai disengagement agreements, in 1973 and 1975 (Kissinger also negotiated an Israeli-Syrian disengagement agreement in 1974). Sadat was hoping that continuation of this process would lead rapidly to a separate Egyptian peace with Israel. His Arab allies during the 1973 war deeply feared such an outcome, as it would take the strongest Arab country out of the military equation, and leave them to fend for themselves in dealing with what would, and did, become an even more powerful Israel. No one dreaded this outcome more than the weakest of the Arab parties, the Palestinians. In view of the Egyptian president's hopes for more special attention to his needs from Washington, he was dissatisfied with signs that the newly inaugurated Carter administration in early 1977 was unwilling to continue on the path charted by Kissinger's disengagement accords toward a separate Egyptian-Israeli bilateral peace. Sadat was particularly frustrated that the new American administration instead appeared to be trying to launch a comprehensive process to address the concerns of all the parties, not just those of Egypt and Israel.

An impatient and exasperated Sadat finally took action when the joint American-Soviet communiqué of October 1977 showed unequivocally that Carter's team preferred to embark on negotiations with all the parties to the Arab-Israeli conflict for an overall Arab-Israeli settlement in collaboration with the Soviet Union to another US-brokered Egyptian-Israeli deal. As his behavior since early in 1971 had consistently shown, what the Egyptian president wanted was a separate peace with Israel, and a privileged relationship with the United States. He did not want to drag along with him all his fractious Arab partners, especially the Palestinians, whose problems with Israel were so intractable, or to deal any further with the Soviet Union in any guise. After clandestine negotiations between his representatives and those of Menachem Begin in Morocco, Sadat paid his famous surprise visit to Jerusalem in November 1977, which led in turn to the Egyptian-Israeli Camp David accords, setting out the basis for the separate Egyptian-Israeli peace he had always wanted. Far from facilitating a comprehensive Middle East peace, this measure, which ended the state of war between Egypt and Israel, a step of enormous significance in and of itself, also made the core elements of the conflict even more intractable. It heralded and indeed contributed to far greater violence than before in both Lebanon and Palestine, violence that has now been ongoing for thirty-five years.

There are many reasons the 1978 autonomy accords were stillborn. One of them, as just discussed, was the exclusion from Camp David and subsequent talks of the Palestinians' chosen representative, and the PLO's subsequent boycotting of a process that it saw as violating the Palestinians' inalienable rights by imposing "autonomy" under continued Israeli occupation as a ceiling on their aspirations. (Israel and Egypt had agreed that selected Palestinians were to be included in a Jordanian delegation, but the Jordanians themselves, never having been consulted on the matter, stayed away, while representative Palestinians, offended by the exclusion of the PLO, never considered attending.)[28] Another reason for this failure was the absurdity of any discussions on Palestinian autonomy between Egyptians, Israelis, and Americans in the absence of the Palestinians themselves. This was especially the case given the intransigent and restrictive Israeli position on a range of important features of such autonomy, an intransigence that the record shows was constantly indulged by American negotiators.

A 1979 meeting on Palestinian autonomy between Israeli minister Yosef Burg and US presidential envoy Robert Strauss provided an early instance of peace-process-speak: the two sides talk about "progress" when in fact none was being made, and showed that both sides were happy in keeping the Palestinians away from the negotiating table. Thus Strauss stated: "For the moment, for the next few months, we can get along without Palestinians," and US ambassador to Israel Samuel Lewis added, "There is no need for Palestinians at the table, but we, yourselves and ourselves, can talk to residents of the West Bank and Gaza." Burg then told his American interlocutors: "If the US woos the PLO less, their appetite will be smaller." The transparent Israeli intention here was to dissuade the Carter administration from dealing with the PLO. The comments of Strauss and Lewis indicate that this was not very difficult to do. The Israelis apparently also had little problem with Sadat on this score: as Burg noted, "In Haifa Sadat said several times that we can manage without the Palestinians. . . . Sadat said that perhaps we can go ahead for the moment without the Palestinians."[29]

A final reason the autonomy accords were never implemented was Sadat's near-total isolation in the Arab world as a result of his making a separate peace with Israel, and thereby in effect abandoning the Arab countries that had supported Egypt during the 1973 war. Paradoxically, his abandonment of the Arabs did not increase Sadat's freedom of maneuver on issues of pan-Arab import, quite the contrary: he was even more constrained than before. To comprehend this paradox it is necessary to understand that in preceding years, following the 1973 war, the various Arab parties, including the PLO leadership, had expected a comprehensive multilateral peace effort with Israel on the basis of Security Council Resolution 242 and Resolution 338, which called for implementation of 242 "under appropriate auspices."

They had hoped such an effort would involve both the United States and the Soviet Union, along the lines of the brief and abortive Geneva conference of December 1973.[30] Instead, as we have seen, from 1974 until 1976 what took place were a series of Kissinger-brokered separate disengagement accords. These agreements had the effect intended by American policy of weakening the position of the Soviet Union in the region, reinforcing the mutual suspicions of many of the Arab states aligned with the Soviets, and setting Egypt well on the way to the separate peace with Israel under US auspices that was the objective of both Sadat and the United States.[31] The PLO and other Arabs had been elated in October 1977 when the Carter administration revived the prospect of a multilateral international conference to be cosponsored by the USSR, and with the involvement of the Palestinians. They were deeply displeased when, as we have just seen, the Carter administration was forced by Israeli pressure to back away from that plan. They were then shocked when Sadat soon afterward flew to Jerusalem to cut out the insufficiently enthusiastic American middleman and deal directly with the Israelis, a process that culminated at Camp David in 1978 and thereafter in the 1979 peace treaty.

While Sadat was willing to sign a separate peace, his discomfort at his subsequent isolation within the Arab world inhibited him from going along fully and publicly with the Begin government's insistence on an extremely restrictive interpretation of the Palestinian autonomy provisions of the Camp David Accords. Doing so, he estimated, would have embarrassed him further with Arab public opinion, which was already vilifying him for abandoning the Palestinians, and indeed still does decades after his death. Needless to say, Sadat never allowed problems on the Palestinian-autonomy track to block his headlong normalization of relations with Israel or his honeymoon with Washington. However, in spite of his unctuous cooperation with most American initiatives, Sadat's position was not helped by either President Carter or his successor, Ronald Reagan, who refused to weigh in with forceful support of the formal Egyptian view on Palestinian autonomy. They may well have realized how little conviction lay behind it.


Until 1982, little had been achieved in the way of implementation of the Palestinian-autonomy portion of the Camp David Accords, in spite of a series of American-Israeli-Egyptian tripartite negotiating sessions over several years.[32] The Reagan administration, which came into office in January 1981, was ideologically much more predisposed toward close alignment with Israel than had been that of Carter, and therefore was even less inclined to put pressure on Israel. This was in part because of its hard-line anti-Soviet posture, into which Israel fit perfectly, as the main local opponent of so-called Soviet clients such as Syria and the PLO. Israeli leaders like Begin and his defense minister, Major General Ariel Sharon, constantly played up to the Reagan administration's strong ideological predisposition. They did so notably with regular references to the danger of state-sponsored international terrorism to the "free world," a danger on which the neoconservatives around Reagan were fixated. Thus, in 1978 Begin invoked the term in the preliminary notes he penned for his Palestinian self-government scheme, wherein he described a prospective Palestinian state as "a grave peril to the free world."[33] The irony in the use of the term "free world" by Israeli leaders who maintained arbitrary military rule over millions of un-free Palestinians under occupation, or who were planning to install a puppet regime in Lebanon against the wishes of the majority of Lebanese, was apparently lost on their terrorism-obsessed American interlocutors.

Another factor in the increased closeness between the two countries was the fact that the upper ranks of the Reagan administration were filled with neoconservatives like Jeane Kirkpatrick and Eugene Rostow. These individuals were both fiercely anti-Soviet and pro-Israel, and they served to bring the American and Israeli positions ever closer in myriad ways.[34] As a dogged defender of Israel's policy of establishing settlements in the occupied Palestinian territories, it was Rostow, a former dean of Yale Law School, who concocted the quaint and obtuse legal argument that the Fourth Geneva Convention did not apply to these lands, and that they therefore were not "occupied." This led the Reagan administration to cease considering Israeli settlements as "illegal," which had formerly been the position of presidents from Johnson to Carter. Now they were described only as an "obstacle to peace," the much milder formulation that has been the official US position under every subsequent president.

Events during the Israeli invasion of Lebanon, which was launched on June 6, 1982, led the Reagan administration to shift course. This occurred even though Israel had secured American approval for its incursion, specifically that of the secretary of state. Haig's proclivities were made clear during a meeting with Israeli Defense Minister Sharon in Washington on May 25, 1982, eleven days before the war started. Although he had proposed to the Israeli cabinet that the operation inside Lebanon would be "limited," the aims that Sharon laid out to Haig and other American officials for the war were sweeping: to clear Lebanon of Palestinian "terrorists," shift Lebanon to the "free world" by fostering the establishment of a pliable client government, and eliminate Syrian forces and Syrian influence from the country. Haig's only response to Sharon's preview of such a massive military operation was to say that it must be a "proportionate" response to a provocation.[35] The wording utilized is interesting: if such an operation was "limited," one wonders what an unlimited one might have looked like.

The shift in the administration's position occurred in the wake of the replacement of the militantly pro-Israeli Haig by George Shultz as secretary of state on June 25, 1982, at the height of the fighting in and around Beirut. Haig's erratic and headstrong behavior tried the patience of those around the president, who finally asked for his resignation.[36] Following the defeat of the PLO, the Syrian forces in Lebanon, and their left-wing Lebanese allies during the war, the Reagan administration decided to launch a new Middle East peace initiative, which came to be known as the Reagan Plan. This decision was the result of a reassessment of the situation in the region by the president's closest advisors, notably the new secretary of state. George Shultz and his subordinates at the State Department had become disaffected from Israel because of the brutality of its siege and bombardment of Beirut, as had President Reagan. They perceived that it was essential for the United States to take advantage of the conjuncture resulting from the Israeli invasion to push through a solution for the Arab-Israeli conflict that would at the same time cement America's paramount influence throughout the Middle East. Among the elements of this conjuncture were, first, the grave weakening of the position of the PLO and Syria, as well as that of their leftist allies of the Lebanese National Movement (LNM), after their resounding military defeat by Israel in the preceding months, and second, the concomitant increase in the influence of Israel. An additional factor was that at this time both Iran and Iraq were almost totally distracted by their savage, fratricidal war.

The decision to launch a US initiative also came partly in response to pressure from the United States' Arab allies, all of which had been castigated in Arab public opinion for their passivity in the face of Israel's ten-week war on Lebanon and its siege of a major Arab capital. Their embarrassment led them to urge the United States to do something about the Palestine question, to counter what Israel was doing with respect to Lebanon and the Palestinians. Taking the lead was the Saudi monarchy, which more than thirty-five years after its founder Ibn Sa'ud had broached the matter with President Roosevelt, hoped to see the Palestinian issue finally resolved on an acceptable basis. To that end, in 1981 the Saudis had issued a peace plan at the Arab summit meeting in Fez in the name of Crown Prince Fahd ibn 'Abd al-'Aziz Al Sa'ud. This was the first occasion since the 1940s that the Saudi royal family had taken such a bold initiative over Palestine. The plan called for a complete Israeli withdrawal from all occupied Arab territories and the dismantling of Israeli settlements, the creation of a Palestinian state after a short transitional period, for return or compensation of refugees, and for all states in the region to be able to live in peace.[37] Shultz, who had spent the eight years before he became secretary of state working for the Bechtel Corporation, had extensive experience in dealing with Saudi Arabia, which was a lucrative market for the company. All around, it seemed a perfect moment for the Reagan administration, which had revived the Cold War rhetoric and outlook of the 1950s and 1960s, to capitalize on the resounding victory of its ally, Israel, over what it saw as three Soviet proxies in Lebanon.

On August 24, 1982, a few days before the Middle East peace initiative known as the Reagan Plan was issued, however, a confidential National Intelligence Council memo entitled "US-Israeli Differences over the Camp David Peace Process" was produced for the director of central intelligence.[38] This document laid out in precise detail for US policymakers the extraordinarily restrictive interpretation placed by the Begin government—and every government that has followed it in Jerusalem—on the concept of Palestinian "autonomy." As we shall see, this term was crucial in all that followed. The memo also revealed how daunting would be the task of the Reagan administration (and all of its successors down to the present) in trying to put forward a credible plan that would resolve the Arab-Israeli conflict by ending Israel's occupation of Palestinian land and halting Israeli settlement expansion, both of which Begin was firmly committed to continuing. The final outcome of this showdown was decisively in Begin's favor. It foreshadowed the complaisance, or political cowardice, that would be shown by Washington in trying to overcome the obstacles raised by Begin and his successors—to the point that this feebleness became complicity with their aims—whether this was in the early 1980s, the early 1990s, or the second decade of the twenty-first century.

The perceptive CIA analyst responsible for this memo, whose name and title are redacted from the declassified document,[39] was blunt in laying out the Israeli prime minister's bottom line. He wrote: "Begin asserts that the C[amp] D[avid] A[ccords] rule out the emergence of a Palestinian state. In Begin's view, the agreements 'guarantee that under no condition' can a Palestinian state be created. In practice Begin effectively rules out any exercise of Palestinian self-determination except one that continues Israel's preeminent position in the West Bank." This is a striking assertion, and it is accurate in every respect as a reflection not only of the views of Begin and his government, but of the enduring position of every Israeli government since. It is also accurate as a reflection of the outcome thus far of the entire twenty-two-year process that began many years later at Madrid in 1991. It is notable that these conditions were meant by Begin to apply, and indeed still do apply, not only to the "interim period" of several years foreseen in both the Camp David and the Oslo Accords, but indefinitely. In spite of the obvious acuity of its author and the precision of his analysis, however, the memo did not try to explain how any form of "Palestinian self-determination" that involved actual self-determination was in any way compatible with the maintenance of "Israel's preeminent position in the West Bank."

The American intelligence analyst argued further that "there is no reason to accept Israeli arguments that the US is prohibited from putting forth its own interpretations" of the Camp David Palestinian autonomy provisions. However, his assessment of the many crippling conditions and restrictions that Begin and his government would insist on placing on Palestinian autonomy indicated that these would not be easy arguments to refute. He noted: "Begins's view is that the S[elf-] G[overning] A[uthority] should be a *solely administrative authority* regulating the affairs of the Arab inhabitants and leaving control of the territory and all key security issues with Israel. In sum, *autonomy is for people not territory* [emphasis in the original in both cases] and therefore does not prejudice Israel's territorial claims to the West Bank."

Again, this was a completely faithful rendition of Begin's stated views, indeed of the precise phraseology that the Israeli prime minister consistently used. It also mirrored perfectly the structure of the autonomy accords that the governments of Yitzhak Rabin and subsequent Israeli prime ministers later negotiated with the PLO and that produced the still extant, and exceedingly feeble, Palestinian Authority.

The memo for the CIA director explained further:

Israel has already defined its views on all the key issues, and in each case makes a narrow interpretation:

- Jewish settlements are to remain under Israeli control and not be subject to the SGA. The SGA could not prevent new settlements and territorial expansion of existing ones (115 settlements currently).
- Water rights would be allocated by joint Israel-SGA agreement. If agreement is not reached, the status quo—which benefits Israel—prevails.
- Land rights would also be under joint control (Israel currently controls 1/3 of West Bank land).
- Security issues, internal and external, would be under sole Israeli control, with only minor police rights given to the SGA.
- East Jerusalem is not considered part of the West Bank and its Arab inhabitants are not eligible to vote for the SGA.

Three things leap out from this extraordinarily prescient intelligence assessment. The first is that in keeping with the principles enunciated in the March 1977 Likud electoral platform, cited as the epigraph to this chapter, this scheme was meant to preclude *permanently* any form of Palestinian national self-determination. This is clear as well from Begin's handwritten notes sketching out his ideas for Palestinian autonomy prepared around the time of the Camp David summit in 1978. They conclude with a "Unilateral Declaration by Israel": "Under no circumstances will Israel permit the establishment in Judea, Samaria and the Gaza district of a 'Palestinian State.' Such a state would be a mortal danger to the civilian population of Israel and a grave peril to the free world." Another such declaration reads: "After the end of the transitional period of five years Israel will claim its inalienable right of sovereignty in the areas of 'Eretz Israel': Judea, Samaria and the Gaza District."[40] Begin's language could not have been clearer: all of Palestine, including the West Bank and Gaza, was part of "Eretz Israel," which was the exclusive, inalienable, and "eternal" property of the Jewish people. The Arabs in consequence had no rights to any part of this land, irrespective of any internal administrative arrangements that might be granted to them under the dishonest rubric of "autonomy." For what kind of autonomy could there be for people who did not control, or even have any rights to, the land they stood on?

The second thing apparent from this assessment is that the position of Israel on most of the core issues surrounding its relationship with the Palestinians in the context of "Palestinian autonomy" has in substance remained the same under more than half a dozen different governments of every political stripe for nearly thirty-five years. There has been near-total continuity in terms of these basic tenets, with most of the differences mere matters of detail. As we shall see, this was true even of the three years of the government of Yitzhak Rabin, in spite of its departure from some of Begin's intractable ideological principles as expressed in his party's 1977 platform.

The third thing that follows from this analysis is that in practice Israel's intransigent position with respect to Palestinian autonomy has defined virtually every important outcome in the West Bank and occupied

Arab East Jerusalem since 1977. The only thing that took place under the various Israeli-Palestinian accords signed during the mid-1990s that differed in any significant manner from Begin's schema is that Israel eventually did allow East Jerusalem residents to vote in elections for the Palestinian Legislative Council. However, with special urgency since 1991, Israeli policy has systematically worked to detach East Jerusalem from the rest of the West Bank via a series of draconian measures. These have included illegally settling more than two hundred thousand Israeli citizens in East Jerusalem and the areas of the West Bank annexed to it after 1967 in massive blocs that surround the city on three sides, from the north, east, and south. They have included as well the construction of a vast complex of walls as part of a closure regime that has cut off what is left of the Arab Eastern part of the city from its West Bank hinterland. These physical realities have given the most concrete possible meaning to the view attributed to Begin by the anonymous CIA analyst that "East Jerusalem is not . . . part of the West Bank."

The analyst's memo is therefore not simply a catalog of Begin's intransigent, ideologically extreme positions insisting on the continued subjugation of the Palestinians to Israel's will, and on Israel's right to sovereignty in and effective control over all of the land of former Mandatory Palestine. It is Menachem Begin's wish list, but it is also much more than that. It is an accurate preview of how Begin would exercise his iron will where the issue of Palestine was concerned, and a road map for the acquiescence of the United States on virtually every one of these positions. It is consequently also a description well before the fact of every significant aspect of the regime that has prevailed in the occupied Palestinian territories since an interim self-government autonomy scheme was negotiated and implemented there in the 1990s. In fact, the memo serves as an accurate definition of the reality of the "interim self-governing authority" that was set up under the provisions of the Oslo Accords of 1993.

In accurately summing up Begin's position, this 1982 intelligence memo, written well over a decade before Oslo, thus delivers a precise description of the tight limitations on the so-called Palestinian Authority that has now been in place for nearly two decades. An Israeli-devised and -dominated scheme like this, which guarantees the continuation and expansion of settler colonialism and alien military control, does not amount to "self-rule," or "autonomy." Neither of these lukewarm euphemisms correctly describes the new reality that has been created since 1993. To see why, it is essential to understand that this scheme was firmly grounded in concepts expressed in the 1977 Likud platform and which constituted unshakable core beliefs of Begin and his followers: "The right of the Jewish people to the Land of Israel is eternal and indisputable. . . . Between the sea and the Jordan River there will be only Israeli sovereignty." Anyone taking these words seriously would understand that a scheme based on them could not produce anything that could be described as genuine self-determination for the Palestinians. Instead it is most honestly described as a colonial or, at best, a neocolonial regime.

As they showed by their behavior during the fruitless autonomy negotiations, which dragged out over the subsequent several years, Menachem Begin and his successor as prime minister, Yitzhak Shamir, were unwilling to agree with Egypt and the United States to grant the Palestinians even this less than a half loaf. It would take the enormous shock caused by the massive popular uprising of the Palestinian population living under occupation in the West Bank and the Gaza Strip—the first intifada, of 1987–91—and a subsequent change in the Israeli government in 1992 to transform this situation. The unarmed and largely nonviolent uprising forced Israelis, and eventually also the new Rabin government, into a realization that the status quo of naked occupation was not sustainable, and that a new regime would have to be offered to the Palestinians. However, although Yitzhak Rabin and a new set of Israeli leaders may not have subscribed to all of the ideological underpinnings of Begin's scheme, as we shall see in the next chapter, the regime they ultimately imposed on the Palestinians in the 1990s was one of veiled occupation, precisely along the lines of Begin's restrictive "autonomy" plan.

Finally, and perhaps most strikingly for our examination of US policy on Palestine, over time the very low ceiling established by Menachem Begin and his successors for what the Palestinians under occupation would be allowed to obtain by Israel has become the continuing limit on what American policymakers will allow, or even foresee, for them. These limits were imposed on US policy in spite of the apparent discomfort of the unnamed US intelligence analyst who produced the prescient memo setting forth Begin's position. This discomfort could be seen both in the analyst's assertion that Begin's was not the only possible interpretation of the Camp David Accords, and from the title of his assessment, which asserts that there were "US-Israeli Differences over the Camp David Peace Process." Other much more senior policymakers at the time and afterwards shared the same discomfort: Shultz and many of his aides disagreed fundamentally with Begin's views on the Palestine issue.[41] In practice, however, since then what has counted most were not the interpretations of the Camp David Accords of Reagan or Schultz or later American presidents or secretaries of state; it was rather Begin's interpretation that became the fixed policy of the state of Israel under every subsequent government. In the end, all on the American side were obliged to acquiesce in this interpretation, with good or ill grace. Even those presidents like Carter, Reagan, George H. W. Bush, Clinton, and Obama, all of whom initially appeared as if they might be inclined to take a more enlightened and less harshly restrictive position on Palestinian rights, ended up bending to the will of the Israeli government on this issue.

When Ronald Reagan finally promulgated his Middle East initiative in a televised speech on September 1, 1982, a few days after the issuance of the CIA's intelligence assessment of Begin's position, he offered the Palestinians little more than had the Israeli prime minister at Camp David. While referring to "a just solution of their claims," the Reagan Plan balanced the Palestinians' "legitimate rights" against "Israel's legitimate security concerns." As already explained, the latter has traditionally been a highly elastic term used to cover a multitude of ever-expanding demands and requirements, which invariably trump all else, including especially Palestinian rights. Reagan stated that he opposed "Israeli sovereignty or permanent control over the West Bank and Gaza," but he also excluded "the formation of an independent Palestinian state," and insisted that "self-government by the Palestinians . . . in association with Jordan" was the maximum they could hope for. How the Palestinians could enjoy "self-government" under the aegis of a nondemocratic, monarchical Jordanian regime traditionally hostile to their national aspirations was not explained by the president. Given the tortuousness of this position, which was far below the minimal threshold of Palestinian demands for self-determination and statehood, it is not surprising that the Reagan Plan was unacceptable to the Palestinians, especially in the immediate aftermath of the PLO's traumatic defeat and evacuation from Beirut.

The ambiguous language of Reagan's initiative was incidentally not the only way in which his administration had addressed the Palestinians at this time. Starting soon after the launching of the Israeli invasion in early June through August 1982, Ambassador Philip Habib had brokered the withdrawal of PLO forces from Beirut, thereby essentially facilitating the achievement of one of Sharon's major aims in his war on Lebanon. This was the result of a lengthy series of highly complex indirect negotiations about the PLO's evacuation from Beirut involving France, several Arab countries, and Lebanese leaders as intermediaries, since by its 1975 self-denying ordinance the United States could not directly contact the PLO. In August 1982, Habib had finally sealed the deal by giving the PLO guarantees for the safety of the Palestinian refugee camps in Beirut after the withdrawal of its forces. PLO negotiators had persistently demanded these guarantees as a condition for withdrawal. The American envoy had offered explicit assurances that Palestinian noncombatants left behind after the PLO withdrew from Beirut would not be harmed, and could live in "peace and security."[42]

Obtaining these American assurances had been of utmost importance to Palestinian leaders who negotiated the departure of the PLO's forces, which had previously protected the inhabitants of the refugee camps from their many enemies in Lebanon. These leaders had good reason for insisting on such guarantees in light of the ferocity of the Israeli assault on the city and the camps bordering it over the preceding ten weeks.[43] They were especially concerned given the historical background of massacres of Palestinians and others in Karantina and Maslakh, and in the Dbaye and Tal al-Za'tar refugee camps during the 1975–76 phase of the Lebanese war by the same Lebanese right-wing militias that were now openly partnered with Israel. Their fears were not misplaced. A few weeks later, after the entry of Israeli troops into West Beirut in mid-September following the assassination of president-elect Bashir Gemayel, many hundreds of unarmed and helpless Palestinian and Lebanese civilians were slaughtered in the Sabra and Shatila camps over three days by Lebanese militiamen allied to and armed by Israel. They were introduced into the camps by the Israeli forces ringing them, who provided illumination for their clients' ghastly work with star shells.[44] The massacres showed these American assurances to be utterly worthless.[45] Clearly, some American pledges, such as the two major ones made to Israel by Kissinger in 1975, were more reliable than others. We shall see in the next chapter that this was not the last time that critical US assurances to the Palestinians proved to be utterly unreliable.

Notwithstanding the unacceptability of the Reagan Plan to the Palestinians, it was also wholly unacceptable to Begin, as it deviated in a number of crucial respects from his core desiderata, as previously laid out. Regarding Israeli settlements, Reagan's speech called for a halt to their expansion, and requested "the immediate adoption of a settlement freeze." Reagan said this although his had earlier been the first US administration to cease describing Israeli settlements as "illegal," a change of position that had manifestly delighted Begin at the time.[46] In his speech of September 1, 1982, Reagan also stated of the settlements that the United States "will not support their continuation as extraterritorial outposts." Begin and his colleagues were infuriated by all of these points, and by Reagan's assertion that "further settlement activity is in no way necessary for the security of Israel and only diminishes the confidence of the Arabs that a final outcome can be freely and fairly negotiated."[47] Finally, the president proclaimed US opposition to Israeli sovereignty or permanent control over the West Bank and Gaza Strip.[48]

Not surprisingly, in view of the Reagan Plan's major divergences from the firmly held positions of the Begin government (and from some of the terms Carter had accepted at Camp David), it provoked a firestorm of Israeli criticism. Begin was enraged that there had been no effort to gloss over these differences. Although Reagan had been careful to inform Begin of the provisions of the speech just before he gave it, it was apparent that there had been prior consultations with Arab countries. The substantive aspects of the Reagan Plan were galling to this right-wing Israeli government. Equally galling, perhaps, was the fact that, in a possible gesture at evenhandedness, it had not been previously submitted to them for prior vetting and approval, as per what had become the firm Israeli interpretation of the secret 1975 Kissinger Memorandum of Understanding. In consequence, Begin spared American leaders none of the self-righteous invective for which he was renowned. His sulfurous reply to the US president concluded with words from Isaiah 62: "For Zion's sake I will not hold my peace, and for Jerusalem's sake I will not rest."[49] As usual, Begin was as good as his word. A subsequent Israeli cabinet resolution summarily rejected the Reagan Plan, detailing seven points of irreconcilable difference with it.

The US initiative, like the Camp David autonomy provisions, was in any case stillborn. It was unacceptable to the Palestinians (although some Arab governments were apparently satisfied with it), but it foundered primarily on Begin's unyielding insistence on holding fast to every detail of his stance. This was combined with the remarkable feebleness with which American policymakers defended their positions and pushed back against Begin's intransigence. They had been amply warned what to expect by their own intelligence professionals, in the memo cited earlier. But like the Carter administration after the issuance of the American-Soviet joint communiqué, the Reagan administration seemed almost unnerved when faced with the full-throated opposition of the Begin government and its Washington supporters. The Reagan Plan thus sank almost without a trace, except in the historical record.

The beauty of Begin's point of view, as it was accurately summarized by the unnamed intelligence analyst I have cited at length, is that it is straightforward and candid. More than thirty years on, and in the wake of Begin's demonstrated ability in the end to force both Presidents Carter and Reagan to back down, it should be clear that one still ought to take Begin's positions very seriously. The assertion that the only kind of autonomy arrangements he or his successors would permit "'guarantee that under no condition' can a Palestinian state be created" is infinitely more honest than the disingenuous statements since then of a procession of Israeli and American officials. In recent years, American presidents and Israeli prime ministers have asserted publicly their acceptance of a Palestinian state, but sotto voce they have added crucial caveats and conditions. Thus, what they are actually referring to amounts to a mini-"state" that meets Begin's restrictive definition, and ensures enduring occupation and the denial of self-determination to the Palestinian people. Whether in regard to control over land, water and security, the status of Jerusalem, the refugee issue, or any other major point of contention, the long-term regime that was envisaged and actually imposed on the ground in the West Bank and East Jerusalem by Israel is in its essentials bluntly described in the 1982 intelligence summary of the position of Menachem Begin.

What is most striking in this episode is not that the father figure and revered icon of the modern Israeli right wing has come to define Israeli practice and much of Israeli discourse. After all, the Revisionist Zionist "Greater Land of Israel" line incarnated by the movement's founder, Zeev Jabotinsky, and his successors Menachem Begin and Yitzhak Shamir has almost completely dominated Israeli politics for more than thirty-five years. It is rather that the United States has acquiesced in and effectively supported this radical and uncompromising position. It has come to define the bottom line of American policy, or rather what I call the low ceiling of what the United States envisages as allowable for the Palestinians. This reality is concealed by a veil of deceitful, Orwellian verbiage, as feeble thought corrupts language, and dishonest language corrupts thought. I will go on to describe how this bottom line became even more fixed as a feature of American policy during the Madrid-Washington negotiations of 1991–93. In the process, further violence was done to language, more deceptions were perpetrated on the Palestinians, and the notion that a United States closely allied to Israel and hamstrung on this issue by its domestic politics could act as an impartial intermediary between Israel and the Palestinians was utterly disproved.

# THE SECOND MOMENT:
# THE MADRID-WASHINGTON
# NEGOTIATIONS, 1991–93

*We want to assure you that nothing [done] . . . in this phase of the pro-*
*cess will . . . be prejudicial or precedential in the outcome of the nego-*
*tiations. . . . We encourage all sides to avoid unilateral acts that would*
*exacerbate tensions or make negotiations more difficult or preempt their*
*final outcome. . . . The United States has long believed that no party should*
*take unilateral actions that seek to predetermine issues that can only be*
*resolved through negotiations. In this regard, the United States has opposed*
*and will continue to oppose settlement activity in the territories occupied in*
*1967, which remains an obstacle to peace.*

— US LETTER OF ASSURANCES TO THE PALESTINIANS,
   OCTOBER 18, 1991[1]

Much like President Reagan and George Shultz before them in 1982,
President George H. W. Bush and his secretary of state, James Baker,
saw the upheaval produced by a major regional war in 1991 as an opportunity for American self-assertion in the Middle East via a new initiative
to resolve the Arab-Israeli conflict. In reaction to Iraq's August 1990
invasion and occupation of Kuwait, the United States had fashioned a
broad international coalition that, starting in mid-January 1991, took
less than two months to expel Iraqi forces from Kuwait under the ban-
ner of a UN Security Council resolution.[2]

Like the outcome of the 1982 Lebanon war, the first Gulf War of
1991 was seen in Washington as a triumph for the United States and its
allies. But it came not in the context of a revived Cold War, as in 1982,

but rather in the waning days of the American-Soviet competition, and just before the dissolution of the Soviet Union. Indeed, the breakup of the Soviet empire seemed a harbinger of an entirely different era, one of unipolar American global dominance that President Bush dubbed a "new world order." There were other contrasts. Israel had played the central role in the 1982 war, and in the Reagan administration's conception of a post-1982-war Middle Eastern system. However, Israel had been marginal to the 1990–91 war over Kuwait, and appeared to have a more modest place in the Bush-Baker vision for the post–Gulf War, post–Cold War world than it had had under the Reagan administration.

In service of this changed American vision of a reorganized Middle East under renewed American preeminence, James Baker undertook many months of arduous Middle Eastern shuttle diplomacy before and after the 1991 allied ground offensive to liberate Kuwait. He was attempting to do what the Reagan Plan had failed to do after the 1982 war: cement America's place as the paramount Middle Eastern power through a comprehensive peaceful resolution of the Arab-Israeli conflict. Such a resolution would formally reconcile the main two American allies in the region, Saudi Arabia and Israel, resolving a latent tension in the US relationship with the Saudis that we have seen had existed since 1945. The Bush administration hoped to capitalize on America's greatly enhanced global post–Cold War status by exploiting a number of conditions created by the war in the Middle East. These included the participation of three major Arab states, Saudi Arabia, Egypt, and Syria, alongside the United States in the military campaign against Iraq; the annihilation of the offensive capabilities of what had been the strongest Arab military power, Iraq: and the grave weakening of the PLO as a result of its having aligned itself with a now-defeated Iraq. The decision of the Palestinian leadership to align itself with Iraq was extremely ill-advised, because it had deeply alienated the Arab Gulf states, on which the PLO and its constituent groups depended for much of their financing. The Gulf was moreover the site of large and well-established Palestinian communities that were highly supportive of the PLO and that now became vulnerable to retaliation. Indeed, the largest and most prosperous of them, the half million Palestinians in Kuwait, suffered mass expulsion after the country's liberation. The PLO was thus greatly weakened in consequence of its strategic blunder in supporting Saddam Hussein, and because of the decline of its erstwhile patron, the USSR.[3] These were among a number of regional factors that appeared favorable to the strategic position of the United States in the Middle East as a consequence of the Gulf War.

As in the wake of the 1982 war, the profoundly flawed assumption in Washington was that yet another dramatic improvement in Israel's strategic situation in 1991 resulting from yet another crushing Arab military defeat might lead it to adopt greater flexibility as regards a resolution of the Arab-Israeli conflict. This assumption drew on the long-standing, widely held, and equally flawed premise that Israeli governments could be expected to make concessions only when their country was in a position of strength, a premise that had led one American administration after another to give Israel virtually whatever it asked for, only to meet with unbending rigidity in its negotiating position. The post-1991 case was to be no exception, in spite of the fact that the end of the Cold War and Israel's virtual irrelevance during the Gulf conflict seemed to many to have diminished its strategic value to the United States.

To their credit, President Bush and his secretary of state were attempting to exploit the unique opportunity provided by the end of the Cold War and the resounding victory over Iraq to risk a major departure from earlier approaches. Indeed, they were trying to do something that had never before been achieved in the entire history of the international dispute over Palestine that began with the issuance of the Balfour Declaration in 1917. This was to bring all the protagonists together at an international conference table in order to achieve a comprehensive resolution of the conflict.[4] Since 1967, all Israeli governments, and most American administrations, had strongly resisted a comprehensive approach, preferring piecemeal, bilateral efforts. The only brief exception had been the Carter administration, which had proposed just such an approach with the 1977 American-Soviet joint communiqué, as noted earlier, only to see it spurned by both Sadat and Begin.[5]

At the end of October, 1991, Bush and Baker took the first major step toward their goal, convening a peace conference in Madrid, again under nominal American-Soviet joint sponsorship, with representatives of Israel and all the most important Arab countries present. Insufficiently appreciated at the time or afterward was that simply holding this meeting was a historic achievement in and of itself, however little may have come of it in the end. The conference's two-day plenary session, which started in Madrid on October 31, 1991, and all subsequent bilateral and multilateral meetings, took place on the basis of ground rules laid down in a joint Letter of Invitation from the two cosponsors to all the concerned regional parties.[6] Given the precipitate decline of the nominal Soviet cosponsor—indeed, the Soviet Union itself was dissolved in December 1991, leaving Russia as an even feebler nominal cosponsor—it was not surprising that the conference and much of what followed was effectively under American management, as evidenced by the separate "Letters of Assurances" issued by the United States alone to Israel, Syria, Jordan, Lebanon, and the Palestinians.[7] These letters were to take on particular importance in the eyes of the Palestinians, as we shall see. The predominant American role was evidenced as well by the fact that after the ceremonial plenary opening session involving all the parties in Madrid, the essential negotiations were to take place on a separate bilateral basis between Israel and the Arab parties, which since 1967 had been the preferred American-Israeli structure for negotiations. Perhaps the best proof of the preeminent US position in the negotiations was that these bilateral sessions took place in Washington, DC, inside the US State Department, and essentially under exclusive American auspices.

There was one exception as regards the participation of the representatives of all the concerned regional parties in these negotiations. The Palestinians were allowed to be present at Madrid—the first time in their modern history that they were permitted to take part in direct international negotiations with their adversaries.[8] However, because of the adamant insistence of the Shamir government, they were allowed to participate neither via a separate delegation representing them as a separate people, nor with delegates of their own choosing. The Letter of Invitation contained no mention of a "Palestinian people" (nor needless to say of the PLO), referring simply to "consultations with Palestinians," and to negotiations "between Israel and the Palestinians." It did not define who these "Palestinians" were to be, which is a peculiar omission in a formal diplomatic document. Instead, the letter stated that "Palestinians will be invited to attend as part of a joint Jordanian-Palestinian delegation," which was to be headed by a Jordanian. This was in deference to the fixed Israeli position that there was no such thing as a Palestinian people with a right to national self-determination and statehood in its own homeland, Palestine. This position had, as we have seen, long been enshrined in the terms of Israeli political discourse, through references to all of Palestine as "Eretz Israel" and to the Palestinians as "Palestinian Arabs" (thereby implying that they were generic Arabs and denying them a separate national identity), or as "Arabs of Israel."

Again at the Shamir government's insistence, and after months of consultations by Baker with both sides, any individual identified with the PLO was barred from the Palestinian component of this joint delegation. As for Palestinians from the West Bank and Gaza, only those with no links to the PLO were allowed to take part. Also excluded were prominent Palestinians residing in the diaspora or in Jerusalem. The latter group included Faysal Husayni and Dr. Hanan Ashrawi, the former the preeminent Fateh leader in Jerusalem and one of the most important political figures in all of the occupied Palestinian territories, and the latter an academic and intellectual. Over the many months of intense negotiations with the Americans that preceded Madrid, Husayni and Ashrawi had played the primary role as intermediaries with the ultimate Palestinian decision-makers in the PLO leadership in Tunis. Their exclusion from the negotiations and that of various other categories of Palestinians was a direct reflection of deeply rooted Israeli views. One was the insistence, which as we have seen was particularly strong among partisans of Likud, that not only was there no "Palestinian people," but that the entire problem was one restricted to managing the internal administrative affairs of the "Arabs of the Land of Israel" in the regions referred to as "Judea and Samaria." A second was that the Palestinian refugee problem had been created by the Arabs and not Israel, and was none of its concern, and thus that the majority of Palestinians who had been driven from their homes had no standing in the negotiating process, nor any stake in its outcome. Yet another was that the PLO was no

more than a bunch of terrorists who had no place at the negotiating table, and the last was that Jerusalem, Israel's "eternal, indivisible" capital,
belonged to it alone. Irrespective of whether US diplomats subscribed
to these views in principle, they deferred to them in practice in framing
the conditions for Palestinian participation in the peace negotiations.

In response to the persistent demand of the Palestinians for broader
representation, and over the strong protests of the Shamir government,
Baker finally acquiesced in selected individuals from Jerusalem and from
outside Palestine serving as "advisors" to the Palestinian delegation.[9]
These individuals, however, were not allowed to take part in face-to-
face talks with the Israeli side; only "official," Israeli-vetted Palestinian
delegates could do so.[10] The "official" Palestinian delegates who met the
restrictive Israeli preconditions were for the most part professionals,
academics and businesspeople, some of them loosely identified with the
various PLO factions, but none of whom had any legal background or
experience in international diplomatic negotiations. The Israeli government was adamant in rejecting the direct participation in the negotiations of the somewhat more knowledgeable and politically experienced
"advisors." It was not until after the defeat of Yitzhak Shamir and his
replacement as prime minister by Yitzhak Rabin in mid-1992 that these
debilitating restrictions were gradually lifted.

More significant in the long run than these humiliating conditions
limiting the representation of the Palestinians was the structure of the
negotiations imposed by the United States on the Palestinians alone.
Both these limitations and the way the talks were organized impaired
the effectiveness of the Palestinian negotiators at the outset. The architecture for the Madrid and Washington meetings as devised by Baker
and his advisors (as usual, in consultation primarily with the Israeli government), provided for three bilateral tracks for negotiations with Israel,
one for Syria, one for Lebanon, and one for the Jordanian-Palestinian
delegation. The latter was eventually separated into two subtracks, one
Jordanian and one Palestinian. There were in addition several multilateral tracks on topics such as refugees and water, in which all the parties
to the bilateral talks participated, as did other regional states, the European Union, the UN, and other concerned parties. But whereas in their

bilateral tracks the Syrians, Lebanese, and Jordanians were meant to resolve all the outstanding issues in dispute between them and Israel while negotiating the terms of a final lasting peace—in the event, Jordan and Israel did this in 1994, with Syria and Israel coming extremely close in the following year—as a result of this American-imposed architecture the Palestinians were not allowed to do the same thing.

At the insistence of the Shamir government, and very much in line with the Begin-inspired Camp David framework, the United States imposed ground rules whereby initially the Palestinians were only allowed to negotiate what were called transitional "interim self-government arrangements." The Letter of Invitation stated that this was because "a transitional period is necessary to break down the walls of suspicion and mistrust and lay the basis for sustainable negotiations on the final status of the occupied territories." The American intermediaries argued incessantly that what was needed was "confidence-building measures." Such prescriptions proceeded from the assumption that the problem was simply "mistrust and suspicion" and lack of "confidence" between two implicitly equal sides, rather than that one was in illegal military occupation of the territory of the other, and in effect had its boot on the other's neck. In any case, this and other justifications for the transitional period proved to be patently false: as was predicted by the Palestinians, this period created widespread mistrust rather than confidence. Aaron David Miller, who was deeply involved in the Washington negotiations and subsequent talks, several years later admitted as much. He told Palestinian officials: "I know that your experience with transitional periods has been unhappy. Rather than building trust, it has eroded it."[11] Far worse, the transitional period ultimately served the purpose of strengthening Israel's hold on the occupied territories. Whether the American officials involved sincerely believed at the time in the false remedies and deceptive language that they were purveying is a moot point: as we shall see, many Israeli leaders certainly understood that these "interim" measures bought them time to further entrench their occupation and settlement enterprise. This should not have been so hard to perceive: after all, that was the whole point for Begin, who thought up the entire scheme in the first place.

To understand why this was the case, it is necessary only to relate what actually happened, as opposed to what is supposed to have occurred. The talks to devise the arrangements for this five-year transitional period were meant to be completed within one year, or by the end of 1992. The Letter of Invitation stated that "beginning the third year of interim self-government arrangements," or supposedly by 1995, negotiations were to commence on "final status issues," with the aim of concluding them by the end of the five-year period. If all had gone according to the plan laid out in this letter, that would have meant an end to the interim period and a final peace agreement by the end of 1997. Only during so-called "permanent status" talks were the Palestinians at last to be allowed to deal with the most crucial issues between them and Israel: ending the military occupation, removing settlements, control of land and water, the status of Jerusalem, the refugee issue, and sovereignty and statehood. Until then, the American-Israeli-imposed ground rules stipulated that all these crucial matters were off the table and could not be discussed: all that could be negotiated were interim arrangements. So as far as the Palestinians were concerned, at this stage the "peace process" did not encompass the basic elements of a real, lasting and just peace, or a resolution of any of their basic problems. By contrast, from an Israeli perspective an interim period relieved some of the burdens of occupation, giving the illusion that Israel was moving toward peace with the Palestinians, while leaving in place and indeed allowing for the reinforcement of all the fundamental elements of Israeli occupation and settlement in the occupied Palestinian territories. Thus, from the start the terms of the negotiations were gravely deficient and profoundly biased in favor of Israel and against the Palestinians.

Even had everything gone as projected with respect to this timeline, while all the other Arab parties could immediately begin to negotiate a final peace agreement with Israel in the fall of 1991, for the initial few years the Palestinians were only permitted to quibble over the details of the 1978 interim self-government autonomy plan that Begin had bequeathed to Shamir, and Shamir then bequeathed to Rabin. But in fact, none of this went according to plan. In the meantime, the Palestinians, by making the fateful decision to accept this skewed architecture, found themselves in a straitjacket, one in which they are indeed confined to this day.

The protracted nature of the process amounted to an enormous victory for Israeli partisans of the status quo in the occupied territories. It meant that for an indeterminate period (in practice, for the over twenty years from 1991 until the present day), the Palestinians would be restricted to talking about and eventually living under the extremely low ceiling of Begin's scheme for "autonomy" for the people, but not the land, all the while continuing to suffer under a regime of continued occupation. Israel could, and eventually did, drag out the negotiations over the details of autonomy for many years, thereby repeatedly postponing any consideration of "final status issues." Meanwhile, it vastly increased the settler population while creating other "facts on the ground." Israel later refused to budge on the final status issues, further prolonging what was supposed to have been an "interim period." It was in fact an infernal trap for the Palestinians, as they soon found out to their regret. Shamir said after his electoral defeat in 1992, "I would have conducted negotiations on autonomy for 10 years and in the meantime we would have reached half a million people."[12] Both this time period and the number of Israeli settlers implanted in the occupied territories have since been egregiously exceeded by Shamir and his successors.

In fact, far from beginning in 1995, the first serious substantive negotiations over "final status" issues took place five years after that, in July 2000, at the hurriedly convened, poorly prepared, and ultimately abortive Camp David summit.[13] Previous talks that nominally dealt with final status issues were really just an extension of the autonomy talks, with Begin's 1978 bottom line as the constant subtext. For evidence that this was the case, it is necessary only to look at minutes of a meeting held in June 2000 between the American side, headed by Dennis Ross, and the Palestinian side, led by Abu al-'Ala, as part of the so-called "Permanent Status Negotiations." The minutes show that after nine years of an unsuccessful "transitional period," the main effort of the American side was to try to persuade the Palestinians to accept yet another "transition," and continued Israeli control. Thus Ross's first question was "Can you see circumstances under which they will have control over territory and you have sovereignty over it?"[14] That Ross could talk of "sovereignty" without control shows the degree of corruption of language by this stage, and also how deeply the United States subscribed to an Israeli agenda, rooted in Begin's scheme promulgated back at Camp David in 1978.

The subsequent "final status" negotiations that took place in Washington, DC, and at Taba in Egypt, at the end of 2000 and in early 2001, in the final days of both the Clinton administration and the government of Ehud Barak (which had come to power in 1999), were equally hurried and equally abortive. In any case, by this late stage all three of the top leaders concerned—Clinton, Barak, and ʿArafat—had lost most of their political support and much of their legitimacy: indeed, the first two left office very soon afterward. Moreover, the entire negotiating process was about to collapse in the violence of the second Palestinian intifada and the Israeli army's reoccupation of the very limited areas of the West Bank from which it had withdrawn a few years earlier under the provisions of the Oslo Accords. The intifada was a direct result of the disillusionment of most of the once-hopeful Palestinian population of the occupied territories with nine years of a "peace process" that had deferred statehood indefinitely while in practice allowing for the consecration of occupation, the expansion of Israeli settlements, and increasingly severe new restrictions on the movement of the Palestinian population.[15] While many of their leaders apparently continued to be deceived by "peace process talk," most Palestinians by this point saw clearly the trap they had been led into, and they eventually reacted with fury in the second intifada, in what became one of the most violent episodes inside Palestine in the entire post-1967 history of the conflict.

Surprising as it may sound, serious and properly prepared "final status" negotiations along the lines supposedly envisaged in October 1991 have in fact never taken place, in spite of a few subsequent attempts that were similarly abortive, as we shall see below. Nevertheless, the grotesquely misnamed "peace process" that emerged from this fatally flawed negotiating architecture has been rolling along majestically ever since. It is still going strong, at least notionally, recently entering its third decade, and providing glittering careers for an entire generation of American diplomats. "The East is a career," said Benjamin Disraeli: what was true of the East in the heyday of the British Empire has become true of the so-called "peace process" at the apogee of the era of American global dominance.[16] Or, as James Baker dryly said to Aaron David Miller, one of the chief officials responsible for the management of this process over many years, "I want you to know, Aaron, if I had another life, I'd want to be a Middle East specialist just like you, because it would mean guaranteed permanent employment."[17]

I will not lay out the entire complex history of the series of negotiations in Madrid, Washington, Oslo, Taba, Wye Plantation, and many other sites the world over that have continued sporadically ever since, and which produced a set of "interim" Palestinian self-government arrangements that have proven anything but temporary. This history is a worthwhile topic that has not yet been treated comprehensively and critically, but it is beyond the limited scope of the present book.[18] Rather, in what follows I will focus on a few key interactions between the Palestinians and their American-Israeli interlocutors during the 1991–93 Madrid-Washington negotiations that are particularly illuminating. I will examine briefly the striking continuity between what preceded and what followed in terms of the ultimate acceptance by the United States of an exceedingly low, Israeli-defined ceiling on Palestinian rights and expectations, once again after abortive attempts to resist by the Palestinians themselves and by some American officials.

A note on the sources I have used and on my own role is necessary at this point, at the risk of interrupting the flow of the narrative. A number of accounts of these events have been produced by key participants. I have drawn on several of them in the writing of this book.[19] The reader should know, however, that I do not come to this task solely as a historian, but also as a participant in many of the events I describe in this chapter in particular. My participation started while I was in Jerusalem during the spring and summer of 1991 doing research for a book on modern Palestinian history, and was meeting various Jerusalemites to obtain access to family records in their possession.[20] During one such meeting, Faysal Husayni asked me in passing whether I would serve as one of a group of advisors to the Palestinian delegation should the mooted Arab-Israeli peace conference take place. At that time Husayni, Hanan Ashrawi, and other leaders from the occupied Palestinian territories were deeply involved on behalf of the PLO leadership in discussions with Secretary of State James Baker about the composition of the Palestinian negotiating team. When Faysal Husayni asked me to participate, I believed that there were scant prospects for any such conference ever eventuating, in view of the Shamir government's firm opposition to any serious Palestinian participation. I agreed to allow my name to be considered, without seriously expecting that it would ever amount to anything. Back at home in Chicago in mid-October, I was surprised to learn that the conference would indeed take place, and that my name and those of the other advisors were being hurriedly processed by the US State Department for inclusion in the delegation, under the restrictive ground rules I have already described. I was also told that I would have to leave in a few days for Amman and then Madrid to take part.

There followed nearly two years during which I served as one of several advisors to the Palestinian delegation at Madrid in October–November 1991. I participated in every one of the subsequent rounds of bilateral Israeli-Palestinian negotiations in Washington, DC, doing so alongside my own research and teaching. There were ten such bilateral rounds after an initial pro forma meeting in Madrid, some lasting as long as several weeks, spaced out between December 1991 and June 1993. Our role as advisors included helping draft Palestinian proposals, and analyzing those of the Israeli side, as well as meeting with State Department officials, all of which I did. In the final phase of these negotiations, advisors including myself were permitted to participate in meetings with the Israeli side. In the course of this work, I accumulated a large collection of documents, which is the basis for the core of this chapter, supplemented by materials and recollections I obtained from some of my colleagues at the time and thereafter, and other documents. This is essentially a personal archive, which although extensive, is far from being complete, even for the period of less than two years during which I was intensively involved.[21]

One day, it will be possible to use a full range of declassified official records to write a comprehensive history of the entire range of negotiations from 1991 until the present, including the decisions taken by all the concerned parties. Such a history will treat notably the historic opportunities that were missed by the United States and Israel for a just and lasting settlement not only with the Palestinians but also with Syria and Lebanon, and also the critical errors made by the Palestinians themselves. It will be possible to undertake such a task only on the basis of a far more complete and comprehensive documentary record than I have at my disposal, presumably after the opening of all the relevant archives and the writing of memoirs by more of the participants. In the meantime, what I propose to do in this chapter is much more modest. The materials I have at hand, which mainly reflect the interactions and documents I had access to as an advisor to the Palestinian delegation, are fully sufficient to illustrate the limited range of issues I am focusing on: the US role in this process, how it related to Israeli positions, and the extraordinary continuity, in both cases, with previous and subsequent experiences.

A few of many episodes I was involved in or that are reflected in the documents in my possession will suffice to give a sense of the extraordinary degree of coordination of the American and Israeli positions, and how extensive was the carryover from what has been described in earlier chapters. Two of these episodes set the tone very early on in the Madrid and Washington negotiations. The first and most crucial American-Israeli collaboration had in fact already taken place by the time the peace conference formally began at Madrid: that relating to the restrictive ground rules previously detailed for curtailing Palestinian representation and limiting what could be discussed by the Palestinians to the narrow question of a self-government regime for the occupied territories under continuing Israeli control. As we have already seen, in its essentials this amounted to no more than warmed-over ideas left over from Begin's notions of "autonomy" from the Palestinian portion of the Camp David Accords. This meant uninterrupted occupation, with a promise of "final status" negotiations at some time in what turned out to be an indeterminate future. "Final status," of course was another of the slippery, dishonest terms that have characterized the entire history of this "peace process." "Final status" proved to be anything but final, amounting to an ever-receding mirage. Prepared well ahead of time, this proposal for autonomy talks with a promise of other negotiations in the distant future was all that was on offer to the Palestinians at Madrid on a take-it-or-leave-it basis. It was reluctantly accepted by the PLO, and became the basis of all subsequent negotiations and agreements.

If we believe the accounts produced since then by a number of participants and analysts, James Baker apparently had the intention of expanding Palestinian representation, and of pushing the ultimate result that emerged from the negotiating process beyond Begin's restrictive concept of self-rule for the Palestinians under overall Israeli control.[22] Baker certainly seemed to have seen the issue of settlements as crucial, and to have had some sympathy for the plight of the Palestinians under occupation.[23] In a letter to Faysal Husayni, Baker wrote the following:

I was struck in Moscow by your description of the hardships on the ground which you and your colleagues face. We have raised these concerns, many of which we share, at the highest levels of the Israeli government with the view to reducing, if not eliminating, the most severe burdens of the occupation. I also share your concern about the accelerated pace of settlements activity, a problem which remains high on my agenda.[24]

However, whatever Baker's intentions and sentiments may have been, in the end he and President Bush were rigidly constrained by the exceedingly low ceiling regarding the Palestinians already accepted by the Carter and Reagan administrations, to which Shamir insisted on holding the United States. They were also hampered by their unwillingness or inability to force Israel to stop settlement activity, which they indeed did try to do, as we shall see. Baker had bluntly told Husayni in a meeting in February 1992: "I told you in the first meeting, I cannot wave a wand and stop the settlements."[25] This language is revealing, and constitutes a frank admission of the limits of the power of the US executive branch when it comes to exerting pressure on Israel, limits that had already frustrated several previous administrations.

Moreover, it frequently transpired that attempts of the secretary of state to go beyond the restrictive framework that bound United States policy were further sabotaged by a mode of thinking ingrained in a fixed set of terms derived mainly from Israeli political discourse that had subtly taken root among his subordinates. This was premised on the idea that the United States could not, indeed *must not,* put pressure on Israel to go beyond these subordinates' assessment, however flawed it might be, of the Israeli domestic political consensus on a given issue. Thus if these officials (quite wrongly, as we shall see) determined for example that Israel's internal political balance meant that its government would *never* agree to negotiate with the PLO, then the United States could not reasonably demand such a thing of Israel. Beyond this, what was presumed by these "experts" to be acceptable to the Israeli domestic consensus often came to be seen as the limit of what the United States itself was permitted to do. This was eventually erected into the current doctrine, rooted in Kissinger's secret 1975 commitment to consult with Israel before launching any initiative, that there should be no surprises between the two allies (or at least that the United States should not surprise Israel; the latter has always felt free to unleash unpleasant surprises on the United States), and that their positions should be seen as identical. A further extension of this doctrine is that there should be "no daylight" between the two allies, in a phrase Mitt Romney used on the presidential campaign trail in 2012. This is the current stance of outspoken supporters of the Israeli-AIPAC line in the US Congress, notably among Republicans, but with broad bipartisan support.[26]

We have seen the beginnings of this process with the banning of US contacts with the PLO from the mid-1970s onwards. Although some American officials such as Kissinger independently opposed such contacts for their own reasons, the United States followed suit essentially because conventional wisdom in Israel was adamantly opposed to the PLO and abhorred the idea of contacts with it. In any case, the Israeli government held the United States firmly to the terms of Kissinger's second 1975 commitment. However, many American officials chafed at these restrictions imposed on their country's freedom of action. Moreover, in highly charged security conditions like those of Beirut during the Lebanese civil war, it proved to be vital that the United States undertake contacts with the PLO, albeit clandestinely to avoid angering the Israelis. As we have seen, even under Kissinger these developed well beyond the original narrow pretext of "security."

The delicate sensibility regarding the internal politics of Israel was directly linked to the fact that Israelis were generally seen by Americans as "like us." Israel was and is widely regarded in American political discourse as an exemplary ally: famously, it was supposedly "the only democracy in the Middle East." This shibboleth, endlessly and mindlessly repeated, ignores Israel's nearly half a century of military rule over millions of voiceless Palestinians in the occupied territories, many within a few minutes' drive of its main population centers. Like the more than half million Jewish settlers in their midst, they live in what the Israeli government considers to be "Eretz Israel," all of whose land is under Israeli control; but only the settlers have full democratic, legal, human, and civil rights. It ignores as well the fact that elsewhere in the Middle East Kuwait and Lebanon have for decades both been functioning, albeit flawed, democracies, as is Turkey today.

Notwithstanding these anomalies, which remained invisible to most, Israel was broadly admired in the United States for its democracy (and for other reasons), and thus the Israeli domestic political consensus was in some measure considered sacrosanct by many American officials. Such consideration was almost invariably absent from the way the United States dealt with other countries, including established democracies that were long-standing allies, but Israel was clearly considered special. This led it to be treated specially. Speaking of several officials, including himself, Aaron David Miller, who played key roles under presidents from Carter to George W. Bush, said, "If you wanted to succeed in Arab-Israeli peacemaking, you must be an advocate for both sides. Far too often the small group with whom I had worked . . . had acted as a lawyer for only one side, Israel."[27] Until James Baker left the State Department to run President Bush's flagging reelection campaign in the summer of 1992, he balanced this one-sided tendency of his subordinates to some extent by providing what Miller himself called "adult supervision."[28] Since Baker's departure from Foggy Bottom over twenty years ago, there has not been such mature, evenhanded oversight either at the State Department or the White House. Partly in consequence, a partisan and unbalanced spirit has animated the policy of the United States vis-à-vis Israel and the Palestinians to this day.

A second important example of how the United States' close collaborative relationship with Israel negatively affected its treatment of the Palestinians was summed up in how the key passages of the Letter of Assurances, cited in the epigraph to this chapter, were ultimately interpreted by the United States government. Among these passages was the letter's warning against actions that were "prejudicial or precedential" to negotiations, or against "unilateral acts that would exacerbate tensions . . . or preempt their final outcome." This was combined with the assertion that the United States opposed "unilateral actions that seek to predetermine issues that can only be resolved through negotiations." Taken at face value, these injunctions seemed to mean that the United States would vigorously oppose measures like continued settlement expansion or the isolation of Jerusalem from the rest of the West Bank that started in earnest in 1991, acts that had a permanent impact on the very issues whose resolution was postponed—by American-Israeli fiat—until the "final status" negotiations. To their lasting regret, the Palestinians initially assumed as much. Events proved that they were gravely mistaken.

It is true that in the fall of 1991 and the spring of 1992 the Bush administration took the unprecedented step of holding up $10 billion in loan guarantees to Israel until the United States could be assured that the money would not be used for the building of settlements in the occupied territories. In doing this, Bush openly singled out the Israel lobby as an obstacle to his policy, and obtained some public support in so doing. Bush challenged AIPAC and Congress directly, stating:

I'm up against some powerful political forces. . . . we're up against very strong and effective, sometimes, groups that go up to the Hill. I heard today there were something like a thousand lobbyists on the Hill working the other side of the question. We've got one lonely little guy down here doing it. . . . But I'm going to fight for what I believe, and it may be popular politically but probably it's not. But that's not the question here, that's not the question, is whether it's good 1992 politics. What's important here is that we give this process a chance. And I don't care if I get one vote, I'm going to stand for what I believe here, and I believe the American people will be with me, if we put it on this question of principle.[29]

The effort to curb the building of Israeli settlements came to naught, however, since after Yitzhak Rabin's Labor coalition came to power in June 1992, and as the November 1992 American presidential elections approached, Bush chose to take a less confrontational approach. The result was that settlement expansion continued. Clearly, there was no "magic wand" for stopping the Israeli settlement enterprise.

This principled American action over the loan guarantees, short-lived although it proved to be, may well have helped in alienating Israelis from the hard-line Shamir-led Likud government, and in inducing them to vote in a Labor Party government headed by Yitzhak Rabin in June 1992.[30] And it provoked much self-congratulation from American officials, one of whom, Daniel Kurtzer, reprimanded Palestinian negotiators for their ingratitude in February 1992: "You have only given criticism of the US role, instead of saying never in US history has . . . the US been so willing to take on the Israelis and been such an honest broker."[31] But it is crucial to stress that even under Rabin, who was not particularly favorable to the settlement enterprise, its expansion did not stop.[32] His new government pledged to complete ten thousand housing units that were already under way, including in Arab East Jerusalem, and was allowed to do so without hindrance by the Bush administration. And so the larger trend of unfettered settlement expansion and the separation of West Jerusalem from the rest of the West Bank continued. Thus between 1991 and 2000, at the height of negotiations, the number of Israeli settlers in the West Bank and East Jerusalem more than doubled to over four hundred thousand, while Arab East Jerusalem was completely cut off from its West Bank hinterland by movement restrictions, new settlements, and a huge wall.

———————

For all of its occasional tough words about settlements, perhaps the toughest of any administration before or since,[33] in the end the first Bush administration was unwilling or unable to give any concrete meaning to the assurances offered to the Palestinians in October 1991. Confronted with profound transformations engineered by Israel that with monotonous regularity established concrete new facts on the ground and changed the very contours of the most important issues that the Palestinians were not allowed to discuss, but that were eventually supposed to be subject to negotiation, at the end of the day the United States did nothing at all. This was essentially a consequence of two of the three patterns that as we have seen led the Truman, Carter, and Reagan administrations to back off from difficult decisions on Palestine and Israel. The first related to domestic American politics, and the second to the notable absence of pushback from Arab states that proclaimed their devotion to the cause of Palestine but did nothing to further it in practice. Whatever protests, feeble or otherwise, about Israeli settlement expansion the United States did make from time to time had little or no effect on the ground. They were drowned out by the incessant roar of bulldozers, cement mixers, and dump trucks building infrastructure for new settlements and expanding old ones all over the occupied West Bank and East Jerusalem, and were studiously ignored by a succession of Israeli governments.

To their credit, the Palestinian negotiators in Washington realized very early on that something was profoundly amiss as Israeli settlement activity continued unabated and Arab East Jerusalem was progressively cut off from its West Bank hinterland, and they made attempts to redress the situation. Memos of Palestinian working meetings with US State Department personnel during the first and second rounds of the bilateral negotiations in December 1990 and January 1991 are replete with the insistence of Palestinian participants that by the terms of reference for the negotiations Israel could not be allowed to continue its settlement activity or to close off Jerusalem from the West Bank while the talks were going on. There was little response from the Americans beyond one senior State Department legal official, who echoed Baker's comment about his having no "magic wand" where settlement expansion was concerned: "I can't debate the logic of what you are saying. The US opposes settlement. It is difficult to get Israel to stop."[34]

During the second round of negotiations in Washington, in January 1992, the leaders of the Palestinian team protested to Secretary Baker himself that Israel was refusing to freeze the expansion of its settlements, and was sealing off Jerusalem to Palestinians from the West Bank. It was thus acting in ways that closed off options supposedly left open for a later stage, were in violation of the ground rules for the negotiations, and were contrary to specific American assurances to the Palestinians. Dr. Haydar 'Abd al-Shafi, the distinguished nationalist leader and physician who headed the Palestinian delegation, later said of his discussions with Baker:

> I asked him how we could engage in a process when the other party was violating the basic terms of reference from the very beginning. That's where the Americans did not honor their commitments and responsibility as the party that had called for the peace negotiations. They violated their trusteeship by allowing Israel to continue to violate the ground rules that they themselves had established.[35]

It became clear after several fruitless meetings with Baker and his aides that these protests were having no effect, and that the United States would not or could not make good on its assurances and was unwilling to impose anything on Israel insofar as settlements or Jerusalem were concerned. After extensive consultations with members of the delegation, 'Abd al-Shafi determined to fly to Tunis to place the issue before the PLO leadership. There he recommended, on the basis of a consensus among the Palestinian team in Washington, that the Palestinians suspend participation in the negotiations. The reason was simple: they had been invited to join in talks via an invitation and ground rules that had proven to be couched in false terms. After listening to 'Abd al-Shafi, the PLO leaders decided against this course of action, and were adamant about pursuing negotiations without ever insisting that

the United States remain faithful to its commitments. They took their fateful decision although this duplicity by the United States had fatally undermined the negotiators that they themselves had selected.[36] With Israel able to expand its settlement enterprise and continue the absorption of Arab East Jerusalem with impunity in the absence of an effective American response, the Palestinians were negotiating from a position of even greater weakness than they originally suspected. The deal ultimately reached in 1993, in Oslo rather than Washington, reflected this weakness, as well as Israel's obduracy in sticking to the essential lineaments of Begin's original autonomy scheme.

This was not the first, nor would it be the last, of the mistakes that Yasser 'Arafat and his colleagues would make in the course of these negotiations, but it was one of the gravest. In effect, it allowed Israel to continue gobbling up the pie, the partitioning of which the two sides were, eventually, supposed to negotiate. The issue of freezing the expansion of Israeli settlements remains deeply divisive to this day. It was the subject of continuing contention between President Obama and Prime Minister Netanyahu from 2009 until Obama was forced to back down starting in late 2010, as I will discuss in the next chapter. However, in the previous chapter I reviewed briefly the Likud Party platform of 1977; the first handwritten notes on the subject of autonomy made in 1978 by Menachem Begin, the patriarch of the Israeli Right, setting out the concepts that became central to the Camp David Accords; and a 1982 US intelligence assessment of the Israeli position. On the basis of these documents alone, it should by now be crystal clear that the sanctity not only of the continuity of the settlement enterprise, but of uninterrupted settlement expansion, in occupied Arab East Jerusalem and the West Bank, was at that time an absolutely nonnegotiable Israeli bottom line. During the Washington negotiations and for several decades since it has continued to be the case, and no American president since 1967 has been willing or able to breach it, although some have tried.

In the face of this rock-solid Israeli position, American determination and US assurances to the Palestinians proved to be utterly ephemeral in 1991–93. The brief discussion in chapter I of US guarantees for the security of Palestinian refugee camps in Beirut in 1982 showed that

this was not the first time such solemn American assurances had proven not to be worth the paper they were written on. This unfaithfulness regarding what the Palestinians believed were binding American pledges undermined the very structure of the negotiations that began in Madrid. It also fatally undermined the standing of the PLO in front of its own people. Seeing the ceaseless activity of Israeli bulldozers and dump trucks, they watched the uninterrupted expansion of settlements, and of Israeli control over the occupied territories, in spite of all the empty talk of progress in a "peace process." It is from this juncture that one can date the emergence of Hamas as a serious political rival to the PLO. Its rise was rooted in a profound skepticism among many Palestinians about the value of the approach that eschewed any forms of resistance to ongoing occupation and settlement expansion and relied exclusively on ultimately futile negotiations in terms of actually changing the situation on the ground inside Palestine. It was devastating for the standing of the PLO that the day-to-day situation of most ordinary Palestinians was actually getting worse while PLO and Israeli negotiators ostentatiously hobnobbed with one another all around the world.[37]

From that very early point onward, failure of the entire negotiating process, built on the unstable foundation of these skewed terms of reference, was assured, not only at Washington but also at Oslo and at every point afterward. Successive Israeli governments could with impunity fashion on the ground the final arrangements they desired regarding West Bank settlements and Jerusalem. All the while they could simultaneously ensure that the endless futile negotiations that were falsely described as a "peace process" went on and on without result and without end. These arrangements were ultimately to guarantee that at least until the present, there was to be no Palestinian state, no end to occupation, and no peace between Palestinians and Israelis, in spite of the promising beginnings of the Madrid Peace Conference, and the best intentions of many of those who participated.

We now turn to the denouement of the Washington bilateral talks after their ill-omened, if not fatal, beginning. Of course, the 1991–93 negotia-

tions ultimately produced no agreement between the two sides—one was only reached as a result of the direct talks between the PLO and Israel that took place secretly and on a parallel track in Oslo and elsewhere starting in January 1993. Nevertheless, it is important to examine briefly some of the specific topics over which the talks in Washington foundered, since they remained unresolved in the Israeli-Palestinian Oslo talks, nor have they been resolved in endless rounds of American-mediated negotiations since. These very issues thus illustrate clearly the reasons for the ultimate failure of the Oslo Accords and the entire "process" built around them, to bring about peace between Israelis and Palestinians.

There is nothing in the least surprising about the questions over which the Palestinian and Israeli sides reached an impasse in Washington from 1991 until 1993. They were without exception related to central features of the Begin plan that were at the core of what both the United States and Israel insisted was all that was on offer for the Palestinians. Although the Palestinian negotiators in Washington labored mightily to reach an agreement while escaping the constraints of the intellectual straitjacket fashioned fifteen years earlier by the iron-willed Likud prime minister, they were ultimately unable to do so. The two sides clashed in Washington over several key points related to an autonomy regime for the Palestinians of the occupied territories. One of them is most revealing of the unbridgeable gap between what the Israeli negotiators—faithfully and almost invariably supported by their American colleagues—were willing to offer, and the minimum that the Palestinians were able to accept. This was related to the "jurisdiction," territorial and otherwise, of the Palestinian interim authority that was supposed to emerge from the negotiations. The issue of jurisdiction was especially problematic because it related to land, specifically the "Land of Israel," which was central to Begin's vision and that of his nationalist and religious followers.

When, after many frustrating delays, negotiations finally got to the stage of the presentation of proposals, the first substantive Palestinian paper, put forward on January 14, 1992, during the second round of negotiations, was exceedingly clear and far-reaching regarding the jurisdiction of its proposed "Palestinian Interim Self-government Authority"

(PISGA). It stated: "It covers all the Palestinian territories occupied since 1967. The jurisdiction of the PISGA shall encompass all of these territories, the land, natural resources and water, the subsoil, and their territorial sea and air-space. Its jurisdiction shall also extend to all the Palestinian inhabitants of these territories."[38]

By contrast, everything the Israeli side had presented the Palestinians from the very beginning of the negotiations lacked this central component of jurisdiction over land, not to speak of real control over anything substantial, let alone any aspects of sovereignty (which were supposed to be deferred to "final status" talks). Simple reference to the core Begin-derived concepts that governed Israeli thinking, like "autonomy for the people but not the land," explains why this was the case. Thus, one of the first formal Israeli presentations, delivered during the third round of bilateral negotiations in February 1992, proposed that interim arrangements "must deal with people, not with the status of the territories." It further stated that "the jurisdiction of the I[nterim] S[elf] G[overning] A[uthority] organs will apply to the Palestinian Arab inhabitants of Judea, Samaria and the Gaza District." Nowhere in this document is there any mention of land, or of the territorial limits of the area over which this authority would have control or jurisdiction.[39] The accompanying letter to Dr. ʿAbd al-Shafi from the chief Israeli negotiator, Ambassador Elyakim Rubinstein, was more explicit. In a peremptory tone, Rubinstein wrote: "The arrangements will apply to the Palestinian Arab inhabitants of the territories under Israeli military administration. The arrangements will not have a territorial application, nor will they apply to the Israeli population in the territories. They will not apply to inhabitants of Jerusalem." Read carefully, this is the wording of a directive being dictated to subalterns, lacking only the imperative mode and exclamation points. It is not the language of one side putting forward its position in a negotiation between equals. The arrogance of its tone aside, the reason for this unyielding position was that the territories in question were part of "Eretz Israel," for Rubinstein and his superiors. They had no authority to give it away, for as the 1977 Likud program, cited as the epigraph to chapter I, intoned: "The right of the Jewish people to the Land of Israel is eternal."[40] Rubinstein added tartly that the Palestinian model of January

14 "is a far cry from acceptable interim self-government arrangements and . . . basically represents a Palestinian State in all but name, considered by Israel a mortal security threat."[41]

These contrasting positions perfectly illustrate the gap between the two sides over this crucial issue, one that was never resolved, in spite of efforts by the Palestinians in particular to craft a formula that would provide the PISGA with jurisdiction over a specified territory without crossing any Israeli red lines. Thus the Palestinians argued in response to Rubinstein's strictures in a paper delivered to the Israeli side in the same round in early March 1992: "A self-governing authority cannot exercise its powers for the benefit of the inhabitants without having an exclusive territorial jurisdiction."[42] This argument for a territorial basis to the jurisdiction of the interim Palestinian authority was repeated in every Palestinian position paper and proposal presented to the Israeli side, and was pressed vigorously in meetings with Israeli negotiators. As one Palestinian negotiator stated in frustration to the Israelis in a working group during the tenth (and what proved to be the final) session of the bilateral talks over a year later, in June 1993:

Very simply you have an authority which by agreement is going to be created. In our view there can be no such thing without some geographical scope. That's all. It's inconceivable. We will never be able to explain it. We don't think it exists. We believe it's not logical. There is a fundamental difference. You seem to feel that functions can be transferred without any delineation on the ground of where those functions are. We feel that's impossible, illogical, unworkable. It's not a matter of final status. We think if you have some scope, geographic, territorial, it does not prejudge: we're not drawing frontiers, if that's what you're worried about; that's for final status. The extent of our authority has to have some geographical dimension. People won't understand it for one thing. I don't know if you have tried to explain it to Israeli public opinion, but Palestinian public opinion will never understand.[43]

Such efforts were still being made at the very end of the negotiations when the Palestinian negotiators, by now including previously excluded "advisors," among them myself, continued to press their territorial approach on the unyielding Israeli negotiators. In one of the last sessions in Washington, on June 23, 1993, the Palestinians finally elicited a semi-positive response from the chief Israeli negotiator, Elyakim Rubinstein, who asked, "In your model, which I have been asked about by my government, in the territorial model, what will be the legal status of Israelis and the legal status of Israeli armed forces in the territories?"[44] The Palestinian negotiators in Washington recognized that this query constituted a sort of breakthrough, coming as it did at a special joint session of the two working groups that Rubinstein himself had requested, and particularly since he repeated twice that he was speaking at the instructions of his government. However, it was too little, too late. This breakthrough, if breakthrough indeed it was, came in what proved to be the last round of the American-mediated bilateral talks, at a point when neither the PLO leadership in Tunis nor the Rabin government was focusing on the Washington negotiations. As we shall see in more detail below, the two sides had already initiated backchannel contacts that had culminated in January in direct talks in Oslo and elsewhere between envoys of Israel and the PLO, and by June these talks had already made significant progress. Thus, by this point the real locus of negotiations had already shifted away from Washington. It remains only to detail highlights of the final stage of the Washington talks in order to show how the very same issues recurred in the secret Oslo meetings, and to illustrate important ongoing features of the US role.

The issue of the clandestine negotiations between Israel and the PLO arose in dramatic fashion at a special session with two senior American officials on June 22, 1993. Several Palestinian negotiators had been instructed by the PLO leadership to communicate some of the initial understandings regarding security that emissaries of the PLO had already reached in its secret backchannel talks (elsewhere than Oslo) with representatives of the Rabin government.[45] They provoked only consternation among their American interlocutors by informing them, as they had been explicitly instructed to do by the PLO in Tunis, that

"Palestinian external resources" including possibly "officers in the P[alestine] L[iberation] A[rmy]" might play a role in keeping security under an interim autonomy regime. This statement caused amazement among the American officials, one of whom blurted out, "Well, for the first time we are speechless!" In response, the Palestinian side tried to reassure them of what was in fact the case: that the PLO had already reached an informal but solid understanding to this effect with senior Israeli officials connected to their own security establishment,[46] saying, "We think that Israeli security managers think that for things to work out there have to be experienced and respected [people] who can maintain public order." The astonished response of another American was: "This security presentation is otherworldly."[47]

The reason this presentation was so hard to absorb for these two highly experienced American diplomats—Daniel Kurtzer and Aaron David Miller—was that it went directly counter to the firmly fixed preconceptions of the core group of American officials involved in the negotiations about the utter unacceptability of the PLO to the Israelis, and indeed the undesirability of the involvement of the PLO. At this point, Kurtzer continued by saying that he was going to "put on an Israeli hat. Now I am Joe Israeli and I think how this is going to affect my security, and I'll say forget it." In the face of this incredulity (and this completely faulty misreading of the Israeli scene), one of the Palestinians tried again to reassure the Americans that there were in fact already understandings with the Israeli government on this matter, saying, "We don't think we'll have a problem agreeing [with the Israelis] on this," but it was to no avail. The American diplomats were skeptical, disbelieving, and visibly irritated. They apparently were angered because they realized that if the PLO and the Israeli government were secretly in contact, the two parties had in effect gone behind the back of the United States government, and cut the Americans out of the loop. For representatives of what in 1993 had just become the world's sole superpower, this was a bit much to take. Worse, in doing so, the PLO and Israel had just done what these officials had believed was impossible and undesirable. Indeed, their boss Dennis Ross soon afterward had been overheard to say, "I was never convinced that the PLO should be involved in this process."[48] Worse still, negotiating directly with the PLO was something they and Ross had always confidently, and wrongly, assured their superiors that Israel would never do.

This of course is exactly what had happened. The two sides had persevered with their clandestine direct negotiations at Oslo and elsewhere because they were frustrated with the slow progress in the Washington talks under American tutelage, which the Palestinians and the Israelis blamed largely on the American mediators—whom both came to see as more royalist than the king.[49] Both the PLO and the Rabin government might have come to this understanding as a result of such American initiatives as a "bridging proposal," presented with much fanfare in May 1993 to break a deadlock in the talks, which was *less* forthcoming in several important respects than Israeli proposals previously made directly to the Palestinians. The American mediators' misplaced zeal to avoid antagonizing the Israeli negotiators provoked barely disguised contempt on the part of the Palestinian delegation, members of which spent over three hours in another meeting with Kurtzer and Miller listing the deficiencies of the "bridging" proposal. Ashrawi stated tartly: "We did have a problem with the document reflecting Israeli substance and an Israeli linguistic bias."[50] Having worked so closely for so long with the Israelis, not only the thinking but even the language of American officials had been affected.

The clandestine direct contacts between the PLO and Israel produced full-fledged negotiations in Norway, which were preceded by other important secret, direct contacts between the two sides elsewhere, including those that produced the aforementioned security understandings, which have since gotten much less attention. These eventually resulted in the Oslo Accords, and in formal recognition of the PLO by Israel, both major events in the history of the conflict. However, although it has been claimed that the PLO negotiators in Oslo benefited from the copious work done by the Palestinian delegation in Washington,[51] the result shows unequivocally that this was simply not the case. Quite the contrary, those in Oslo ignored the expertise and experience accumulated by the latter group. Indeed, the Oslo negotiators fell into traps their Palestinian colleagues in the bilateral talks in Washington had been aware of and carefully avoided, notably regarding jurisdiction. The failure of the Oslo team to avoid these pitfalls, and their lack of appreciation of the valence of some of the terms involved, is clear if one assesses the "Declaration of Principles" (DOP) negotiated in Oslo solely in terms of the key issue of jurisdiction.

Notwithstanding the stubborn insistence of the Palestinian delegation in Washington on the projected Palestinian authority's territorial jurisdiction over the entirety of the West Bank, Gaza Strip, and East Jerusalem, the relevant language of the DOP finally agreed upon shows that the negotiators at Oslo failed utterly to achieve this purpose: "Jurisdiction of the Council will cover West Bank and Gaza Strip territory, *except for issues that will be negotiated in the permanent status negotiations* [author's emphasis]. The two sides view the West Bank and the Gaza Strip as a single territorial unit, whose integrity will be preserved during the interim period."[52] The wording relating to the West Bank and Gaza Strip constituting "a single territorial unit" was an advance on previous Israeli positions, but it had originally been offered by the Israeli side in Washington.[53] More importantly, however, the phrase "except for issues that will be negotiated in the permanent status negotiations" had only one meaning in the Israeli lexicon: settlements, military installations, land, and much else that were considered by them as "final status" issues were excluded from the purview of the Palestinian authority's jurisdiction. This was just what Begin had demanded at Camp David and afterward and what Ambassador Rubinstein had always insisted on in the Washington talks. The DOP therefore amounts to a capitulation to a key Israeli demand, disguised in innocent-sounding terminology.

Much more could be said about the flaws of the DOP negotiated in Oslo and signed on the White House lawn in September 1993. In the eyes of those members of the Palestinian delegation in Washington who were the most deeply involved in its everyday work, it was beyond question that the PLO negotiators in Oslo had frittered away the results of their many months of efforts. Raja Shehadeh, the highly respected lawyer who was the main Palestinian legal advisor in Washington, was categorical: "Little use was made during the Oslo talks of the work done by the Palestinian Delegation to the Washington talks."[54]

In light of their experience in Washington, they saw further that the Oslo negotiators had failed to hold out for the essential minimum in an interim accord that might have halted the inexorable march of Israel's occupation-settlement complex and could have provided the basis for a final outcome that would have amounted to Palestinian sovereignty and statehood.[55] This would necessarily have included: formal Israeli acceptance in principle of Palestinian self-determination and of the applicability of international occupation law to the West Bank, Gaza Strip, and East Jerusalem; a halt to settlement expansion; and the full jurisdiction—at least in most essential respects—of the new Palestinian interim authority over the entirety of the occupied territories.

The DOP agreed upon between 'Arafat and Rabin achieved none of these things. It thus was essentially little more than a restatement of the original inflexible ideas that Begin had come to Camp David with fifteen years before. The main difference was that this gloss on Begin's profoundly anti-Palestinian concepts had now been formally accepted by the PLO itself. It proved to be a disastrous beginning to a long string of bitter disappointments for the Palestinians, and to a period that saw the disappearance of the possibilities for peace which had seemed so bright to some in 1991 when the Madrid Peace Conference convened.

The fatal flaws in this agreement were ignored by many Palestinians and others in 1993 because in certain respects Oslo appeared to mark an achievement for the Palestinian national cause and an advance over what was on offer at Madrid and Washington. This could be seen in the willingness of the Rabin government finally to talk directly to the PLO, and later to recognize it in the Oslo Accords as the "representative of the Palestinian people."[56] This recognition signified a shift of great importance in the official position of the state of Israel, which now recognized that there was such a thing as a Palestinian people. It is worth mentioning here, although it is little remarked upon, that the PLO had already recognized the state of Israel in 1988 in its Declaration of Independence. Israel's belated reciprocal recognition that the Palestinians were a people meant, moreover, that it would no longer dictate who could and could not represent the Palestinians. This ended the charade produced in Washington by the artificial Israeli-imposed rules for negotiations involving separation of advisors (from Jerusalem, the diaspora, or with links to the PLO) from the actual delegates, while the PLO itself was forced to remain behind the scenes, even as it actually pulled all the strings. Now, the Israeli government could talk directly to its main adversaries at the highest levels, which in principle was clearly preferable. (Soon afterward, with the rise of Hamas, the old Israeli-American litany about "not talking to terrorists," and thereby deciding who could and could not speak for the Palestinians, reemerged.)

However, Oslo did not put an end to two other fundamentally objectionable features of the Madrid-Washington process for the Palestinians that I have already detailed. The first was Israel's refusal to agree to halt actions like settlement expansion that prejudiced or predetermined "final status" issues, actions that indeed decided some of these issues finally and in the most concrete possible way: with the pouring of huge amounts of concrete annually in settlement-building activity all over the West Bank. The second of these objectionable features was Israel's insistence on remaining within the constrictive linguistic and conceptual framework of Begin's autonomy scheme. Even though Yitzhak Rabin was the first Israeli prime minister to accept formally the idea that the Palestinians were a people, he never officially conceded that this people had the right of national self-determination and statehood. These terms consequently occur nowhere in the 1993 agreements. Thus, although they nominally accepted that the Palestinians were a people, the Oslo accords in fact did no more than formally consecrate Begin's scheme: we have seen that the canny Polish-born lawyer understood that the terms he had obdurately insisted on at Camp David in 1978 "'guarantee that under no condition' can a Palestinian state be created." Even worse, Oslo gave this dogmatic construct produced by the mind of the most resolute opponent of the cause of Palestinian national self-determination the seal of legitimacy of the endorsement of 'Yasser Arafat himself, the very symbol of that cause.

Why did the PLO leadership accept such a terrible bargain? One of the key leaders responsible for the Oslo deal (and its main negotiator), Ahmad Quray (Abu al-'Ala), justified his actions at length in his three-volume memoirs.[57] Other justifications, most of them equally feeble, have been offered by other PLO leaders and analysts sympathetic to them.[58] Considering the situation at the time, two main sets of real reasons can be adduced for these profoundly flawed decisions. The first set had to do with these leaders' essentially accurate assessment of the grave situation of the PLO itself. The organization was growing ever weaker in exile in Tunis and other out-of-the-way places distant from Palestine, and cut off from any Palestinian population center. Since leaving Beirut, its cadres, military forces, and militants, who had just fought and lost the third-longest Arab war with Israel,[59] had been trapped in enforced idleness. After their return to Palestine following the Oslo Accords, subsequent events revealed that over a decade of inactivity had had a debilitating effect on many of them. Moreover, due to its leaders' ill-thought-out decision to side with Iraq during the 1990–91 Gulf War, the PLO had been deprived of the crucial financial support of the Arab Gulf countries. The PLO's chiefs had little remaining leverage or credibility among the Arab states, and had clearly worn out their welcome in many Arab host countries.

'Arafat and his colleagues were therefore eager to move to what they hoped would be a safer base of operations, in the midst of their people. They saw the agreement that Rabin offered them, which would allow them and the core of their followers in exile to return to their homeland, as a way out of this pressing dilemma. They mistakenly hoped that once inside Palestine, they might go beyond the political and legal limits that Israel sought to place on them. Moreover, they were obsessed with the symbolism of recognition of the PLO, after so many decades when the very existence of the Palestinian people and the representativity of the PLO were denied by Israel and its supporters. In consequence, at Oslo and in subsequent negotiations brokered by the United States they ignored the most crucial features, based essentially on Begin's 1978 bottom line, of what Israel was willing to offer, seeing them as unimportant "details." They had little appreciation of, or patience for, the linguistic and legal aspects of this offer. Ironically, these features, such as the denial of jurisdiction to a Palestinian authority, were the very ones which the Palestinian delegation in Washington—which they had selected—had rightly balked at.[60] As we have seen, these "details" meant that from the Israeli point of view, essentially acquiesced in thereafter by the Americans, the agreements they signed guaranteed that the Palestinian people would be prevented from achieving even their minimum national aspirations.

The second set of reasons does the PLO leadership even less credit. Immured in Tunis, and having operated for most of their adult lives in the environment of inter-Arab politics, they had lost touch with the situation in Palestine. They utterly failed to appreciate the grave long-term implications of issues like a settlement freeze or Israel's closure and separation of East Jerusalem from its West Bank hinterland. None of them had been anywhere inside any part of Palestine for over twenty-five years when they signed the Oslo Accords. None of them had any idea of what Israel's occupation regime and its vast settlement project actually looked and felt like, even if some of them had an intellectual understanding of their import. Israel's assassination of Abu Jihad in Tunis in 1988 had deprived the PLO of the leader who was the most engaged with and aware of the situation of Palestinians under occupation.[61] The assassination of Abu Iyyad three years later by a gunman from the Abu Nidal terrorist group deprived 'Arafat of the last of his peers who could stand up to the increasingly autocratic *khityar,* or Old Man, as his associates increasingly called him.[62] The remaining PLO leaders were fatally unaware of just how deeply Israel was entrenched in the occupied territories. Hanan Ashrawi put it bluntly: "It is clear that those who initiated this agreement have not lived under occupation."[63]

The PLO leaders were also insufficiently aware of the degree to which successive Israeli governments were committed to the Begin autonomy formula, or of the absolute rigidity of this scheme. Moreover, they initially underestimated the high degree of coordination between successive US administrations and Israeli governments, suspicious although they were of both. Their failure to benefit from the expertise and experience that the delegation in Washington had painstakingly accumulated was a grievous mistake, as was their naïve dependence on biased Norwegian mediators at Oslo.[64] So was their failure to employ in Oslo the kind of legal, diplomatic, linguistic, and technical expertise essential to a diplomatic negotiation that was accumulated over twenty-one months in Madrid and Washington. All these factors contributed to the fiasco of the Oslo Accords for the Palestinians.

If one can understand some of the reasons, many of them discreditable ones, that led the PLO leadership to make these decisions, it is often difficult to understand why Yitzhak Rabin took some of the decisions he did. He retained Begin's inflexible framework for autonomy, although he made other changes that Shamir and Begin would never have made, such as negotiating with and ultimately recognizing the PLO, and allowing PLO forces into the occupied territories to perform police functions. However, as evidence of how Rabin himself perceived these police functions and Palestinian autonomy generally, we have the words of Major General Shlomo Gazit, former chief of military intelligence and a close associate of Rabin's. Gazit was also the lead negotiator, on behalf of Rabin, in the confidential backchannel pre-Oslo talks regarding the security arrangements for the occupied territories involving the PLO discussed earlier in this chapter. At a later public event, Gazit responded as follows to a question about Yasser 'Arafat that appeared to irritate him: "Arafat has a choice: he can be a Lahd or a super-Lahd."[65] The reference was to General Antoine Lahd, puppet commander of the collaborationist South Lebanese Army, which performed colonial police functions for the Israeli army of occupation in South Lebanon. Like France's Algerian *harki* auxiliaries in 1962, this force collapsed when Israel abandoned its occupation of the region in 2000. These were presumably similar to the functions Gazit and Rabin foresaw 'Arafat's PLO forces playing in the West Bank and Gaza Strip in the context of Palestinian autonomy (later formally dubbed the Palestinian Authority [PA]). In view of this revealing comment, it is worth reflecting on what kind of "autonomy" the two men envisioned for the PA.

Further dooming any possibility of change, Rabin kept in place the personnel chosen by the Shamir government to negotiate with the Palestinians, notably the pro-settler Beginist lawyer, Ambassador Elyakim Rubinstein, today at the top of his profession as an Israeli High Court justice. Rubinstein was a constant source of Palestinian complaints for his bland coldness toward everything the Palestinians put forth, and his fierce, unbending ideological rigidity (he declared to the Palestinians during one round of negotiations that "a Palestinian State [was] considered by Israel a mortal security threat").[66] By way of contrast, Rabin changed the Israeli personnel dealing with Syria, installing as head of that negotiating team his newly appointed ambassador to the United States, Itamar Rabinovich, who was a close personal friend and sometime tennis partner. Rabinovich was a noted academic whose expertise was on Syria under the Ba'th Party, and was also a senior reserve officer in Israeli military intelligence. His appointment had an immediate positive effect on negotiations with the Syrians, which came very close to an agreement during Rabin's tenure in office.

As far as negotiations with the Palestinians were concerned, meanwhile, with Begin's basic framework unchanged, and Shamir's personnel in place, Rabin shackled himself (perhaps willingly?) to a rigid recipe. This was drawn in part from Rabin's own unique military and security background, as well as from Begin's ideologically rooted concepts and the language rooted in them, but in any case it guaranteed failure in dealing with the Palestinians.[67] 'Arafat, for his part, in the end refused to "be a Lahd." As the manner of his decline and demise shows, he paid dearly for his temerity in insisting on going beyond the circumscribed and humiliating role that Rabin, Gazit, and their senior colleagues in the Israeli security establishment coldly envisioned for him and his fellow leaders of the PLO.

While the Rabin government and the PLO leadership were largely responsible for this outcome, the main burden of this chapter has been to show that it was also very largely the result of long-standing positions taken by several US administrations. These included support of an inflexible Israeli stand regarding the Palestinians, support that has wavered little now for several decades. Such support was often extended largely because of concern about domestic American political considerations. This was linked to an excessive attentiveness by American officials to the domestic dynamics of Israeli politics, which, as has been shown, these "experts" in fact often poorly understood. But their insistence on not pushing beyond what they wrongly perceived to be unbreachable Israeli "red lines," in keeping with the spirit of Kissinger's secret 1975 memo, had the effect of hamstringing US diplomacy. Indeed, as a result of their excessive solicitude with respect to Israel's position, we have seen that at times American officials took a more "Israeli" line than even the Israelis themselves. One example of the excessive zeal of American mediators, discussed previously, was the wording of their so-called "bridging proposal" of May 1993. That essentially very little has changed in American policy on Palestine over multiple administrations can be seen from a confidential PLO memo prepared twelve years later, before a 2005 meeting during the George W. Bush administration. Referring to a draft American paper, the PLO memo stated: "It is almost verbatim the Israeli non-paper submitted November 9th 2005 just before the Agreement on Movement and Access [AMA] was agreed, with which Palestinians adamantly disagree. In fact, Israel had moved well beyond these positions by the time the AMA was concluded."[68] Twelve years later, American negotiators were once again so reluctant to be seen as out front of the Israeli position that they were even less forthcoming toward the Palestinians than the Israelis themselves.

These factors were coupled with what had become almost routine American unconcern about the possible reactions of Arab states. This unconcern was fully justified. At no point during the negotiations I have just discussed was there any evidence of serious pressure from the Arab states to move the United States to be more flexible with the Palestinians or tougher with the Israelis. Often, it was quite the contrary: at one point during the 1991–93 negotiations in Washington, an American diplomat told his Palestinian interlocutors that if they did not accept a specific offer, the United States could ask its Arab "friends" to put financial pressure on the PLO.[69] Whether this was a bluff or just routine diplomatic blackmail is not apparent, but the implication is clear: the Gulf Arab regimes, which had in the past helped finance the PLO, were closer "friends" of the United States than they were of the Palestinians. This was undoubtedly true in any case, and had been since at least 1945.

The United States' demonstrated bias in favor of Israel was rarely matched by concern for (or indeed knowledge of on the part of its supposed "experts") the acute political constraints on Palestinian leaders. There was constant pressure on the Palestinians to accept Israeli positions, evidence of which can be found in virtually every set of minutes of every meeting between Palestinians and Israelis to which I have had access.[70] Their bias in favor of Israel and disregard for Palestinian aims and constraints led American policymakers to lose sight of the forest for the trees, and thus to ignore the basic elements necessary for a lasting peace, even as they obsessed about details of the negotiating process. Indeed, process became a substitute for real movement toward peace. This is not new in American policy and frequently reached the level of outright deception. The words of Richard Nixon speaking of the Arabs to Henry Kissinger in 1973 could have been spoken by many of his successors, had they been as brutally frank as the thirty-seventh president of the United States: "You've got to give them the hope. It's really a—frankly, let's face it: you've got to make them think that there's some motion; that something is going on; that we're really doing our best with the Israelis."[71] Precisely the same obsession with process and creating the false impression of movement can be found in the handiwork of policymakers from Kissinger through Dennis Ross and Condoleezza Rice.

The Oslo Accords and their sequels, erected on the flawed basis and using the skewed language that emerged from the American-brokered Camp David negotiations in 1978 and the Madrid/Washington talks in 1991–93, thus not only failed to produce a just and lasting peace between Palestinians and Israelis. This sequence of agreements arguably made achieving such a peace much more difficult. By indefinitely delaying a resolution of any of these core issues, while allowing uninterrupted expansion of Israeli settlements and of Israel's control of the occupied territories—as all the while the cumbersome wheels of the "peace process" never ceased to turn—these accords gravely exacerbated the deepest problems between the two sides. American policy thus helped measurably to squander any possibilities for peace that might have been opened up by the historic convening of the Madrid Peace Conference.

III

# THE THIRD MOMENT: BARACK OBAMA
# AND PALESTINE, 2009-12

*But understand this as well: America's commitment to Israel's security is
unshakable. Our friendship with Israel is deep and enduring. And so we
believe that any lasting peace must acknowledge the very real security concerns that Israel faces every single day.*

*Let us be honest with ourselves: Israel is surrounded by neighbors that
have waged repeated wars against it. Israel's citizens have been killed by
rockets fired at their houses and suicide bombs on their buses. Israel's
children come of age knowing that throughout the region, other children
are taught to hate them. Israel, a small country of less than eight million
people, looks out at a world where leaders of much larger nations threaten
to wipe it off of the map. The Jewish people carry the burden of centuries
of exile and persecution, and fresh memories of knowing that six million
people were killed simply because of who they are. Those are facts. They
cannot be denied.*

—BARACK OBAMA, BEFORE THE UN GENERAL ASSEMBLY,

SEPTEMBER 21, 2011[1]

In the past, zealots have castigated a number of American presidents for
their alleged lack of sufficient enthusiasm for the cause of Zionism and
Israel. Presidents Eisenhower, Nixon, Carter, and the elder George Bush
were all accused at one time or another of sharing this supposed failing.
But no chief executive has been reviled in this regard quite as viciously
or as systematically as has Barack Obama. In part, this is a function of
garden-variety bigotry. Obama is the first American president of African ancestry, he is the first to be descended from a parent of Muslim
heritage, and he is the first to bear Muslim names: Barack, meaning

blessed in Swahili (from the Arabic word *baraka,* or "blessing"), and Hussein, the name of the grandson of the Prophet Muhammad. To those for whom identity explains everything, these three "incriminating" facts are more than sufficient to brand him as irreconcilably anti-Israel, or perhaps even anti-Semitic.

Beyond the issues related to Obama's identity, there were his allegedly ominous links during his Chicago days to a range of supposed radicals, from his pastor, the Reverend Jeremiah Wright, to University of Illinois Professor Bill Ayers. He was familiar with such individuals when he was their neighbor in Hyde Park, an Illinois state senator, and a member of the University of Chicago Law School faculty. As the representative in the Illinois Senate of a district including much of the South Side of Chicago, he had also frequented and solicited support from local community groups, including those of the Arab community, a part of which resided in his constituency. These relationships—suitably distorted, inflated, and exaggerated by the popular media—were the basis for a barrage of vituperative attacks on Obama (and on these individuals and groups) from the outset of the 2008 presidential campaign. Sad to say, not all of these onslaughts came from the usual suspects: right-wing Zionists, the increasingly dominant radically conservative wing of the Republican Party, and the privileged podium both enjoy in the Rupert Murdoch–owned media; indeed, they started with Democrats.[2]

To Obama's detractors, I was one of these "suspect" individuals, linked to Obama because I was a colleague of his at the University of Chicago, lived in the same Hyde Park neighborhood, and because our families at times socialized together. The fact that I am of Palestinian descent, and that I had frequently publicly expressed opinions supportive of Palestinian rights and critical of Israeli policies, was more than enough for them to brand Obama by association as a fervent opponent of Israel, tainted by bad company. I have avoided as best I could this fetid swamp of seamy insinuations in the past, and will refrain from wading into it here or elsewhere. Most of these allegations are falsehoods that do not withstand even the most cursory investigation,[3] and a few of them are downright ludicrous. I described them to the *Washington Post* as an "idiot wind" toward the end of the 2008 presidential campaign, and that description still stands.[4]

However, I think it is important to stress that the barrage of partisan accusations against Obama for being insufficiently "pro-Israel,"[5] of which the instances mentioned above are just samples, has succeeded in distracting many from an underlying reality that is quite important. As we shall see, it has in fact served to mask the high degree of continuity in a number of basic respects between Obama's positions on Palestine and Israel and those of four of his five immediate predecessors in the Oval Office (the notable exception in several, but not all, respects was George W. Bush, about whom more later).

Careful examination of the record shows that the Obama administration in fact followed very much the same trajectory in dealing with Palestine and Israel as most previous administrations over the past thirty-five years, specifically those of Carter, Reagan, the senior George Bush, and Clinton, which were discussed in greater or lesser detail in the previous two chapters. There are considerable differences in this regard between the actions of Obama and his four immediate predecessors and those of the George W. Bush administration.[6] Many changes have taken place in the situation on the ground in the Middle East and in US policy over these decades. But with the singular exception of the last Bush administration, there was a high degree of similarity in how each of these presidents and their advisors initially assessed the situation in the Middle East, and came to the conclusion that certain key adjustments in US policy were necessary, notably vis-à-vis the Palestinians.

All four of these administrations and that of Obama attempted to push in some small way beyond the cocoon of platitudes reassuring to the Israeli government and its American supporters. They all sought to go ever so slightly beyond the core immobilism in American policy that is basically devoted by its proponents to maintaining the status quo of Israeli domination over the Palestinians—all of this couched in flatulent rhetoric about the sanctity of the "peace process." As they attempted to challenge at the margins this rigid set of policy prescriptions, senior officials in all these administrations were frustrated by the same obstacles we have seen arise since the time of Truman. Beyond dogged resistance from a succession of Israeli governments, these obstacles included solid backing in Congress and much of the media for the status quo of US support for whatever Israel considers to be in its all-important "security" interests, whether this facilitated peace or not. They included as well consistently poor advice from high-level "experts" within the government, much of it designed to avoid rocking the boat and thereby maintain this pernicious status quo. Perhaps the most important obstacle was the old problem of the absence of any significant counterweight, whether within the American political system or internationally, that could overcome the powerful inertia that for decade after decade has kept US policy on essentially the same tracks leading toward futility and failure where peacemaking between Palestinians and Israelis is concerned. No domestic group, and no foreign actors, whether Palestinian, Arab, or other, proved able to exert countervailing pressures to match this increasingly formidable constellation of obstructionist forces. The situation of the Obama administration differed little from that of four of its five predecessors in all of these respects.

In Obama's case, he faced a number of specific obstacles to an attempt to recalibrate policy toward the Palestinians. The first was the arrival in power in Israel in February 2009 of a strongly pro-settler coalition government dominated by the Likud Party and headed by Binyamin Netanyahu. This took place just a month after Obama's inauguration, and his administration thereafter floundered in its attempts to deal with the very hard line taken by Netanyahu. Another obstacle was the Republicans' victory in the House of Representatives in the 2010 midterm elections. Their capture of the House considerably strengthened Netanyahu's ability to resist the president, in view of the ideological proximity between Likud and the right-wing Tea Party and neoconservative agendas that now had significant sway in the Republican Party. A third was the enduring, profound, and destructive split in Palestinian ranks between Fateh and Hamas, and therefore between the West Bank and the Gaza Strip, dominated by rival "Palestinian Authorities." American and Israeli policy had in the past worked tirelessly to exacerbate this division, on the pretext, by now fully enshrined in US law, that Hamas was a "terrorist" group and therefore beyond the pale. This split made a unified consensus on Palestinian strategy, and therefore successful ne-gotiations, impossible. It's easy to see why a divided and feeble Palestin-ian leadership was useful to Israeli governments: that weakness made it easier for the Israeli side to win concessions from the Palestinians dur-ing negotiations, or to postpone them. It is harder to see how it served the stated American interest in a negotiated solution to the conflict. A final obstacle was the continued unwillingness of the conservative Arab coalition headed by Saudi Arabia to exert itself over the Palestine ques-tion in any significant positive way. The situation was exacerbated by the growing divisions, instability, and discord throughout the Middle East as a result of the Arab Spring, the Syrian civil war, and the bur-geoning controversy over the Iranian nuclear program. These troubling and interconnected developments preoccupied the US administration and complicated its efforts to focus on Palestinian-Israeli matters. I will return to the specific obstacles the new president faced.

However, delving into the Obama administration's performance re-garding policy over Palestine constitutes a very different challenge than was posed in discussing previous administrations. The events I have analyzed so far took place relatively far back in the past—1991, after all, is a full generation ago, before nearly all of the undergraduate students I teach today were born. By contrast, from here on in I will be discussing primarily events that are still in progress, and the policy of an adminis-tration that is still in office as these words are being written, and whose performance is still evolving, with outcomes that can only be guessed at. That performance will ultimately be judged historically on the basis of events and actions that very well may be far in the future. In other words, while the administrations of Truman, Carter, Reagan, Bush senior, and Clinton are already well in the past, and can with relative ease be subjected to at least an initial historical assessment, the Obama administration is in some measure still a work in progress. It is thus something of a moving target for a historian, even one like myself with some experience in dealing with peculiar problems of understanding the modern and contemporary periods.

Secondly, my discussion of the policies of earlier administrations was mainly grounded in unpublished or recently published official sources, which were either publicly available after declassification, or were in my possession as a participant in the events I described. What follows is almost entirely dependent on the public statements of leading officials of the Obama administration, and journalistic interviews with them.[7] Notwithstanding both of these caveats, there is a sufficient basis to posit certain preliminary conclusions about the track record of the Obama administration regarding the Palestinians and its efforts to achieve peace between them and the Israelis. This in turn will make possible a brief extrapolation of certain broader lessons about the United States, Israel, and Palestine from that record and those of the five previous administrations.

In its essentials, the entire public record of Barack Obama on the Palestine question and Israel is quite limited: it basically goes back to his campaign for election to the US Senate in 2004, in which year he burst upon the national scene with a keynote speech at the Democratic National Convention. Before this date, although Obama taught at the University of Chicago Law School and had other professional experience, his political resume included only seven years as an Illinois state senator and an unsuccessful 2000 Democratic primary run for the US House seat of incumbent Bobby Rush in Illinois' First Congressional District. These were not situations that required him to take a public position on any aspects of US foreign policy, and with rare exceptions—like his by now famous speech opposing the Iraq war in October 2002—he did not do so.[8] So before his campaign for the US Senate in 2004, this was a man with very few publicly expressed views on Palestine, Israel, or Middle Eastern issues generally.[9]

Obama's public record from that point onward can be roughly divided into three phases. The first encompasses the five or so years of his career spent as a candidate for the US Senate, as the junior United States senator from Illinois, and as a presidential candidate, from roughly 2003 until he was elected president in November 2008. The second phase includes the first year and a half of his presidency, when Obama appeared to be trying a new approach to the problem of Palestine and Israel, in parallel with aspects of what we have seen that Presidents Carter, Reagan, Bush senior, and Clinton had tried and failed to do. That effort lasted roughly until the Republican Party's capture of the House of Representatives in the midterm elections of November 2010. That victory significantly changed the political situation in Washington where Israel was concerned, measurably strengthening both Netanyahu and Israel's lobby there, and thereby effectively stymieing the president. By the time of the midterm elections, the Obama administration had already entered its third phase, one of retreat from the mildly adventurous positions on Palestine it had taken in its first two years, and a return to the unthinking orthodoxy that normally prevails in Washington where Palestine is concerned. This phase extends down to the moment of this writing, in the fall of 2012.

Before around 2004, therefore, Barack Obama had no foreign policy record to speak of, let alone a record on Palestine and Israel.[10] This was the case although he was knowledgeable about the world in certain important respects, indeed considerably more so than some previous US presidents (emphatically including his immediate predecessor in the White House). Very simply, this was because unlike many US presidents, who had little knowledge of the world and were relatively insular in terms of their experience and worldviews when they came into office,[11] Barack Obama had not only seen the world, he had lived in the world. More than that, he had personal experience of cultures other than that of the United States, and he had immediate relatives, such as his half sisters and brothers, who had grown up in different countries around the world. And the parts of the world he had seen and was familiar with were not just the standard ones for most Americans: western Europe, Canada, Mexico, and the Caribbean. Thus not only was he the first American president of African descent, he was also perhaps the first (since the founding fathers, who grew up under the British crown) who had spent some of his formative years living outside the United States of America, notably four years in Indonesia.

However, although Barack Obama from his early years had a certain sense of the world that constitutes an unusual background for a US president, his experiences thereafter were almost entirely within the United States, and all of his adult political experiences were restricted to the American domestic sphere, up to and including his seven-year tenure as an Illinois state senator. Where Palestinian-Israeli issues are concerned, all there is to examine, therefore, is a record dating back for a relatively brief period of no more than five or six years before he became president.[12] For historians to analyze the policies of this presidency as it should be done,[13] and eventually one day will be done, would require the declassification of official documents and access to those individuals closest to Obama over the past eight or nine years, combined with their willingness to see their recollections and assessments published.[14] Neither of these things seems imminent at this moment. Since we ordinary mortals cannot see into people's souls, we are restricted to the on-the-record declarations on this topic by this president and by those speaking on his behalf over a period of a few short years.

Much has been written and said in the media about the striking contrast between Obama's approach during the second and third phases I have outlined, that is to say between his first year and a half in office, and then the most recent period, broadly since the 2010 elections. This commentary has focused on the new president's supposed willingness to modify radically US policy on Palestine immediately after he came into office, as symbolized by his giving speeches in Istanbul and Cairo during his first months in office, although as we shall see, these speeches actually contained little or nothing that was really new as far as US policy on Palestine was concerned.[15] Many observers have contrasted this approach with Obama's subsequent retreat from his earlier posture, leading to his administration's return to a more conventional "pro-Israel" stance over approximately the past two years. However, before examining this contrast, which was less dramatic than some pretended, but which does mirror the abortive reassessments of Palestine policy we have seen with the four previous administrations already discussed, it is necessary to say a few words about those earlier years when US senator Obama and presidential candidate Obama had not yet given way to the man who became the forty-fourth president of the United States. This is important because even a brief recap reveals a high degree of continuity in some of Obama's publicly enunciated views on key issues throughout the entirety of the past nine or so years, from the moment when he first came to have a public record on aspects of the Palestinian-Israeli issue. This is particularly true of those of his opinions that are clearly rooted in core elements of the Israel-centric narrative about the Middle East that permeates and dominates public and political discourse in the United States.[16]

Crucially, since Barack Obama first publicly stated his views on this topic, he has always accepted a constant, central element of Israel's self-presentation: its victim status, to which it has always clung fiercely and aggressively. In his public statements he has always accepted as well a related proposition, dear in particular to the heart of Binyamin Netanyahu, the Israeli right wing, and its followers in the United States, but widely believed farther afield: that the state of Israel and the Israeli people, indeed the entire Jewish people, are in a state of perpetual existential danger. For many of those who hold these views, it always seems as if another Holocaust is just around the corner, new Nazis lurk everywhere, successors to Neville Chamberlain are alive and well and stalk the land, and another Munich is always imminent. In this charged atmosphere, which evokes and keeps alive past episodes of danger and dread for the Jewish people, Iran is continually portrayed as being on the point of acquiring nuclear weapons that it would not hesitate to unleash against Israel, along with a hail of missiles fired from Lebanon and the Gaza Strip by Iranian proxies. In such a context, not only Israel's security, but its very existence, is viewed as perpetually in the balance.[17] Such propositions retain their currency for some irrespective of real-world strategic balances and rational assessments of material factors. They would include, but not be restricted to, Israel's potent deterrent capabilities based on its possession of hundreds of nuclear warheads married to lethal air-, land-, and sea-based delivery systems that also have impressive conventional capabilities; its thriving first-world economy and enviably advanced world-class technological base; and its seemingly unshakable and uniquely close alliance with the greatest economic and military power in world history.

If we were to try to determine where Obama's own views on these matters came from, we would likely find that they are a result of his interactions, especially since he began his bid for US Senate, and in some cases before, with major political and financial supporters who are strongly committed to Israel's well-being.[18] These backers ensured that in 2006 and 2008 he took carefully organized guided tours of Israel, of the kind deemed obligatory for politicians aspiring to higher office: in the words of a *New York Times* article, "The trips have a reputation as being the standard-bearer for foreign Congressional travel. 'We call it the Jewish Disneyland trip,' said one pro-Israel advocate."[19] Many of these backers, and others with whom Obama associated as he became more and more of a national figure, sincerely believe in this apocalyptic vision of the dangers facing Israel. These are the deep-rooted beliefs of a broad segment of Americans, including much of the American political class, notably the right wing of both parties, and especially of a large and growing number of evangelical Christians. Those who hold them seem to be unaware of, or ignore, the fact that Israel today is not a tiny, vulnerable island amid seas of disciplined, fanatical, competent Arabo-Muslims, if ever it was. It is rather a formidable regional superpower bristling with lethal weapons in the hands of an army with great expertise, and much experience, in using them. Far from being defenseless, Israel has for most of its existence struck fear into its weak, relatively poorly armed, underdeveloped, and disorganized neighbors. None of these neighbors, *without exception,* singly or united, are particularly dreaded by Israel's tough and seasoned generals, however much fear-mongering Israeli, and American, politicians may engage in.[20]

Those who hold these beliefs certainly do not perceive that however daunting may be the actual dangers Israel faces, many of them are of its own creation.[21] More to the point, *none* of the bogeymen most advertised in this regard—whether Iran, terrorism, Islamic fanaticism, Hizballah, the "demographic threat," or the much-touted menace of "delegitimization/lawfare," about which more later—are in fact truly existential threats to it, since they do not have the capability to end the existence of the people and state of Israel. This is because of the simple fact that none of these menaces has anything like the capability to "destroy" Israel, whatever the ill intentions of those animating them may be. Nevertheless, the specter of Israel's imminent destruction, against a background of earlier episodes of extermination and genocidal violence against Jews ranging from the depredations of Nebuchadnezzar and Titus to those of Hitler, is incessantly and obsessively invoked by those for whom these ideas are central to their worldview. Centered around the seminal event of the Holocaust,[22] this has become a key trope in the socialization and indoctrination of Israelis, visitors to Israel, and others.[23]

It is important to recognize that these anxieties, exaggerated though they may be, are linked for many (especially in the older generation) to profound, deeply rooted, and genuine fears, fears that flow from an acute consciousness of the tragedies that have marked Jewish history over millennia. Zionism is, among other things, a response to these fears. No one would seriously deny that even if irrational or inflated, fears can become powerful political realities and must be dealt with as such. But they are notoriously susceptible to exploitation by politicians, and they must *never* be confused, as they are by too many people, with the situation in the real world. Barack Obama may or may not share the depth with which some of the more fervent supporters of Israel hold such beliefs (his equanimity and his cool affect in these matters—as in others—may indicate that he does not). This is not particularly relevant, however, since in any case he has publicly professed, with monotonous regularity, the view that Israel is at existential risk—doing so for the past four years from the bully pulpit of the presidency of the United States of America—and more importantly, he has taken actions that are based on this view.

Thus the trope of a tiny, vulnerable Israel constantly faced with annihilation has recurred again and again in Obama's public utterances, including notably the 2011 speech he delivered before the United Nations General Assembly, and from which is taken the epigraph to this chapter. In one paragraph of that speech he stated that "Israel is surrounded by neighbors that have waged repeated wars against it," and that "leaders of much larger nations threaten to wipe it off of the map," and he referred poignantly to the long years of persecution of the Jewish people culminating in the Holocaust. The same theme figured in Obama's speech in March 2012 to the leading formation of the Israel lobby, the American Israel Public Affairs Committee (AIPAC). In that speech, Obama used the evocative and emotional phrase "Israel's destruction" twice in two consecutive sentences.[24]

It is important to stress that this emphasis is not new, and that it has in fact been a staple of Obama's rhetoric on the Middle East since he became a national figure. Similar language featured prominently in most of his other public pronouncements on the topic, going all the way back to his first speech to AIPAC, in June 2008, just a day after he had clinched the Democratic presidential nomination. That speech movingly invoked the Holocaust while repeating key variations from the Israeli playbook on the theme of a tiny, beleaguered Israel. These included references to "leaders committed to Israel's destruction," "textbooks filled with hate for Jews," "rockets raining down on Sderot," and Israeli children needing to "summon uncommon courage every time they board a bus."[25] Needless to say, the passage, and indeed the entire oration, contained not a word about the Palestinians or any unpleasant things that may have happened, or may be happening, to them.

In this respect, the numerous speeches that Obama gave to such pro-Israel domestic audiences were different from the more "balanced" discourse of his Cairo speech. And yet however balanced it may have been, the Cairo speech, while designed to reach out to Muslims, told its Egyptian listeners much more about the awful things that had befallen Israel and the Jewish people than about the sufferings of the Palestinians. Obama said in Cairo:

America's strong bonds with Israel are well known. This bond is unbreakable. It is based upon cultural and historical ties, and the recognition that the aspiration for a Jewish homeland is rooted in a tragic history that cannot be denied. Around the world, the Jewish people were persecuted for centuries, and anti-Semitism in Europe culminated in an unprecedented Holocaust. Tomorrow, I will visit Buchenwald, which was part of a network of camps where Jews were enslaved, tortured, shot and gassed to death by the Third Reich. Six million Jews were killed—more than the entire Jewish population of Israel today. Denying that fact is baseless, it is ignorant, and it is hateful. Threatening

Israel with destruction—or repeating vile stereotypes about Jews—is deeply wrong, and only serves to evoke in the minds of Israelis this most painful of memories while preventing the peace that the people of this region deserve.[26]

The subsequent section setting out the travails of the Palestinians was shorter and far less impassioned or detailed. We will come back to other important aspects of the Cairo speech, but it constitutes part of a pattern involving a constant emphasis on the idea of Israel as a victim, irrespective of the audience. By contrast, on the very rare occasions when he has addressed himself to domestic Arab American organizations, Obama has been considerably less forthcoming in saying what his listeners want to hear than he has been in his repeated appearances before AIPAC and similar pro-Israel groups.[27] There is no reason to believe that the familiar trope of an outnumbered, beleaguered, and constantly endangered Israel is not an integral part of Obama's worldview, since he has reiterated it for many years, indeed since the moment he arrived on the national stage, and has acted on this basis repeatedly as a US senator and as president.[28]

It goes without saying that if a country is considered to be so vulnerable as to be confronting perpetual existential danger, and as having teetered on the brink of imminent destruction since the moment of its creation, almost anything is permitted to it, and much can be forgiven it. It is vital to emphasize that this trope, although it may be sincerely believed by many of those who incessantly invoke it, is based on an essentially false understanding of history. Notwithstanding the fears of many Israelis and their supporters (and the fierce but hollow rhetoric of some Arab leaders), it is rarely noted that contemporary American military and intelligence officials dispassionately considered that excepting the desperate 1948 conflict, which it nevertheless handily won in the end, Israel did not face destruction in any of its five subsequent major wars. This was not the case in 1967, nor even in the closely fought war of 1973, and certainly not in the 1956 Suez War, the 1969–70 War of Attrition, and the 1982 invasion of Lebanon.[29]

Similarly, in spite of the current fears about Iran that have been cynically stoked by Israeli politicians and that are constantly amplified by their political allies on the American Right, US intelligence and military assessments about the real dangers posed to Israel by Iran are sanguine and decidedly nonalarmist.[30] (They are echoed by the assessments of most of their professional Israeli counterparts).[31] Why are such distortions spread so assiduously, assuming that political leaders in power are capable of reading the reports, present and past, of their intelligence services and their top military brass? It is partly because some genuinely subscribe to the apocalyptic worldview that sees the survival of Israel and the Jewish people as perpetually threatened. But it is also perhaps partly because this trope of imminent destruction effectively constitutes a sort of free pass for Israel that covers a multitude of sins, and allows it to get away with behavior that otherwise would universally be considered outrageous and impermissible. Whether Obama believes these distortions or not, by repeating such profoundly false ideas, the president has considerably exacerbated his own dilemma in dealing with the Palestine-Israel issue.

As a graduate of Columbia and Harvard, who formerly taught constitutional law at the University of Chicago Law School, and as a consummate communicator, the president himself is undoubtedly fully aware of the valence of his words. Given his worldliness, he also is unquestionably able to see the gap between the fantasies he has been repeating about Israel's purported vulnerability and the hard truths on this matter conveyed in the confidential assessments he has been getting from US government agencies. It goes without saying that it is the weight of domestic political realities—and the fact that in consequence of these political realities, falsehoods have been erected into eternal verities in the mind of much of the public—that brings Obama to say what he says, in spite of what he may know, on this and other matters pertaining to Palestine and Israel.

Obama's ability to reflect what his permanent officials tell him, and to use his words carefully, was apparent in an exclusive interview the president gave to Jeffrey Goldberg that was published in the *Atlantic* in March 2012, on the eve of the annual AIPAC national meeting and a crucial visit by Israeli prime minister Netanyahu to Washington. This visit came at the height of yet another of several waves of pressure on the president from Israel and its supporters to take an even more aggressive posture against Iran. It coincided with a moment when public threats to launch a preemptive attack on Iran were being made with almost monotonous regularity by both Netanyahu and his hawkish defense minister, Ehud Barak. Obama's intervention at this time was intended to accomplish a specific vital goal, that of countering this mounting pressure, and to reach a specific set of key audiences. The president and his advisors may have estimated that this could only be achieved by an exclusive interview given to a journalist to whom Obama had spoken before, and whose street credibility (and limitations) where this topic was concerned was in part derived from his previous service as an Israeli Army prison guard over Palestinian detainees.[32] Referring to his 2011 UN speech, Obama told Goldberg: "It's hard for me to be clearer than I was in front of the UN General Assembly, when I made a more full-throated defense of Israel and its legitimate security concerns than any president in history—not, by the way, in front of an audience that was particularly warm to the message."[33] Obama went even further in his "full-throated" defense of Israel's security interests in a speech to AIPAC a few days later, in March 2012, when he said: "Four years ago, I stood before you and said that, 'Israel's security is sacrosanct. It is nonnegotiable.' That belief has guided my actions as president. The fact is my administration's commitment to Israel's security has been unprecedented."[34] This is a very far-reaching remark, involving extraordinary language (e.g., "sacrosanct"). It is particularly striking given how elastic and all encompassing Israel's definition of its "security" has always been, and the wide range of forms of domination it has practiced under that rubric, as discussed at the outset of this book. In this light, it is worth reflecting on Edmund Burke's remarks about a colonial situation with not a few parallels to that of Palestine, and where the subjugation of one people by another was also justified by a claim of insecurity: Ireland. Speaking of British rule over that country, he wrote: "All the penal laws of that unparalleled code of oppression . . . were manifestly the effects of national hatred and scorn towards a conquered people, whom the victors delighted to trample upon, and were not at all afraid to provoke. They were not the effect of their fears, but of their security."[35]

As we have seen from the passage from his 2011 General Assembly speech quoted in the epigraph to this chapter, Obama was absolutely right in his estimation of the fervency of his "full-throated defense" of Israel. Of dozens of US presidential speeches to the UN General Assembly referring to the Middle East (including two earlier ones by Obama himself), it was unquestionably the one that most completely and ardently reproduced the core elements of the Israeli master narrative. Such boilerplate language, meant to resonate deeply with all those who shared that narrative view, is normally reserved for highly partisan American audiences like AIPAC conferences, for select political campaign events, even for the US Congress and most of the mainstream media. As we have seen, in his first few years on the national stage, Obama had repeated such rhetoric regularly, but mainly in these entirely domestic contexts. It is true that important elements of it were present in his Cairo speech, but that was there alongside much else, as we shall see. Now, in September 2011, Obama had made this essentially domestic discourse the international line of the United States. As he himself stated to AIPAC on March 4, 2012, regarding his UN speech: "No president has made such a clear statement about our support for Israel at the United Nations at such a difficult time. People usually give those speeches before audiences like this one—not the General Assembly."[36]

Obama's defense of his own much-attacked record where Israel is concerned, from the interview with Goldberg, is worth quoting at length:

I actually think the relationship is very functional, and the proof of the pudding is in the eating. The fact of the matter is, we've gotten a lot of business done with Israel over the last three years. I think the prime minister—and certainly the defense minister—would acknowledge that we've never had closer military and intelligence cooperation. When you look at what I've done with respect to security for Israel, from joint training and joint exercises that outstrip anything that's been done in the past, to helping finance and construct the Iron Dome program to make sure that Israeli families are less vulnerable to missile strikes, to ensuring that Israel maintains its qualitative military edge, to fighting back against delegitimization of Israel, whether at the [UN] Human Rights Council, or in front of the UN General Assembly, or during the Goldstone Report, or after the flare-up involving the flotilla—the truth of the matter is that the relationship has functioned very well.[37]

It should be clear from careful study of this litany of quite considerable accomplishments in support of Israel that the Obama administration may have been just as ardently pro-Israel (if not more so) as the last several of its predecessors where actual policy initiatives are concerned. This is true notwithstanding the disaffection that developed between the president and the vocal ultra-zealous element of the pro-Israel community in the United States—a disaffection that has been eagerly exploited by opportunistic right-wing Republicans. The alienation from Obama of a major segment of outspoken supporters of Israel has been measurably increased by a nakedly partisan spirit fanned by avid supporters of Israel like the Virginia Republican Eric Cantor, who since January 2011 has been the influential House majority leader. One might ask why these fervent advocates of Israel are so critical of Obama if he was in fact so supportive of Israel. To understand these criticisms and also the disaffection of a large number of Israelis from Obama, it is necessary to go back to the early moves that Obama made on the Palestine question, which alarmed these constituencies, and also to look at some of the profound shifts that have taken place in the interstices of American and Israeli domestic politics in recent years.

Despite his strong and unequivocal support for Israel, Obama is frequently portrayed as not having done enough for this American ally. Many Republicans and other fervent supporters of Israel espouse rhetoric demanding that there be "no daylight" between the United States and Israel, on top of the assertion that the president has "thrown Israel under the bus."[38] The latter phrase was used repeatedly by Mitt Romney, notably during the Republican presidential primary debates in Florida in January 2012, in regard to the Obama administration's assertion that the 1967 frontiers were the basis for any negotiation of frontiers—a heretofore utterly conventional US policy position.

It is worth reflecting on precisely what is being said and done here. Some Republicans, in close coordination with the Israeli government and its Washington lobby, are saying that a Democratic administration should follow exactly the same line as does an American ally and not allow any visible differences between the two. They are in effect supporting a foreign government over their own on questions of foreign policy, indeed on weighty questions of war and peace. Further, attempts by the United States government to assert traditional US policies are described by them as amounting to a hostile act against this ally. It is becoming increasingly clear from these and other instances that Israel represents a realm where politics does not stop at the water's edge, as has traditionally been the case with foreign policy: quite the contrary, the domestic politics of the United States and Israel are today deeply intertwined. Indeed, the two political systems are becoming interpenetrated. This should be no surprise, in view of the two-way flow between the two countries of political, media, and strategic consultants, contributions to political campaigns,[39] funding for think tanks,[40] and the influence of big money on the media.[41] There is thus almost no longer a significant distinction between "foreign" and "domestic" policy where Israel is concerned (Truman's handling of the Palestine issue suggests that already in 1945–48 there never was such a distinction in some respects).

It has long been the case that the United States was heavily involved in the internal politics of many Middle Eastern states, including Israel, as we have seen in a couple of cases. This current now flows both ways, with a shrewd Israeli politician like Netanyahu in effect inserting himself into American politics, as is evidenced by his increasingly partisan speeches to an ever more welcoming US Congress. His speech before a joint session of Congress on May 24, 2011, received thirty-five standing ovations.[42] It is reported that Democratic Congresswoman Debbie Wasserman Schultz raised her arm to signal her colleagues to rise and applaud when the Republicans did.[43] Netanyahu spoke to Congress on the same date a year later, and was similarly rapturously received, in both cases at times when his relations with the president were tense: Netanyahu was thus playing a supine and complicit legislative branch, with bipartisan support, against the executive branch.

The disaffection of some on the Right with Obama over his policies on Israel and Palestine is also partly a result of the striking rightward lurch of both Israel's internal politics and its domestic and security policies, and of the increasingly conservative leadership of the large American lobby that supports Israel. This is as true of the lobby's Christian Zionist evangelical wing as it is of the wing rooted in the leading institutions of the American Jewish community.[44] Both Israel and its most outspoken American supporters have gone so far to the right that American "support for Israel" is now taken by them to mean unquestioning support for expanded colonization of the West Bank and Arab East Jerusalem; for legitimizing overt legal discrimination against the nearly 20 percent of Israeli citizens who are not Jews, and for the permanent exclusion from Israel of Palestinian refugees and their descendants, both under the rubric of "Israel as a Jewish state"; and for military actions outside Israel's borders that are more and more difficult to describe in terms of self-defense. It is hard to reconcile the fealty to increasingly extreme positions that Israel and its supporters have come to expect from Congress and the US government since this rightward turn with traditional official American positions. It is even harder to reconcile it with the aspirations for a resolution of the conflict with which Barack Obama and several of his predecessors began their presidencies.

Leaving for a moment the febrile atmosphere created by this new concatenation of an Israeli polity that has shifted steadily to the right and the increasingly hawkish politics of the Republican Party and the Israel lobby, the achievements Obama claimed in his interview with Goldberg are nevertheless significant, and deserve careful examination. The actual value of American military and intelligence support to Israel since 2009 may never be known. The dollar figures for aid are of course public (and massive).[45] However, Israel has come to get special treatment in so many ways, from exemption from "buy-American" provisions normally attached to economic and military aid, to various kinds of unique financing, such as getting its aid at the beginning of the fiscal year instead of in quarterly installments like other recipients, that the real value of this aid is hard to quantify fully or in a meaningful fashion. And because of the covert nature of intelligence cooperation and high-tech collaboration between the two countries in the fields of cyber warfare, drones, artificial intelligence, and other related fields (in some of which expertise and technology are undoubtedly flowing both ways), even in what is nominally a democracy, ordinary citizens can only with great difficulty find out what their government is actually doing. If murky media reports about computer viruses jointly directed against the Iranian nuclear program by the US and Israeli intelligence services can be believed, a great deal is going on surreptitiously in these realms.[46]

However, the level and the value of the diplomatic support the Obama administration has extended to the most right-wing pro-settler government in Israel's history, over the Goldstone Report, the *Mavi Marmara* incident, at the United Nations, and on other occasions and in other venues, is highly visible and is impressive by any standard. Such unstinting support has been offered by this administration since the moment it came into office in January 2009, when it refrained from censuring Israel for the atrocities of the "Cast Lead" assault on Gaza. This massive offensive, which left fourteen hundred Palestinians in Gaza dead, the overwhelming majority of them civilians, was ended by the Israeli military just before Obama was inaugurated. The new administration thereafter assiduously shielded Israel from condemnation over the Gaza attack, notably through rejecting the conclusions of the UN Human Rights Council's Goldstone Report, which was savagely criticized by Israel and its partisans but was otherwise widely regarded as authoritative and unbiased.[47]

The Obama administration's diplomatic support in this and other contexts included an extraordinarily active and aggressive American effort to counter what was called the "delegitimization" of Israel. The president himself utilized this term in his *Atlantic* interview with Jeffrey Goldberg and in his March 2012 AIPAC speech. This is a term that issues from the questionable assumption that Israeli actions such as the blockade imposed on the 1.75 million people of the Gaza Strip, or the use of phosphorus shells against civilian areas, or detention without trial, or indeed Israel's forty-five-year occupation of Palestinian territories, are "legitimate" in international law. The international legal consensus, excepting naturally the view of the Israeli (and increasingly the American) government, is that they are not. A related trope regarding "lawfare," another right-wing American-Israeli legal term of art, is gradually being adopted by Israel's supporters within the American government to argue against the use of international law to prevent Israeli violations.[48] The employment of such rhetoric from the president on down is striking evidence of a root-and-branch commitment by all levels of the Obama administration to an Israeli-driven agenda, and Israeli-generated terminology. Thus, during a meeting at the State Department in May 2010 a senior official in the Bureau of Near Eastern Affairs expressed concern that certain measures contemplated at the UN mildly critical of official Israeli actions in Jerusalem might amount to "lawfare" against Israel.[49]

Contrary to the view of partisan commentators, who see Obama as harboring an inveterate hostility to the Jewish state, such exaggerated deference to Israel's desiderata has operated throughout the tenure of his administration, and indeed throughout Barack Obama's national career. These positions are not by any means solely a function of the new situation since the 2010 midterm elections measurably strengthened the Republicans on Capitol Hill, obliging a weaker President Obama to appease Netanyahu and his American supporters. Nor were such stands taken only with a view to the November 2012 presidential election: they are rather in keeping with everything Obama has said and done since he came on the national stage.

Notwithstanding all these considerable forms of material and diplomatic support for Israel, there was no question that by late 2010, before the end of the second year of Obama's presidency, he had thoroughly alienated the right-wing Israeli government of Benyamin Netanyahu and its vociferous American advocates in a number of ways. Among them were atmospheric elements, such as the fact that Obama lacked any apparent emotional warmth even when making his most supportive pronouncements vis-à-vis Israel. Coming from a man who is notoriously cool, this is perhaps not entirely surprising. This coolness was routinely contrasted by his critics with the president's unprecedented effort to reach out to the Arab and Muslim worlds with his address to students in Istanbul and his Cairo speech in April and June 2009 respectively.[50] In them, the president said little that went beyond what had been routine for his predecessors as far as Palestine was concerned; indeed, in Istanbul he said almost nothing on the topic.[51] In Cairo, aside from the passages of the speech already cited, which laid more stress on Jewish and Israeli than Palestinian suffering, Obama called on the Palestinians to abandon violence (with no similar request of Israel), and reiterated the traditional American demands on Hamas. He also said that the United States "does not accept the legitimacy of continued Israeli settlements . . . It is time for these settlements to stop," and stated mildly that "the continuing humanitarian crisis in Gaza does not serve Israel's security." Together with the rhetoric about Israeli and Jewish suffering already cited, the speech put together supportive but by now standard, traditional US views toward the Palestinians to date: the president said that there should be a Palestinian state, that Gaza is a humanitarian crisis that does not serve Israel's security, and that the settlements are not legitimate and should stop. Of these three pieces of boilerplate, only the third had even the possibility of raising a frisson in Israel or among its supporters (and, predictably, it eventually did). However, in sum, there was nothing earthshaking or even very new in the speech. But given their context, as part of a dramatic attempt to improve American relations with the Muslim world, and given their venues, in two of the greatest cities of Islam, these speeches were seen as having great symbolism. Some critics suspiciously saw these speeches as representing the genuine sentiments of a person of Obama's particular racial and religious background, reflecting a troubling essentialism ("it is because he is of Muslim origin that he is doing this") that tells us far more about the blinkered vision of these critics than it does about Obama.

The president's failure to visit Israel while he was in the Middle East on trips to Turkey and Egypt in 2009 was part of the same petulant list of complaints of those who held these views.[52] On reflection, these kinds of petty grievances are remarkably revealing of two phenomena. One is the almost irrationally jealous insecurity regarding the American-Israeli alliance evinced both by Israel's government and by its powerful lobby in Washington. The second involves an element of carefully dosed pressure tactics, whereby no matter how favorable a president is toward Israel, any perceived slippage, however minor, from the high bar set for him by both Israel and the lobby provokes heated charges of betrayal of Israel's security, if not of its very survival. There may be a certain element of sincerity to these histrionics. However, their intended purpose, and certainly their effect, is to bludgeon the offending politician back into line. When Netanyahu yet again renewed his threats over Iran in August 2012, a *New York Times* correspondent implied that this is exactly what the Israeli government's incessant threats about Iran throughout the first eight months of 2012 had been meant to do: "The collective saber rattling is part of a campaign to pressure the Obama administration and the international community, rather than an indication of the imminence of an Israeli strike."[53] For a paradigmatic example of the kind of over-the-top rhetoric used by Israeli Likud premiers on American presidents, one need only go back to Menachem Begin's heated denunciations, with ringing biblical overtones, of perhaps the most pro-Israel president of them all, Ronald Reagan, when the Reagan Plan was announced, as was described in the previous chapter.

More concretely, during Obama's first two years in office, critics in both Israel and the United States were most angered by two specific policy positions he took. These were Obama's insistence on an Israeli settlement freeze as a precondition for negotiations with the Palestinians, and his stating that the basis for a peace settlement between Israel and Palestine should be the 1967 borders, with certain modifications. The fact that these were standard, routine official American positions, and that they have been repeated numerous times by various American presidents, holds no importance for this particular Israeli government. That the Netanyahu government that came to power in 2009 represented the most rightward lurch in Israel's steady political shift to the right since 1977, and was dependent on the votes of strongly pro-settler members of the Knesset, undoubtedly helps to explain the ferocity of its reaction. As regards its American supporters, who include notable Republican leaders, they see absolutely nothing wrong with the hypocrisy of castigating Obama for the very same positions taken by two of the three most recent Republican presidents, including their party's idol, Ronald Reagan.

The fevered nature of the attacks on Obama for taking these perfectly conventional positions undoubtedly was also a function of the fact that Israel had received an unprecedented level of support under the administration of George W. Bush, a phenomenon that is worth discussing briefly here as a contrast to the Obama administration. We shall see, however, that for all the differences between them where Palestine and Israel were concerned, there were also some basic similarities in the approaches of their respective administrations.

The apex of the George W. Bush administration's enhanced alignment of the United States with Israeli positions came with the president's letter to Israeli prime minister Ariel Sharon of April 14, 2004. In it, Bush declared that it was the position of the United States that Israel's "settlement blocs" in the West Bank (they were not even described as settlements, but rather quite neutrally as "existing major Israeli population centers") were "realities" that would have to be taken into account in a final settlement.[54] For partisans of Israel's post-1967 colonial enterprise in the West Bank, this was their greatest victory in terms of changing US policy since Ronald Reagan's administration in 1981 ceased to describe the settlements as illegal.

What the second President Bush did via the stance enunciated in his 2004 letter was not just to endorse a hard-line Israeli position. It was also in effect to toss out the window two cardinal principles of American Middle East policy since 1967. The first was that the United States would leave it to the parties to negotiate the details of a settlement, rather than prescribing its own preferred outcomes. This injunction had admittedly only been nominally obeyed in the past: but in previous cases, such as some of those we have examined, American support for Israeli positions was surreptitious and sub rosa. With Bush's 2004 letter to Sharon, the United States came out openly in support of the Israeli demand for the annexation to Israel of these "settlement blocs" (elastic and always expanding entities, whose size and perimeters have never been delineated either by Israel or the United States). As the Palestinians complained, these blocs were so located (intentionally by decades of Israeli strategic planners, of course) as to make a contiguous, coherent Palestinian state an impossibility.[55] Also under this heading, Bush's letter aligned the United States firmly and officially with the Israeli insistence that Palestinian refugees must not be allowed to return to Israel, and in direct opposition to the Palestinian position that refugees have a right to return and to compensation (a position the United States had originally supported and maintained for several decades).[56]

The second principle of standing American policy that Bush violated was that inscribed in Security Council Resolution 242 of 1967, regarding the inadmissibility of the acquisition of territory by force. This was the basis for the original American stance that the 1967 lines, with minor modifications, should be the basis for the final frontiers in a peaceful resolution of the conflict. It was also at the root (together with Article 49 of the Fourth Geneva Convention[57]) of the US position starting in 1967 that Israel's settlements in the occupied territories were illegal, and for the position as modified under Reagan, that they were "obstacles to peace." With a stroke of his pen, the junior President Bush had swept away both of these long-standing pillars of American Middle East policy. Colonial settlements established in violation of customary international law, and firmly opposed, at least rhetorically, by US presidents for thirty-seven years, suddenly became "already existing major Israeli population centers," whose maintenance and annexation to Israel George W. Bush now formally endorsed.

Further increasing the mutual comfort level between the two allies under the George W. Bush administration, many of its dealings with Israel had been handled by officials like Elliott Abrams, who was a longtime and fervent supporter of extreme Likud positions.[58] Abrams served as senior director for Near East and North African affairs in the National Security Council (NSC). He thus had unparalleled access to the White House, and was deeply involved in handling Palestinian affairs. Abrams was only one of a coterie of far right-wing figures in senior policymaking positions in the Bush administration who dealt with the

Middle East, and who also played a major role in leading the United States to war in Iraq. They included prominent neoconservatives such as Paul Wolfowitz and Douglas Feith, the number two and three officials at the Pentagon under Donald Rumsfeld; Richard Perle, head of the Defense Policy Board; I. Lewis "Scooter" Libby, chief of staff to Vice President Richard Cheney; and John Bolton, US permanent representative to the United Nations. All these individuals subscribed to exactly the same neoconservative/Revisionist Zionist political ideology espoused originally by Vladimir Jabotinsky, as did leaders of the Revisionist/Likud-descended governments that have run Israel since 2001 and that had dominated Israeli politics for over two decades before that. Indeed, several of these individuals and others who played key Middle East–related roles in the Bush administration had in the past given belligerent and radical advice to the Likud Party on policy issues.[59] This was yet another instance of the overlap between the Israeli and American domestic and foreign policy spheres.

Meanwhile, as national security advisor and later as secretary of state, Condoleezza Rice reinforced these proclivities to be uncritically supportive of Israel and its regional objectives. She showed these tendencies, and incidentally demonstrated her callous insensitivity, most notoriously when she described the massive destruction to Lebanon's infrastructure and the death of more than twelve hundred people, most of them civilians, inflicted during Israel's savage attack on that country in 2006, as "the birth pangs of the new Middle East." At the same press conference, Rice refused to endorse an immediate cease-fire to bring the ongoing Israeli assault to a quick end, declaring, "I have no interest in diplomacy for the sake of returning Lebanon and Israel to the status quo ante. I think it would be a mistake."[60]

Notwithstanding these and many other weighty tokens of the strong and unwavering support it extended to Israel, it is noteworthy that in many crucial respects the Bush administration followed precisely the same patterns as did its predecessors. This can be seen from revelations contained in confidential Palestinian negotiating documents from this period that have been leaked to the public.[61] Thus, Rice told Palestinian negotiators during a bipartite meeting at one point in 2008 that she did not want to harm "my role as the 'honest broker,'" while insisting that she played that role "the same with the Israelis." This was a clear echo of the function supposedly played by American mediators under previous administrations, as they ostentatiously attempted a display of "evenhandedness" as between the United States' closest ally and the Palestinians. This posture of equidistance between the two sides is preposterous, given that, as we have seen, Israel is in some ways virtually part of the US domestic system, and has always been favored over the Palestinians.

The relationship between the United States and Israel is so close, indeed, that the former has in some respects become the "metropole" for the Israeli colonial enterprise in the West Bank.[62] This is certainly true in terms of generous (tax-deductible) private American funding of the settlements and the constant movement from the United States to Israel of religious nationalist colonists, many of them aggressive and fanatical, to live in these settlements.[63] The settlement enterprise, together with other key segments of Israeli society and politics, is thus in some ways embedded within and intertwined with American society and the American political system. The contrast between this close identification with Israel and the disdain with which American lawmakers, policymakers, and the media generally regard the Palestinians, holding them at arm's length at best, could not be more stark.

Rice's pose as an "honest broker" actually fell somewhere between high irony and farce, given that at this meeting she was trying to convince the Palestinians to make several significant unilateral concessions to Israel (thus serving as a broker, but certainly not an honest or disinterested one). The concessions she was trying to press on the Palestinian side included accepting a formula that would have allowed Israel to keep large swathes of territory (in "settlement blocs" such as Ariel and Maale Adumim), which would have split a putative Palestinian "state" up into, at a minimum, four separate, easily isolated cantons; in effect abandoning the right of return to Israel proper for Palestinian refugees; and avoiding forcing Israel to accept that it had a formal "responsibility" for the massive expulsions of 1948 that originally produced 750,000

Palestinian refugees. The latter was a seminal event in Palestinian history, one that Palestinians call the *nakba,* or catastrophe.

Displaying the stunning lack of sensitivity that had already become her hallmark in dealing with the Middle East, during these talks with Palestinian negotiators, Rice referred to the refugee issue and urged the Palestinians to ignore the issue of Israeli responsibility for the *nakba,* saying: "Bad things happen to people all around the world all the time. You need to look forward."[64] Coming from someone of her background, that was an astounding statement: it is hard to imagine her saying the same thing to a Jewish American or African American audience about traumatic events that were central to their collective past. During another negotiating session, Rice tacitly supported Israel's position that it would have to keep troops on the territory of a supposedly "sovereign" Palestinian state, comparing the situation of such a state to that of Germany with foreign forces on its soil, and adding disingenuously, "I am not talking about restrictions on sovereignty."[65]

In this and other interactions with the Palestinians revealed in the leaked Palestinian documents (we are not privy to records of Rice's or other American officials' bilateral meetings with the Israelis), Rice appears exactly like her predecessors, which is to say much less like an "honest broker" than as "Israel's lawyer," in the words of Henry Kissinger, as reprised by Aaron David Miller. Thus during a meeting in 2008, Rice urged the Palestinians to ignore continued Israeli settlement expansion, in spite of such expansion being expressly forbidden under the Bush-inspired "Road Map." She thus showed the usual extreme American sensitivity to the constraints imposed by Israeli politics, combined with complete indifference to the domestic political pressures on Palestinian leaders: "There will always be people in Israel who are against ceasing settlement construction, but these activities should not stop you [from negotiating]. You must find a way to continue."[66] This high degree of solicitude with respect to Israeli domestic political constraints was a constant for American policymakers. Thus Stephen Hadley, President Bush's national security advisor, in 2005 responded to Palestinian prime minister Salam Fayyad's concerns about the expansion of Israeli settlement, saying: "If we can help we will, but we must take Sharon's domestic problems into account."[67]

What these revelations indicate is that notwithstanding its exceptional partiality to Israel and the extraordinarily intense pro-Israel bias of some of its key officials, in important respects the Bush administration was not fundamentally different from its predecessors in this regard, and if so, only marginally so. They therefore show that the basic pattern of systematic American favoritism toward Israel during negotiations over the Palestine issue that emerged under Presidents Carter, Reagan, George H. W. Bush, and Clinton, discussed in the previous two chapters, was still solidly in place under George W. Bush. The administration of the younger Bush, however, was unquestionably more forthcoming in its indulgence of the Israeli settlement enterprise, and in operating as "Israel's lawyer," than had been any of its predecessors. Moreover, at no stage did it do what each of these four administrations, including those of Reagan and the president's father, had done in trying at least briefly to reframe American policy in a fashion slightly more favorable to the Palestinians. In these respects it marked a high point in the alignment of American policy on Palestine with the core desiderata of a series of Israeli governments.

Barack Obama came into office against the background of eight years of his predecessor's extraordinarily pro-Israel policies. Beyond not living up to quite the level of unblinking and unthinking support for Israel established by George W. Bush and his administration, where did Barack Obama go wrong? Did he simply choose the wrong advisors in dealing with the Middle East, assess the situation and his options poorly, and then make the wrong policy choices? Or was he doomed by circumstances that were essentially beyond his control? As already noted, these circumstances included Netanyahu's uncompromising coalition government coming to power in Israel in February 2009; the Republicans winning the House in the 2010 midterm elections, leaving Netanyahu in effect with more support on Capitol Hill than the president; inter-Palestinian divisions and the near-paralysis in PA policymaking that resulted; and finally the fragmentation of political power in the Arab world and the rest of the Middle East as a result of the Arab Spring and the Syrian civil war, making a concerted Arab stand over Palestine even less likely than before.

One might conclude that the impasse in US policy on Palestine under Obama was most probably a function of all these factors, plus whatever missteps the administration may have made. Certainly, events such as these and others that occurred in the Middle East and Washington created major problems for the administration, in ways that are largely self-evident. Rather than exploring the impact of these events, important though they were, I prefer to focus on matters over which the president had some control. These included his general approach to the problem of dealing with Palestine and Israel, the individuals he chose to implement his policies, and his specific policy choices.

To begin with his approach, Barack Obama apparently could not see, or was not willing to accept, that the entire Camp David/Madrid/Oslo framework going back to 1978 had run its course. Far from being a process that could bring about peace, it had become a device for the maintenance and management of a status quo that got progressively worse for the Palestinians. Indeed, the procedures followed by previous administrations were intrinsically unsuited to producing—in fact had been crafted in ways that prevented—any kind of just, lasting resolution of the conflict. Obama simply would not, or could not, break away from the stifling conventional wisdom in Washington on this score. Instead he embraced it, rather than boldly trying to adopt a new paradigm. This is what Carter and Vance had tried to do with the American-Soviet joint communiqué of 1977, and Bush senior and Baker with the Madrid Peace Conference (albeit without great success in the end in either case). As we have seen, both presidents were brought back to earth by the steely intransigence of Begin and his successors, and by the absence of any domestic or foreign counterweight to the formidable combination of a determined Israeli government and its energized supporters within the American political system. But Obama did not even really try a bold new approach to peacemaking. This is not surprising, for as anyone who had carefully watched his career before he became a national figure knew, Barack Obama never was a radical, however his most fervent detractors may have portrayed him.

The closest thing to a daring move by Obama in this regard was to appoint former Senate majority leader George Mitchell as presidential special envoy to deal with the Palestinian-Israeli conflict. This was a mildly unconventional appointment, for two reasons. The first was because Mitchell had made his reputation in international peacemaking in Northern Ireland by bringing the IRA, long labeled a "terrorist organization," to the negotiating table. He was able to do this (in the teeth of British and Northern Irish Protestant objections rooted in the IRA's enduring commitment to and practice of violence) once the IRA had committed itself to a peaceful, democratic resolution of the conflict. This achievement led directly to the resounding success of the Good Friday Agreement of 1998, which has so far brought fifteen years of peace and relative normalcy to Northern Ireland after many generations of conflict. It was a not inconsiderable achievement—others have gotten Nobel Prizes for much less—and Mitchell was thus in some ways a good choice.

It was naturally assumed that Mitchell might try to do the same thing with Hamas, bringing it into the negotiating process, moderating its behavior and stances, and thereby modifying the American policy of refusal to deal with it as a "terrorist organization." Mitchell was soon to find that Israel/Palestine was even more treacherous ground than Ireland, and in the end he proved unable to change US policy in any respect where Hamas was concerned.[68] This policy of exclusion of Hamas unless it met several conditions, including renouncing violence and formally accepting Israel's "right to exist" (Israel was not similarly obliged, as a precondition, to renounce violence, nor was it required to accept mutual recognition of two sovereign states, Israel and Palestine, and the "right to exist" of the latter), had long been fixed in stone. It was rooted in nearly identical, earlier, treatment of the PLO. This policy on Hamas had had dramatic effects since at least 2007, when the Islamic movement won a majority in the elections for the Palestinian Legislative Council. Thereafter, the Palestinian Authority governments Hamas tried to form, including in coalition with its rival Fateh, were boycotted and actively undermined and sabotaged by Israel and the United States, with the faithful backing of the European Union. The hard line taken by these powers exacerbated, as it was meant to, the already deep inter-Palestinian division between Fateh and Hamas. This division was abetted by Israeli-American-European policies of supporting one faction and boycotting another,[69] producing a situation that was a huge obstacle to serious negotiations. This should be obvious, as a divided Palestinian polity could not possibly make or implement any of the hard long-term decisions about war and peace that meaningful negotiations would involve. While this division may have suited the Israeli government for various reasons, including its utter disinterest in negotiations that would have required Israeli concessions over settlements, Jerusalem, and refugees, it is hard to see how it benefited the United States and the Europeans, who ostensibly desired successful negotiations for an end to the conflict. The exclusion of Hamas was among the factors that made such an outcome impossible, and that call into question how serious the Americans and Europeans actually were about resolving this conflict.

The second reason Mitchell's appointment was slightly unconventional was that in response to a request by President Clinton to investigate the causes of the second intifada in 2000, Mitchell had the following year issued what came to be known as the "Mitchell Report," calling among other things for an Israeli settlement freeze.[70] This demand had later been incorporated with other elements from the report into the stillborn (or aborted) so-called Road Map for Peace adopted by the George W. Bush administration. In spite of the fact that halting the inexorable progress of the settlement enterprise has always been and still is utterly and inalterably anathema to a long succession of Israeli governments, the recommendations of the Mitchell Report were nominally accepted (with the usual string of grave and debilitating reservations Israel has attached to virtually every accord it has signed with the US and the Arabs) by the government of Ariel Sharon. Needless to say, in spite of its supposed "acceptance" of the Road Map, Sharon's government never implemented such a freeze.

Where the Palestinian-Israeli situation was concerned, Mitchell thus knew the issues reasonably well, and had already taken a clear

position on some of them. Mitchell had the added distinction of being of Lebanese American heritage. Some inflamed partisans of Israel
were suspicious that his background caused him to sympathize with the
Palestinians, which may well have obliged him (as his own background
may have obliged his boss, the president) to bend over backwards to
avoid the impression of partisanship. It certainly seems to have made
the low-key Mitchell take an even more subdued profile on Middle
Eastern issues than he might otherwise have done.

However well (or ill) suited Senator Mitchell may have seemed to
be for this task, several things sabotaged his mission. The first was the
absence of congressional endorsement for the approach he sought to
take regarding Hamas and a settlement freeze, an approach that he knew
would be opposed by the Netanyahu government. When the former majority leader went up to Capitol Hill to seek support for an effort eventually to soften the conditions for bringing Hamas out of the cold and into
the negotiations, he was met with a categorical rejection by his former
colleagues on both sides of the aisle. This was not the first, nor was it to
be the last, time that leading members of Congress sided with an Israeli
government against an American administration. Extraordinarily, this
group included Democrats not afraid of taking a position different from
that of a president who, at that early point in his first year in office, was
still quite popular. Mitchell was told in no uncertain terms by his former
colleagues in the Senate and the House, doubtless with AIPAC looking
over their shoulders, that his proposal was a nonstarter, and that it was
in direct violation of US laws. The fact was that these were laws that the
Israel lobby had assiduously labored to put in place, among other things,
to make sure that Hamas remained beyond the pale and thereby prevent
any such eventuality as Mitchell apparently contemplated.[71]

This was yet another example of an administration that had sound
foreign policy reasons for exploring contacts with a group labeled "terrorist" being prevented from doing so. With the PLO in the 1970s and
1980s, it had been Israel alone that had insisted there be no such contact,
and Kissinger in his Memo of Understanding of 1975 had formally accepted these limitations on US freedom of action (there is little indication that Ford and Kissinger were highly concerned about pressure over

this issue from Israel's supporters on Capitol Hill at that time). Now in 2009 and 2010 it was Israel, vigorously and decisively aided and abetted by its friends in Congress, that opposed such a move, but the effect was much the same. As far as a settlement freeze was concerned, Netanyahu and his government were unyielding, particularly when it came to settlements in the area of Jerusalem. The obduracy of this opposition eventually convinced Mitchell: he told an interlocutor in February 2010, a little over a year after his appointment, that he was convinced that "no matter which government is in power in the Knesset, none is willing to freeze settlement building in East Jerusalem because it would be political suicide."[72]

Beyond these formidable obstacles, which severely undermined Mitchell from the very outset, his mission was being sabotaged in another way: from within the Obama administration. Mitchell was the victim of a prolonged bureaucratic mugging by one of the most skillful survivors and accomplished inside operators in the entire miserable history of the failed so-called "peace process." This was none other than the ubiquitous Dennis Ross, some of whose handiwork I have discussed in the previous chapter. Ross was a Sovietologist by training who had started off his long and glittering career in Washington during the Carter administration working in the Defense Department on Soviet policy in the Middle East. He had served in increasingly prominent positions in every subsequent administration except that of George W. Bush. Ross's last appointment under Clinton had been as a presidential special envoy for Middle East peace. In this capacity, he had in practice taken full charge of the entire Palestinian-Israeli dossier for several years. Much of the richly deserved credit for the dismal overall results of the "peace process" since the early 1990s belonged to Ross. He was later stingingly criticized for his naked pro-Israel bias, and blamed in large part for these failures, by two of the most senior officials who had collaborated with him most closely on this issue for well over a decade, Ambassador Daniel Kurtzer and Aaron David Miller.[73]

Following Bill Clinton's departure from the White House in 2001, Ross took a senior position at the Washington Institute for Near East Policy, a body that had been established by AIPAC leaders to give "academic" credibility to their lobbying effort. There he finished writing a thoroughly self-serving book on his role in the peace process.[74] Obama thereupon found himself in Ross's debt when the latter campaigned for him in crucial states with pivotal Jewish communities late in the 2008 campaign, notably in Pennsylvania and Florida. On the campaign trail, Ross used his great credibility as a devoted friend of Israel to reassure anxious voters that Obama was in fact sufficiently pro-Israel.[75] In later appointing Ross to the State Department with a portfolio covering Iran, the newly elected president was in some measure discharging this debt.

Once at the State Department, Ross ran afoul both of his direct boss, Secretary of State Hillary Clinton, who seems to have learned to distrust him when he worked for her husband, and of newly appointed presidential special envoy Senator Mitchell. Both apparently felt that Ross was trying to insinuate himself into Palestinian-Israeli negotiations, from which he was supposedly meant to have been excluded by Mitchell's appointment.[76] Others have suggested that he was resented because of his direct contacts with the Israeli government, an old Ross habit going back at least to the late 1980s, when his boss James Baker was said to have utilized these private backchannels for his own purposes. Interestingly, the figure on the Israeli side in the backchannel that Ross later affirmed Baker asked him to open in 1989 was none other than Elyakim Rubinstein.[77] Amusingly, in dealing with his old chum "Ely" Rubinstein, the head of the Israeli delegation facing the Palestinians at Madrid and in Washington more than two years later, starting in 1991, Ross was obliged to engage in the charade of being an "evenhanded mediator."

Whatever the reason for the friction with Hillary Clinton and Senator Mitchell, Ross eventually left the State Department, only to land on his feet once again. Indeed, he ended up in an even more influential position, at the NSC as a special assistant to the president and senior director for the Central Region, which included the Middle East.[78] In this post he was in much closer proximity than before to the president. In the subsequent infighting within the administration over policy toward Israel and Palestine, Ross sniped ceaselessly and ruthlessly at Mitchell from his new perch at the NSC. He started from the same flawed assumptions and followed the same old script that he and his colleagues had worked from under previous presidents. According to one account, Ross advocated "pre-emptive capitulation to what he described as the [Netanyahu] coalition's red lines."[79] The Palestinians had seen the very same behavior from Ross again and again in Madrid and Washington two decades earlier, as I discussed in the last chapter.

Worse, when Ross finally triumphed over Mitchell and got complete control of dealings with the Israeli government after the president's climb-down over a settlement freeze had already begun, in the fall of 2010, he was reported to have made an extraordinary offer to the Israeli prime minister. This included twenty much-coveted F-35 stealth attack jets, a US veto of a planned UN Security Council resolution on Palestinian statehood if it came up over the subsequent year, and long-term security guarantees in case of an overall peace settlement. All of this was in exchange for a measly three-month settlement freeze, which would *not* apply to the entire greater Jerusalem region, linked to an unprecedented promise *never* to ask for such a freeze again.[80] Although Netanyahu contemptuously refused the offer, in the scathing words of Ross's ex-colleague, former US ambassador to Israel Daniel Kurtzer, this would have represented "the first direct benefit that the United States has provided Israel for settlement activities that we have opposed for 40 years." Kurtzer went on: "Previously US opposition to settlements resulted in penalties, not rewards."[81] In other words, Israel was being offered a bribe by the United States, represented by Ross, in order to make it stop—very briefly—activities that were themselves illegal, linked to a promise never again to request such a halt. This appeared to be the nadir of the "peace process," although under this sort of direction by American diplomats, enabled by their political superiors, it seems to have had an unlimited capability to plumb ever lower depths, and to move ever farther from real peace. His work seemingly done, Ross left the Obama administration in November 2011, to return to his berth at the Washington Institute.[82]

By the spring of 2012, after a little more than three years in office, the Obama administration had turned 180 degrees where Palestine and Israel were concerned. The president had started off as several of his predecessors had, with what, in American terms, were relatively even-handed declarations about the aspirations and fears of both Palestinians and Israelis, and with an emphasis on the urgency of a resolution of the conflict. As we have seen, in all of his speeches on this topic since the beginning of his career on the national stage, Obama had nevertheless faithfully echoed an Israel-centric narrative. However, in Cairo and in his first speech before the General Assembly in 2009, he also tried to reflect sympathy for some of the grievances of the Palestinians, notwithstanding his greater stress on Israeli suffering. By the time of Obama's 2011 General Assembly speech, any attempt at evenhandedness or balance was long since gone, replaced by a discourse that could have been emitted happily by any Likud minister or AIPAC official. Indeed Netanyahu's super hawkish and openly racist foreign minister, Avigdor Lieberman, was ecstatic about the 2011 General Assembly speech, declaring, "I am ready to sign on [to] this speech with both hands."[83]

Worse than this, having begun his presidency by urging Netanyahu to focus on Palestine instead of Iran, by March of 2012 Obama managed to avoid any reference to Palestine in his statement after Netanyahu's visit to Washington, during which talks between the two men focused almost entirely on Iran.[84] The president had thus been dragged away from what he had started off focusing on, Palestine, and onto ground of the Israeli prime minister's choosing, that of the supposed existential Iranian nuclear threat to Israel. There Obama finally made a stand in March 2012, arguing forcefully against the United States following Israel into an imminent attack on Iran.[85] An element of his resistance to this pressure was his preemptive interview with Jeff Goldberg, cited earlier. The price of this stand, however, was further bribes to Israel in the way of weaponry and military and intelligence coordination, and almost certainly to forget about Palestine and the Palestinians, or at least to stop talking about them. Meanwhile, Netanyahu's coalition government remained remarkably stable, even briefly including the opposition Kadima bloc for a time giving it a majority of 94 of 120 Knesset seats, and he remained very popular with the Israeli public. Moreover, there was no assurance in March 2012 that the Israeli prime minister would not be able to gin up the Iran issue once again at a time of his choosing during an election year, when the president was less able to stand up to him. Predictably, as we have seen, Netanyahu did so again in August and September of 2012, albeit to little effect.

Like most of his immediate predecessors—Carter, Reagan, Bush senior, and Clinton in particular—President Obama had tried and failed to change the course of the American ship of state even slightly where Palestine and Israel were concerned. He was defeated in part because of circumstances beyond his control, partly by his own mistakes and flawed assumptions, and largely because the basic political dynamic in the United States as seen from the Oval Office had not changed since the mid-1940s. As against those numerous, powerful, and organized political forces that, in Harry Truman's words, are "anxious for the success of Zionism," forces which today include importantly a large part of the Christian evangelical base of the Republican Party, there is neither a serious domestic counterweight, nor one among the Palestinians, in the Arab world, or among other international actors. Like other presidents, when Obama faced tenacious opposition on this issue, he eventually did the politically safe thing. A pragmatic, cautious politician, he was not willing to risk his limited stock of political capital to appeal over the heads of these forces to the American people.

As mentioned in the previous chapter, George H. W. Bush had tried to do just this in 1991–92. He had held up billions of dollars in loan guarantees unless and until Israel offered assurances that the money would not be spent on settlements, going so far as to confront the Israel lobby publicly and directly.[86] As we have seen, however, Bush eventually chose to take a less confrontational approach, and Israeli settlement expansion continued unabated. Equally unfortunately, it became conventional wisdom that the president had lost the 1992 election because he crossed the powerful Israel lobby, a piece of faux-history that subsequently served to instill fear into those who might contemplate doing the same thing. There is no evidence that Barack Obama in any case ever contemplated taking on the lobby, which in this day and age would have also meant taking on a Republican Party very different from that of George H. W. Bush, one now driven by its right-wing base, a large part of which is fanatically hawkish and pro-Israel.

As in Truman's day, therefore, and virtually every day in between, the outcome of Obama's efforts was overdetermined. It was an outcome essentially dictated by the contours of the political map in Washington and the rest of the country, and one that could have been predicted in advance. It had little to do with the merits of the policies being followed, and certainly contributed as much to obstructing peace between Palestinians and Israelis as had the failed policies on Palestine of Obama's five predecessors in the White House, going back to Jimmy Carter.

# ISRAEL'S LAWYER

*By [your] stating that this is not a state in the interim, from our point of view it is not enough if we feel it will inevitably become a state. . . . It doesn't mean that you won't raise your wish. What we want to make sure is to find the right balance. We are not hiding anything. One thing a future historian will find is that the tendency, which I don't place, is that so much is being put into the hidden agenda. A historian will find out it is not there. Sometimes I wish maybe we will be such Machiavellians to have such a hidden agenda. We are such an open society that nothing is hidden.*

—ELYAKIM RUBINSTEIN, DURING PALESTINIAN-ISRAELI
  WORKING GROUP MEETING, 1993[1]

Israeli chief negotiator (and current High Court judge) Elyakim Rubinstein was unquestionably telling the truth, in the instance cited in the epigraph above, at least: Israel was not, and is not, hiding anything. Its agenda for the Palestinians, whether Machiavellian or not, was enunciated clearly by Menachem Begin at Camp David in 1978. That agenda has not deviated from its course or changed in any of its essentials since then. If anything is hidden, it is only from those in the United States and elsewhere who cannot see, choose not to see, or are encouraged in their blindness by others who willfully obscure, the realities that Begin and his colleagues never really tried to hide. For Menachem Begin, "'under no condition' can a Palestinian state be created," as long as the strictures he imposed at Camp David were maintained, and they have so far been successfully maintained by his successors. These truths are manifest for those willing to look honestly at the documents I have cited, the facts I have adduced in these pages, and the realities on the ground in a

Palestine that shrinks by the day before the ceaseless attrition produced by ever-expanding colonization and unending occupation.

What I have tried to show in this book is not so much the nature of this cruel regime devised by Israel and imposed on the Palestinians: this is an important topic in itself, which has been well dealt with by others.[2] It is rather the essential American contribution to the imposition of this regime. By refusing to admit these truths to themselves and others as bluntly as did the 1982 intelligence assessment quoted in chapter I, American statesmen and stateswomen have perpetuated a fiction. This is that they can be faithful to solemn commitments made to Begin and subsequent Israeli leaders starting thirty-five years ago at Camp David, while at the same time supporting true Palestinian self-determination and achieving a sustainable, just, and peaceful resolution of the conflict. They cannot.

If one examines them carefully, there can be no question about it: the Camp David agreements, the Madrid framework, and the Oslo Accords on the one hand, and the Palestinian Authority and the permanent occupation and settlement regime that resulted from this structure of commitments on the other, all of these things, summed up in the term "the peace process," are in the end one single construct. This construct is and was always designed by its Israeli architects (and their American subcontractors) to be an impermeable barrier against true Palestinian emancipation, rather than a route in that direction. Thus, this construct does not, cannot, and is expressly meant not to, address the roots of the conflict, which lie in the unending subjugation of the Palestinians, and their refusal to accept their lot. We should not be surprised: all of these elements are inextricably bound to a scheme originally devised by Menachem Begin to avoid such emancipation, and to ensure permanent Israeli control of, and settlement in, the occupied territories, the core of what Begin called "Eretz Israel." Israel's pitiless occupation regime not only guarantees more oppression and Palestinian resistance to this oppression. It also guarantees continued, bitter resentment of the United States for helping to devise, uphold, and defend this regime, a resentment felt particularly acutely in the

Arab and Islamic worlds, in much of Europe, and beyond, where these realities are concealed from almost no one.

This is where we stand today. Although there are many problems with counterfactuals—I have just laid out in the preceding pages many of the reasons why in my view things turned out as they did—it is true that other outcomes might have been possible from the beginning until today. On the American side, Jimmy Carter might have swayed Begin from his single-minded vision. That is hard to imagine, from what one knows of Begin, but Carter might have insisted on doing much more in terms of what he always seems to have intuited about the crucial Palestinian dimension of this problem. He could not. Reagan and Schultz could have held fast to their slightly more liberal interpretation of the Camp David framework outlined in the Reagan Plan. They did not. Instead, they quickly wavered when subjected to a furious verbal assault by Begin and his government. Bush and Baker might have tried even more insistently to force Shamir to be more forthcoming. Or, they could have taken a different tack with the new Israeli government headed by Rabin that came to power in 1992, insisting on a complete end to settlement expansion and a clean break from the Begin-Shamir legacy. None of these things happened, and in any case Bush was defeated in the 1992 elections before the process he and Baker had started in late 1991 could develop fully.

Bill Clinton could and should have insisted on beginning "final status" talks during his first term, as scheduled by the Madrid timetable. Instead he and his two secretaries of state permitted his advisors, headed by Dennis Ross (who was prone to, as we have already seen, what one observer called "preemptive capitulations to [Israeli] red lines"[3]), to run the show and allow interminable delays. These talks only began, with insufficient preparation and a complete lack of trust or confidence on both sides, in the final few months of Clinton's eighth and last year in office.[4] By this stage, the president was already a lame duck, Barak had lost his Knesset majority, and the situation in Palestine was already well on its way to exploding, as Palestinian frustration with the deceptions of Oslo reached a boiling point. These basic facts are often forgotten when analysts lament the "missed opportunities" of the last few weeks and months of Clinton's presidency.

We have just seen that Obama might have done many things differently, among them taking the real measure of Netanyahu, the legitimate and worthy heir of Jabotinsky, Begin, and Shamir. He could have recognized how fatally flawed was the "peace process" framework he inherited from his predecessors, and tried more forcefully to transcend it. He could have avoided reappointing to a high position an official like Dennis Ross, who had spent much of his career as a "lawyer for Israel," and who had already contributed mightily to the awful status quo in Palestine. He did none of these things, for reasons I have attempted to lay out in the previous chapter.

Any American decision-maker, at any stage from Madrid onward, could have insisted on an outcome that would have resulted in a resolution of this conflict, rather than continuing policies that have exacerbated it and perpetuated the status quo. One would have hoped that after over twenty years in which the "peace process" had failed to secure Palestinian-Israeli peace, policymakers would acknowledge that it was utterly dysfunctional, but this sort of "the emperor has no clothes" moment is unheard of in Washington, DC. Accepting that this was the case would have required a willingness to endure not only serious friction with Israel and its lobby, something no president is eager to face. It would have also necessitated soliciting input from officials and experts who were closely attuned to the real situation in Palestine and the Arab world, less wedded to old formulas (which in many cases US officials had helped devise), and less chummy with their Israeli counterparts. But officials capable of providing such input had long since been driven out of top positions (or learned to keep their mouths shut) as a result of a long-running but quite thorough purge of so-called Arabists in the State Department and some other branches of government.[5]

What these presidents and secretaries of state needed and often lacked was policy advice dictated solely by the long-term enlightened American national interest, which would have been served by a rapid, just, and lasting peace settlement in the Middle East. Instead, in the end they were mainly driven by a perceived need to trim to the winds

of American (and Israeli) domestic politics and the politics of big oil
and the big arms industry, all of which favored maintenance of a status quo predicated on preventing a just and peaceful resolution of the
conflict. It would have been hard to take such advice, had it been available. American presidents have less power than some observers think,
but they do have the potential to use their bully pulpit to educate the
public, a process that involves a willingness to expend political capital. I
have shown that several American presidents and their closest advisors
seem to have seen the need for a fundamental, or at least a significant,
change in US policy on Palestine and Israel. However, very few of them
have been able or willing to do so in any sustained fashion, or to expend
their limited stock of popularity and political support on this quixotic
mission. One can indeed question whether in the end any of them saw
that such a difficult and potentially costly course of action was politically feasible in the long term. There were many obstacles to doing so,
and few incentives, especially given the weakness of the Palestinian national movement over the past few decades and the subservience to the
United States of most Arab regimes, led by Saudi Arabia and Egypt, and
their manifest unwillingness to expend their own limited stock of political leverage in Washington advocating on behalf of the Palestinians, or
objecting forcefully and consistently to American policy on this issue.

There are even greater hazards for the United States, and for regional
and world peace, in the current configuration of its broader Middle East
policy than those just outlined regarding Palestine. This is because an
evolution of great importance occurred with the end of the Cold War
in how the United States has defined its regional enemies in the Middle
East, and also in terms of the greater role played by American allies in
defining them. Before 1991, the core concern for American policymakers in the Middle East and elsewhere was the Cold War rivalry with the
Soviet Union, and the process of defining regional objectives was fairly
simple.[6] "Radical" states and movements aligned with the USSR, like
Egypt, Iraq, Syria, the PLO, and the LNM were viewed as Soviet clients
and proxies, and were seen as enemies or as unfriendly actors to be won
over from the Soviet column to that of the United States, as happened
first with Egypt under Sadat. This approach was generally compatible

with the interests of major American allies, whether Israel or the conservative monarchies of the region, as they by and large saw the same states and regimes as enemies. But in this period it was exclusively the United States that defined its regional enemies and goals, while its allies and clients tended to follow suit.

With the end of the Cold War, with the rise of the revolutionary Islamic regime in Iran, and with the alignment of many formerly "radical" Arab regimes with the United States in the war over Kuwait against the Iraqi Ba'th regime in 1990–91, that simple schema changed drastically. Iran increasingly became a focus of American concern, and eventually of a lasting obsession, and that tended to drive a process of defining countries and movements aligned with Iran as unfriendly which was broadly similar to what had happened with clients of the USSR during the Cold War. But another subtle and little-noticed development was at work: this was the extent to which the two states that had been the key American allies in the region for many decades, Saudi Arabia and Israel, began to play a growing part in the definition of America's enemies in the Middle East. For both, the revolutionary Islamic regime in Iran was the main source of concern. This was especially the case after Egypt became an American client state, and after Iraq was destroyed as a regional military power in 1991, and then after 2003 occupied and effectively partitioned on a sectarian/ethnic basis, its existing state structures dismantled.

The increasing role of these two important US allies, Israel and Saudi Arabia, in defining American perceptions of its enemies in the region has accentuated and exacerbated the preexisting American-Iranian rivalry and what I have called Washington's mini Cold War with Tehran, which has essentially been ongoing since 1979. It has also increasingly had the effect of making the enemies of these two states the enemies of the United States. Under several past administrations, this process had the nefarious impact discussed previously in terms of Palestine and Lebanon. Now, however, Hamas and Hizballah have taken the place of the PLO and the LNM as pariah "clients" of the United States' main enemy: then it was the Soviet Union, now it is Iran. In broader terms, Israel's occupation and general oppression of the Palestinians, and its forays into Lebanon, have thereby become largely subsumed in and supported by the all-consuming broader American opposition to "terrorism" and clients of Iran. Moreover, in this larger schema, burning issues for the Palestinians and many other Arabs, like Israeli settlement expansion, can easily be obscured by the adherents of an Iran-focused approach, as Netanyahu brilliantly succeeded in doing in his dealings with the Obama administration, Congress, and the media in 2012.

As a result of this evolution, the bitter hostility toward Iran of both Israel and Saudi Arabia has further envenomed American-Iranian relations, largely thanks to the extraordinary impact on American public discourse and Middle East policy of Israel, its Washington lobby, and the much more discreet lobbying of Saudi Arabia. Equally harmfully, in recent years, this tail-wagging-the-dog tendency has in effect involved the United States in a Saudi-inspired region-wide Sunni-led sectarian campaign against Iran and Sh'ia-dominated states and movements, and indeed often against disadvantaged or oppressed Sh'ia populations in Sunni-dominated states like Bahrain, Yemen, and Saudi Arabia itself. The proxy war in Syria between the United States and its allies on one side and Iran and its protégés on the other that is ongoing as I write is only the most recent example of how deeply American policy has been influenced not only by Washington's obsession with Iran, but also by the calculations and grudges of its two powerful regional protégés.

This has been a subtle process in some respects, but its effects have been quite drastic. For example, in recent years the United States has not really had the option of trying out whether a "grand bargain" with Iran, fashioned in terms of the United States' exclusive definition of its own national interests, was possible or not. Instead, it has not only had to take into consideration the interests of its clients, but has also perforce had to partake in their vendettas, whether those of Israel against Hamas, Hizballah, and Iran, or those of Saudi Arabia against Iran and Shi'a movements and groups throughout the region. From the blinkered perspective of many policymakers in Washington and important lobbies there, this may not seem like a major problem: Iran is their obsessive focus anyway. In addition, the powerful warmongering pressures of the Netanyahu government, the Saudi regime, the Israel lobby, and hawkish Republicans have by now produced a constant anti-Iranian drumbeat for war that all but prevents rational discourse on these issues anywhere inside the Washington Beltway.

But from the perspective of the region, and of the real world—what has quaintly been called the reality-based community—the resulting realpolitik, seemingly driven as much by the interests of American clients as by any carefully defined US strategy, is helping to produce yet another slow-motion tragedy in and around Syria. Because of the brutal stubbornness of the viciously repressive regime of Bashar al-Asad and its foreign backers, combined with the fecklessness, divisions, and potent external influences on the now increasingly heavily armed opposition, Syria in late 2012 has begun to follow the course of Lebanon in the 1970s and 1980s, and of Iraq in the 2000s. This course is leading inexorably down the path of a savage sectarian civil war that is also a proxy war with troubling regional implications; the destruction of Syrian civil society and much of the economy; the degradation of crucial infrastructure and of invaluable national architectural and archaeological patrimony; the weakening of vital state structures built up over many generations; and the forced displacement of millions of people. Beyond these potential consequences inside Syria there is the growing danger of the spillover into Lebanon, Jordan, Iraq, Turkey, and other regional states of unmanageable refugee flows, sectarian and ethnic animosities, and rivalries for influence in a post–civil war Syria. Obsessively concerned almost exclusively with the rivalry with Iran, no policymaker in Washington, let alone in Riyadh or Jerusalem, appears to be particularly concerned about the potential consequences of their actions (and inaction) in Syria. As with Lebanon, Afghanistan, and Iraq in the past, and as in Palestine for many years in the past and into the present, the unintended fallout of the ill-considered policies of the United States and its allies with respect to Syria will be unpredictable, and may be extremely lethal and far-reaching. The consequences will be even worse if the United States is drawn into a catastrophic overt conflict with Iran, toward which its two main Middle Eastern allies and the war chorus in Washington seem to be doing their best to push policymakers. As with all these previous cases, the responsibility for whatever disastrous outcomes may result will be laid in large measure at the door of the United States by Middle Eastern and world public opinion, not entirely without reason. It is the United States, after all, which is the sole global superpower.

From the perspective of the American national interest, moreover, this evolution toward favored allies shaping what the United States can and cannot do in the Middle East, while dragging it toward further engagement in conflict, brings to mind the words of a leader who from lengthy personal experience well understood the calamitous possibilities that can be unleashed by war. In his 1796 Farewell Address, George Washington observed that

> a passionate attachment of one nation for another produces a variety of evils. Sympathy for the favorite nation, facilitating the illusion of an imaginary common interest in cases where no real common interest exists, and infusing into one the enmities of the other, betrays the former into a participation in the quarrels and wars of the latter without adequate inducement or justification.[7]

———

Returning to other outcomes that might have been possible in Palestine over the period covered by this book, on the Israeli side, too, things could have been different. Yitzhak Rabin could certainly have adopted a more expansive vision of Palestinian autonomy, and indeed of Palestinian self-determination, but he seems to the very end to have seen 'Arafat's role in this scheme as no more than a glorified policeman for Israel, a "super-Lahd" in the words of one of his closest advisors, Major General Shlomo Gazit. Whatever modifications Rabin might have been willing to make in Begin's scheme, he maintained in place as chief negotiator with the Palestinians Elyakim Rubinstein. This was an official who had throughout his career always been a loyal servant of Likud's restrictive vision for the Palestinians, and who as we have seen told their delegation in Washington bluntly that a Palestinian state was "considered by Israel a mortal security threat."[8] Nonetheless, in the end Rabin came to be hated and reviled by the powerful settler lobby that is at the core of the Israeli right wing. Indeed, he was assassinated in 1995 by a fanatical supporter of the settler movement out of fear that he would deviate from the vision laid out by Begin, bringing to an abrupt end the possibility of any such departure.

Any subsequent Israeli leader might thereafter have decided that the real emancipation of the Palestinians was in the vital long-term interest of the Israeli people and taken the considerable political risk of forthrightly challenging and facing down this potent lobby. Although two Israeli prime ministers, Ehud Barak and Ehud Olmert, have warned explicitly of the grave long-term peril to Israel itself of the perpetuation of the status quo, no Israeli prime minister before or after them has taken this political risk.[9] Now that the well over half a million Israeli settlers in the occupied West Bank and Arab East Jerusalem, all of whom are citizens and a substantial number of whom are voters, have come to constitute about 10 percent of the country's Jewish population, a proportion that is ceaselessly growing, that eventuality seems ever more unlikely. Israel has thus created for itself (with American help) a situation that has moved inexorably toward the permanent erasure of the "Green Line" between Israel proper and the occupied territories, the elimination of any possibility of a two-state solution, and what amounts to a perverse sort of "one-state solution." In this emerging status quo, a shrinking proportion of Jews are ruling permanently over a growing number of Palestinians suffering from varying degrees of deprivation of basic political rights. Although many Israelis seem unconcerned about this situation, it is not sustainable in the long run.

By no means does all the responsibility for these outcomes lie with decision-makers in the United States and Israel, of course, although they are by far the most powerful actors in the Middle East. The disunited and weak Arab regimes, most of them concerned primarily with staying in power and in the good graces of the United States (and in some cases Israel), have done nothing to help resolve this problem, and many of them have made it considerably worse. This is not just a matter of the exploitation of the Palestine question to divert the attention of domestic public opinion from the authoritarian and corrupt nature of almost all of these regimes, a ruse that cynical Arab rulers have been adeptly employing for decades now. Even more damaging than their disingenu-ously pious lip-service to the cause of Palestine has been the subservient and unhealthy relationship that a broad range of Arab governments has maintained with the United States, in spite of the latter's stand of almost unlimited support for Israel and almost unmitigated opposition to the aspirations and rights of the Palestinians.[10]

As we have seen, this has been the unchanging posture of Saudi Ara-bia since 1945 (King Faysal's oil embargo of 1973 is perhaps the sole ex-ception to this rule). Given its strategic weight and importance to the United States, Saudi Arabia's role in effectively supporting and under-writing the atrocious status quo by giving Washington a blank check (figuratively and sometimes literally) where Palestine is concerned is ab-solutely crucial. Such a posture has also characterized the other conser-vative Arab Gulf principalities, the monarchies in Morocco and Jordan, and Arab states traditionally aligned with Washington. It has also quite frequently been the case for a variety of Arab governments (ranging from the colonels' "*pouvoir*" in Algeria to Syria under the Asads to Iraq under Saddam Hussein) that have posed as "progressive," but for which remaining on good terms with Washington has been vitally important. Certainly for the period we have examined, the thirty-five years since 1978, there is little evidence that any Arab regime has ever put consistent pressure on the United States to take a less unbalanced position on the Palestine question. Certainly, none of them has made its relations with Washington dependent on modifications in US policy on this issue, or worked for a unified Arab stand that might have produced meaningful pressure for a change in US policy. This is the little-understood secret of the US government's enduring bias in favor of Israel: in the face of what since 1967 has increasingly been a Saudi-dominated Arab world, poli-cymakers in Washington are guided almost exclusively by the pressure exerted on Congress, the executive branch, and the media by the Israel lobby, or the stubborn obduracy of Israel's leaders in preserving their regime of colonization and occupation. Because of the Arab regimes' disunity, futile competition with one another, and deep dependence on the United States, there is absolutely no serious Arab counterweight to balance this formidable pressure.

Nor have any major international actors chosen actively to contest American domination of a process that most of them perceive has led to a dead end, and indeed may be endangering their vital interests in a region much closer to many of them than it is to the United States. This is true of both Europe and Russia. When the Soviet Union still appeared to be a formidable challenger to American power in the Middle East, it supported certain nominally "progressive" Arab regimes and the PLO. However, it was never able to prevail in its rivalry with the United States in this region, even given its proximity to the Middle East. We have seen how American policymakers consistently and ultimately success-fully opposed Soviet gains in the region, at times at the expense of the interests of peace. Although the USSR provided a counterweight of sorts to US power, it had little interest in advancing the Palestine question, in part because of its healthy and justifiable fear of US power, and also because the Soviets had other fish to fry in the Middle East, such as fit-fully supporting regional communist parties.

The decline and disappearance of the USSR ushered in the pres-ent era, one of unchallenged American dominance globally and in the Middle East. Indeed this dominance is perhaps felt more forcefully in the Middle East than elsewhere, if the number and intensity of overt and covert US interventions in the region and adjacent areas over the past twenty-plus years, from Iraq in 1991 and 2003, to Afghanistan start-ing in 2001, to Syria, the Horn of Africa, and the African Sahel today, is any indication. There is as yet no sign of any international power or constellation of powers that is able or willing to challenge the United States' dominant role in the Middle East and its environs, particularly where Palestine is concerned. The fact that anger at the unsustainable and unjust status quo in Palestine destabilizes the region, and negatively affects the vital interests of Europe, Russia, and other powers has not moved any of them to obstruct in any meaningful way the serene prog-ress of American support for the status quo there. Indeed, the so-called Middle East Quartet, composed of representatives of Russia, the Euro-pean Union, and the United Nations, together with the United States, and supposed to further the "peace process," has in effect served as little more than an enabling mechanism for whatever Washington sees fit to do at any given moment in support of its close Israeli ally.[11]

Importantly, and finally, at several key junctures the Palestinian leadership could have heeded the entreaties of those who perceived the trap they were letting themselves be drawn into and warned them against it. They might have insisted on basic conditions as a sine qua non for *any* agreement with Israel—such as guarantees for self-determination, statehood, the end of the occupation, and the removal of the settlements—but they did not. This was a fateful choice that Yasser 'Arafat, his colleagues, and his successors made with open eyes, for reasons I have discussed. Notwithstanding the weakness of their negotiating position, they apparently believed that they could later modify the stultifyingly restrictive terms they agreed to in a series of accords starting in 1993, but they were sadly mistaken. And at any stage, they could have rejected the United States as a dishonest broker, and relieved themselves of the burden of having to negotiate not only with their Israeli oppressor, but with their oppressor's closest collaborator and ally.

Moreover, at any point starting with the present, and at any time in the future, a newly unified leadership of the Palestinian national liberation movement could take a stand. It could formally declare to the world that a structure issuing from a purported "peace process," which was supposedly designed to be an interim way station to a future many assumed would include true Palestinian self-determination and independent statehood, has failed to achieve its purpose, and was irremediably bankrupt. The Palestinian Authority was meant to be an *interim* self-governing authority, and that interim period was originally supposed to have ended in 1997. It has been in creaky existence for nearly two decades now, since 1993–94. Palestinian leaders could have simply announced unilaterally that the interim period was long since over, that it had utterly failed in its stated purpose, and that this sham Authority—which has no real jurisdiction, control, or sovereignty—no longer existed and was being dissolved. Municipal functions, health and education and the other basics of self-rule, would remain in Palestinian hands, as they essentially were before Oslo under direct Israeli military rule.

What would emerge again in such a situation is the hard underlying reality of Israeli occupation and control, which has been successfully masked for all these years by the fictions of Oslo. This would constitute a wrenching and perhaps painful shift for some Palestinians, but the past two decades have proven conclusively that the "Authority" exists essentially to serve Israel's occupation and to help maintain it. They have shown as well that an entirely new structure must be developed, or an old one like the PLO must be completely gutted and rebuilt, in order to lead the Palestinian people toward real liberation, self-determination, and equal rights with the Israelis, with whom they must learn to share their homeland in some more equitable future arrangement. Incidentally, under any such arrangement, a much steeper learning curve will be required for the Israeli people, who enjoy almost all of the advantages of today's grossly unequal status quo and are largely ignorant of the brutal realities afflicting their Palestinian neighbors under their control.

A newly unified Palestinian leadership could couple this position with a refusal to participate in any further negotiations based on the Camp David/Madrid/Oslo framework. Instead it could announce that it would be prepared to begin serious negotiations only on an entirely new foundation and under new, less biased, auspices, and exclusively on the basis of Security Council Resolution 242 (with its affirmation of "the inadmissibility of the acquisition of territory by war") and other relevant UN resolutions, such as GA 181 (the partition resolution, especially as it applies to Jerusalem) and GA 194 (which establishes the Palestinians' right to return and to compensation). The objective of these negotiations would be to achieve an immediate end to occupation, self-determination of the Palestinian people including the return and compensation of those desiring to return, and a lasting peace, and nothing less. If this were refused, as it undoubtedly would be, the only remaining option for the Palestinians would be a unified demand for full, equal democratic rights in a single state in all of Palestine/Israel. Doing any of these things of course would require numerous prerequisites that today do not exist, from a unified Palestinian leadership to a Palestinian national consensus on how to proceed. These will not be easy to achieve, given how invested so many actors are in Palestinian weakness and disunity. They would also require uncommon courage in the face of the furious resistance to be expected from the two main pillars, and the sole beneficiaries, of the status quo: the United States and Israel.

If they fail to do these things, or to take similarly radical steps, however, the Palestinians cannot complain about American bias, Israeli oppression, the two-facedness of the Arab regimes, or international indifference, real although all these phenomena are. If the Palestinians do not help themselves, and transform that part of reality which is largely in their own power, nothing can begin to change in their situation, nor can anyone be expected to act on their behalf. Self-reliance of this sort is the essential first step, the sine qua non, required to change the pernicious status quo under which the Palestinian people have suffered for so many years.

Over a period of more than sixty years, beginning in fact many decades before our starting point of 1978, and before even the occupation of 1967, Israel has created for the Palestinian people a unique and exquisitely refined system of exclusion, expropriation, confinement, and denial. Above all, this system is buttressed by a robust denial that any of this is happening or has ever happened. In some ways this denial is the worst part of the system, constituting a form of collective psychological torture. Thus some deny that there is any such thing as an "occupation." Others refuse to call the West Bank, the Gaza Strip, and East Jerusalem the "occupied territories"; they are instead referred to as "the administered territories," or "the territories," or worse, "Judea, Samaria, and the Gaza district," as Begin and his acolytes put it. Arab East Jerusalem is not Arab, it is not "occupied," and it has not been conquered: it has been "reunited." Jerusalem is not a city that has been a center of Arab and Muslim life for nearly fourteen hundred years: it is the "eternal, indivisible capital of Israel," not only now and forever into the future, but also at every moment in the past, back to the dim mists before recorded history. The Palestinians were never expelled from their homeland. A nomadic people without roots in the land, they simply wandered off, or left because their leaders told them to. Violence employed by

Palestinians is "terrorism"; violence employed by Israel, usually producing approximately ten times the casualties, is "self-defense." There is a "peace process." One could go on and on with equally grotesque examples of such Orwellian newspeak, which effectively constitutes a tissue of falsehoods, an enormous web of denial.

These are not just verbal indignities: in this book I have argued consistently that language matters. Such terms and tropes are the essential building blocks of a lofty and solid edifice of denial of an entire narrative, of the existence of an entire people, which is basic to the affirmation of a formidable counterreality. Both the denial and the counterreality are not just based on material power, but enjoy extraordinary discursive potency. This is because both denial and affirmation have been diligently and patiently rooted for many generations in the Bible, in cinema, in popular culture, in racist stereotypes of Arabs, in putatively shared values, and in much else that is nominally outside the realm of politics, as strictly defined. They have moreover been internalized by most of the American political class, by much of the American media, and by many ordinary Americans.

In these pages I have attempted to show that beyond underwriting and defending the process of subjugating the Palestinian people and subjecting them to this system, the United States has played a key historical role in enabling and echoing both counterreality and denial. Without this American echo chamber, extending back for many decades, the entire Zionist project in Palestine could not have been so successful. I began this book with an epigraph from George Orwell's "Politics and the English Language." Orwell tells us there that "political language is designed to make lies sound truthful and murder respectable, and to give an appearance of solidity to pure wind." If I have succeeded, I have shown how in American political discourse, lies about Palestine are made to sound truthful; how crimes—against a people and against humanity—are made respectable; and how the pure wind of terms like "peace process" are given the appearance of solidity.

# ACKNOWLEDGMENTS

Writing even a short book like this one demands a considerable measure of discipline and solitary concentration in the face of the insistent intrusions of daily life and its responsibilities and distractions. It also requires a great deal of help from others. I have benefited from such help from many people in various ways, whether this involved assistance in research, reading and commenting on drafts, offering suggestions, or simply picking up the slack during the many months when I was psychologically or physically absent, as I followed the twists and turns of the past thirty-five years of American policy on Palestine.

Ever since my involvement as an advisor to the Palestinian delegation that took part in the 1991–93 Madrid-Washington peace negotiations with Israel, I had harbored the desire to document and analyze as a historian some of the events in which I had been directly involved. Call it Ibn Khaldun envy: the great historian left us an account of his impressions of Timur (Tamerlane), whom he met when the Turco-Mongol conqueror and empire builder was besieging Damascus in 1401. Ibn Khaldun was uniquely placed to give us such an appreciation, given that he was both an eminent scholar and jurist and had been deeply and actively involved in senior positions in public life in North Africa, Andalus, and Egypt.[1] None of us is Ibn Khaldun (not by a long shot!), and nothing I have experienced is on a par, although I have lived through the lengthy siege of a major Arab city—Beirut, in 1982. But I can understand well his motivation in seeking out this striking historical figure and recording his impressions of him in the midst of earthshaking events.

I had a particular incentive to record and assess a far less momentous and dramatic set of events, since I retained in paper and electronic form all of the extensive documentation I had acquired in the course of the 1991–93 negotiations, including many working documents I had helped produce. These internal materials of the Palestinian delegation, most of them unpublished and unavailable elsewhere, provided the basis for the second chapter of this book. They throw a unique light on the actual role and positions of the United States in these negotiations, as well as revealing much about Israeli diplomacy. I owe thanks to my astute and industrious fellow advisors and members of the official Palestinian delegation, whose dedicated work is represented in this collection of documents, including especially the late Faysal Husayni, as well as Su'ad al-'Amiry, Hanan Ashrawi, Ahmad Samih Khalidi, Ghassan Khatib, Camille Mansour, Nabil Qassis, and Raja Shehadeh. Many of these individuals had at the time forebodings of the grim outcome of the endeavor we were all engaged in, notwithstanding our best efforts.

For a historian, especially one whose business for over four decades has involved analyzing and critiquing diplomatic and policy documents as part of my own research and writing, finally being able to utilize these unpublished and confidential materials as sources was an especially attractive proposition. Several works covering these negotiations have been published over the past two decades, and are mentioned in the footnotes. Some of them are quite perceptive, but none of them provided precisely the perspective I was contemplating, and none drew on this specific range of sources. In the past, however, an opportunity for me to offer my own reading of these documents and the events they reflected never arose.

The occasion to do so, and the trigger for me to reexamine and use these materials, came as a result of the research of Seth Anziska, a graduate student working on his doctoral dissertation under my supervision in the history department at Columbia University. While conducting research in the National Archives, Seth came upon a declassified American document from 1982 that I found extremely revealing of much that has happened since then between Americans, Palestinians, and Israelis. I cite this intelligence memo extensively in this book's first chapter. I was fortunate to be given access to it and several other newly declassified documents that Seth found in the course of his own fascinating research into the Carter and Reagan administration's Middle East policies. With his kind permission, I have gratefully used several of them, after he employed them in conference papers he has presented in a variety of venues.

In the course of my examination of these and other documents, I realized that they revealed significant underlying continuities in American policy on Palestine from the late 1970s and the early 1980s right down to the present. I noticed particular similarities to what transpired during the 1991–93 negotiations, with which I was extremely familiar due to my own involvement, as well as with the Obama administration's performance on the Palestine question. These continuities, it was clear to me, are concealed behind the soporific repetition of a "peace process" mantra, and are obfuscated by superficial policy changes from one US administration and one Israeli government to another. This realization was the genesis of a short book that would focus on three moments during which these continuities were most apparent: 1978–82, 1991–93, and 2009–12, thereby taking advantage of the trove of documents in my possession and other sources available to me.

It is impossible to recall everyone who provided me assistance while I was working on this project, and I apologize to anyone whom I may have inadvertently failed to mention. I owe thanks first to Seth Anziska, whose archival discoveries not only helped set me on the path to this book, but also greatly deepened my understanding of a series of crucial junctures in Middle Eastern history and American Middle East policy. The full results of his examination of these and many other materials will be available to others when his dissertation is completed.

My assiduous research assistant, Sam Klug, has dug up for me primary materials on the policies of the Clinton and George W. Bush administrations, covering the period subsequent to that treated in the documentary collection already in my possession. These came mainly from the Palestine Papers made available electronically by the *Guardian* and al-Jazeera. His work was exemplary, especially for an undergraduate drafted to help me at the last minute. I also received useful tips, vital information and sources, help of various sorts, inspiration, and good advice from Bashir Abu-Manneh, Gil Anidjar, Kai Bird, Jason Brownlee, Rosie Bsheer, Victoria de Grazia, Alvaro de Soto, Graham Fuller, Raja Khalidi, Mahmood Mamdani, Camille Mansour, Jon

Randal, George Salem, Naomi Wallace, and John Whitbeck. Special thanks go to my daughters Lamya and Dima, my niece Monette, and my son Ismail, all of whom helped in usual and unusual ways, as well as to the young Olympian, Tariq, who in his own unique way did his very best to keep his grandfather from obsessing too much about this book.

Among others who helped to bring this work to completion were Professor Henry Laurens, who by his kind invitation led me to present a series of four lectures at the Collège de France in March and April 2012, and with his comments, helped me measurably to shape the argument of this book. My thanks are due as well to the Collège for their warm hospitality while I was in Paris, and to the School of Arts and Sciences at Columbia University for its generous research support. Colleagues of mine at Columbia too numerous to mention listened tolerantly as I exposed to them various stages of my research, and many of them provided useful observations. Several people did me the kindness of carefully reading and commenting on parts of the book. They include notably Jim Chandler, whose acute suggestions and careful reading were invaluable in underlining linguistic aspects of my argument and often in showing me what I was really trying to say; Ahmad Khalidi, whose knowledgeable advice helped me to avoid many pitfalls and guided the manuscript in a much better direction at an early stage; and my toughest and most perceptive critic, the incomparable Mona, who provided invaluable feedback in more ways than I can count or thank her for, including especially a careful, expert reading of the third chapter, on Barack Obama.

In a class of its own is the team at Beacon Press, with whom it has again been a pleasure to work, including Tom Hallock, Pam MacColl, Susan Lumenello, and especially Helene Atwan, the best editor any author could ask for, whose astute readings very much improved the book. My constant changes of the title of this book (originally meant to be "Dishonest Broker," until we found that that title was taken) and slippages in deadlines, were taken by them, as always, with good humor.

In spite of all this help, any remaining flaws or omissions in this book are entirely my own responsibility, and all opinions expressed in it are my own.

I dedicate this book to those who have tried in different ways over the decades to change the pernicious and short-sighted policies just described, which have been so harmful to so many, especially ordinary Palestinians. Far from bringing a just and lasting peace to the Palestinian people, to the Israelis, and to the Middle East, these policies have made realization of such a peace much more distant. And it is "peace" that is supposed to be the point, not "process."

# NOTES

## INTRODUCTION

1. On water issues in the West Bank, see Amira Hass, "Using Water as a Weapon in the West Bank," *Haaretz,* August 1, 2012, http://www.haaretz.com/. For details on the siege of Gaza, see Mohammed Omer, "When the Lights Go Out, Talk," Inter Press Service, August 2, 2012, http://www.ipsnews.net/. The infinitely expansive concept of "Israeli security" is a worthy topic in its own right, and has a lengthy colonial pedigree. Brutal actions ranging from the types of punitive measures described in the articles just cited to military operations such as the 1982 invasion of Lebanon, the 2006 attack on Lebanon, the 2008–9 assault on Gaza, the lethal boarding in 2010 of the humanitarian-aid ship *Mavi Marmara,* and the 2012 attack on Gaza are rationalized via a hermetically sealed train of reasoning whereby once such an action is determined to be necessary for Israel's security, it is automatically seen as fully justified, and is carried out irrespective of legal and international norms. The mindset that makes this possible is discussed further below.

2. Another trope, which sees Israel as "the only democracy in the Middle East," is discussed in chapter II.

3. Introduction to *Blaming the Victims: Spurious Scholarship and the Palestinian Question,* edited by Edward Said and Christopher Hitchens (New York: Verso, 1988), p. 1.

4. Cited in Georges Duby, *Le dimanche de Bouvines: 27 juillet 1214* (Paris: Gallimard, 1973), p. 9; author's translation.

5. For a blatant example of how this process of concealment operates, see note 66 below.

6. Rashid Khalidi, *The Iron Cage: The Story of the Palestinian Struggle for Statehood* (Boston: Beacon, 2006) and *Palestinian Identity: The Construction of Modern National Consciousness* (New York: Columbia University Press, rev. ed. 2010), cover aspects of the modern history of Palestine. Excellent works on the current situation include Saree Makdisi, *Palestine Inside Out: An Everyday Occupation* (New York: Norton, 2008); Raja Shehadeh, *Palestinian Walks: Forays into a Vanishing Landscape* (New York: Scribner, 2008); Eyal Weizman, *Hollow Land: Israel's Architecture of Occupation* (London: Verso, 2007); and Idith Zertal and Akiva Eldar, *Lords of the Land: The War over Israel's Settlements in the Occupied Territories, 1967–2007* (New York: Nation Books, 2007).

7. Among them is notably William Quandt, *Peace Process: American Diplomacy and the Arab-Israeli Conflict since 1967,* 3rd ed. (Washington, DC: Brookings Institution,

2005). See also Laura Eisenberg and Neil Caplan, *Negotiating Arab-Israeli Peace: Patterns, Problems, Possibilities*, 2nd ed. (Bloomington: Indiana University Press, 2010). Both provide links to key documents available online, to which I will refer in these notes.

8. In a speech to pro-Israel campaign donors in Jerusalem on July 29, 2012, Romney failed to mention the Israeli occupation as a factor in Palestinian economic backwardness, a point much commented on in the media, but best made, with typical irreverence, by *The Daily Show with Jon Stewart:* "Democalypse 2012: National Geogaffe-ic—Romney Abroad," July 31, 2012, http://www.thedailyshow.com/videos.

9. Israel's occupation additionally largely explains the yawning gap between Israeli and Palestinian GDP per capita, a fact ignored by Romney in referring to this disparity in his July 2012 speech in Jerusalem, and much criticized even in the mainstream media. See Ashley Parker, "Romney Comments on Palestinians Draw Criticism," *New York Times,* July 30, 2012, http://thecaucus.blogs.nytimes.com, and Scott Wilson, "In Israel, Romney Wows Crowds but Puzzles with Grasp of Palestinian Relationship," *Washington Post,* July 31, 2012, http://www.washingtonpost.com/.

10. For some details of the earliest phases of these traumatic events for the Palestinians, see Khalidi, *The Iron Cage,* pp. 105–217.

11. The AP on September 2, 1982, reported that the Lebanese police had tallied 17,852 people killed and 30,203 wounded in Lebanon over ten weeks of fighting. Of these casualties, nearly 23,000 were Lebanese civilians, but the police noted that figures were not broken out for the high Palestinian civilian casualties, and that those buried in mass graves were not counted. Similar figures, derived from a later Lebanese police report, can be found in Rashid Khalidi, *Under Siege: PLO Decisionmaking during the 1982 War* (New York: Columbia University Press, 1986), p. 22, n. 5.

12. For details, see ibid, pp. 174–76.

13. Redacted author, National Intelligence Council, to Director of Central Intelligence, Deputy Director of Central Intelligence, "Memorandum on US-Israeli Differences Over the Camp David Peace Process, August 24, 1982," Secret, September 24, 2010. CIA-RDP 84B00049R00160401004–1, CIA Records Search Tool (CREST), National Archives and Records Administration, College Park, MD. I am grateful to Seth Anziska, who discovered this document in the National Archives. Fuller details can be found in chapter I.

14. John Mearsheimer and Steve Walt, *The Israel Lobby and US Foreign Policy* (New York: Farrar, Straus and Giroux, 2007), is the basic work on this lobby, although it lacks the historical depth of the late Peter Novick's brilliant *The Holocaust in American Life* (New York: Houghton Mifflin, 1999), which is indispensable for understanding the role Israel has come to play in American Jewish life and in American politics since the 1960s. Also, as Noam Chomsky has argued convincingly in an interview in the *Journal of Palestine Studies* 41, no. 3 (Spring 2012), Mearsheimer and Walt's "realist" international-relations perspective does not recognize that US support for Israel is entirely compatible with many basic American corporate and strategic interests, rather than being mainly the result of the action of this lobby.

15. For the text of resolution SC 242 of November 22, 1967, see Quandt, *Peace Process,* Appendix A, available on the website of the Brookings Institution, http://www .brookings.edu/research/books/2005/peaceprocess3.

16. See Peter Beinart, "Obama Betrayed Ideals on Israel," *Daily Beast,* March 12, 2012, http://www.thedailybeast.com/.

17. The statement declared that while the two "spoke at length about the threat from Iran," with the president stressing that the United States would "prevent Iran from obtaining a nuclear weapon" and would pursue a policy of diplomacy "backed by unprecedented pressure, including the additional sanctions," and that "all options are on the table," they merely "also discussed a range of regional issues, including Middle East peace and the tragic situation in Syria." "Readout of the President's Meeting with Prime Minister Netanyahu," March 5, 2012, http://www.whitehouse .gov/briefing-room/statements-and-releases.

18. Jeff Halper, quoted in Frank Barat, "We've Gone Way beyond Apartheid," Al-Jazeera, May 2, 2012, http://www.aljazeera.com/.

19. This is confirmed by a later White House statement about a call from Obama to Palestinian Authority (PA) President Mahmoud Abbas, which mentions none of the previous points of contention between the United States and Israel, and seems to indicate that their conversation was restricted to pious generalities: "Readout of the President's Call with Palestinian Authority President Mahmoud Abbas," March 19, 2012, http://www.whitehouse.gov/briefing-room/statements-and-releases.

20. Quandt, *Peace Process,* p. 236.

21. This is detailed in Hisham Ahmed, "Roots of Denial: American Stand on Palestinian Self-Determination from the Balfour Declaration to World War II," in *US Policy on Palestine: From Wilson to Clinton,* edited by Michael Suleiman (Normal, IL; Association of Arab-American University Graduates, 1995).

22. There has yet to be a searching historical treatment of these deep affinities along the lines of Novick's *The Holocaust and American Life.* The American cultural historian Amy Kaplan is currently engaged in a study of American Zionism that promises to fill this gap. Noam Chomsky notes the shared American-Israeli "frontier" attitude to indigenous populations in the *Journal of Palestine Studies* interview cited in note 14 above.

23. The United States had a major economic effect on Palestine in the decades before 1948: American contributions to aspects of the Zionist project totaled over $330 million by 1948, plus $55 million in investments. These were considerable sums in an economy whose average annual national income in the 1930s was around $75 million. See the table reproduced in Walid Khalidi, ed., *From Haven to Conquest: Readings in Zionism and the Palestine Problem until 1948* (Washington, DC: Institute for Palestine Studies, 1987), pp. 850–52.

24. According to CIA figures: "Saudi Arabia," *The World Factbook,* https://www.cia .gov/library/publications/the-world-factbook/. These numbers are in dispute: other sources give Russia as the world's largest oil producer, and Venezuela as having the world's largest proven oil reserves.

25. Quoted in Irene Gendzier, "US Policy in Israel/Palestine, 1948: The Forgotten History," *Middle East Policy* 18, no. 1 (Spring 2011): 42–53.

26. Letter from President Roosevelt to King Ibn Saʻud, dated April 5, 1945, United States Department of State, *Foreign Relations of the United States: Diplomatic Papers* (hereafter *FRUS*), *1945*, vol. 8, *The Near East and Africa* (Washington, DC: US Government Printing Office, 1945), and available online via the Avalon Project, Yale Law School, "The Middle East 1916–2001: A Documentary Record," http://avalon.law.yale.edu/. The letter confirmed the US government's commitment regarding Palestine "that no decision be taken with respect to the basic situation in that country without full consultation with both Arabs and Jews," adding that the president "would take no action, in my capacity as Chief of the Executive Branch of this Government, which might prove hostile to the Arab people."

27. During the seven years when Roosevelt was assistant secretary, the US Navy commissioned its first oil-powered battleships, the USS *Nevada* and the USS *Oklahoma,* as part of a fleet-wide shift from coal to oil. For details on the enhanced perception of the strategic importance of oil as a result of the events of World War II, see Rashid Khalidi, *Sowing Crisis: The Cold War and American Dominance in the Middle East* (Boston: Beacon, 2009), pp. 42–47.

28. The incident, which took place in the fall of 1945, is described in John Snetsinger, *Truman, the Jewish Vote, and the Creation of Israel* (Palo Alto, CA: Hoover Institution Press, 1974), pp. 19–21.

29. See Lawrence Davidson, "Truman the Politician and the Establishment of Israel," *Journal of Palestine Studies* 39, no. 4 (Summer 2010): 28–42. Michael Cohen, *Truman and Israel* (Berkeley: University of California Press, 1990), comes to much the same conclusions.

30. Col. William Eddy, *FDR Meets Ibn Saud* (Washington, DC: America-Mideast Educational and Training Services, 1954; repr. Vista, CA: Selwa Press, 2005), p. 31.

31. *FRUS, 1945,* vol. 8, *The Near East and Africa,* p. 17. Snetsinger, *Truman, the Jewish Vote,* p. 18, quotes Truman as saying much the same thing in a private letter in October 1945.

32. *FRUS, 1945,* vol. 8, *The Near East and Africa,* p. 10, n. 2.

33. In the end, the Democrats won handily when the Republican vote was split between two candidates. Nevertheless, Palestine was an issue in the election, as it has often been since then in New York City politics. An expert was quoted in the *New York Times* of March 27, 2012, as saying of a recent political controversy over a Brooklyn co-op's proposed boycott of Israeli products: "New York's neighborhoods have their own foreign policy. . . . The boundaries of New York's mayoral campaigns are infinite. Everything is potentially an issue."

34. *FRUS, 1945,* vol. 8, *The Near East and Africa,* p. 17.

35. In his *Memoirs: Years of Trial and Hope, 1946–1952* (Garden City, NY: Doubleday, 1955), vol. 2, p. 164, Truman explicitly stated of the permanent officials of the State Department that "there were some among them who were also inclined to be anti-Semitic."

36. This is well documented in Cohen, *Truman and Israel.*

37. This tragic story is recounted in David Wyman, *The Abandonment of the Jews: America and the Holocaust, 1941–1945* (New York: Pantheon, 1984), and Deborah Lipstadt, *Beyond Belief: The American Press and the Coming of the Holocaust, 1933–1945* (New York: Free Press, 1945). For an example of the pervasive anti-Semitism of one sector of American society in these years, academia, see the relevant passages of Peter Novick, *That Noble Dream: The 'Objectivity Question' and the American Historical Profession* (Cambridge, UK: Cambridge University Press, 1988).

38. Truman in 1945 told his envoys to the Arab world "that if Palestine could only take some [Jewish] refugees from Europe to relieve the pressure . . . it might satisfy some of the demands of the 'humanitarian' Zionists." *FRUS, 1945,* vol. 8, *The Near East and Africa,* p. 17. Even after the war it proved impossible to change US immigration laws to allow the entry of more Holocaust survivors. On this issue Zionists, who wanted them to go to Palestine, were in accord with those who opposed greater Jewish immigration for other reasons: see Cohen, *Truman and Israel,* and Snetsinger, *Truman, the Jewish Vote.*

39. This is borne out by Cohen, *Truman and Israel,* and by Snetsinger, *Truman, the Jewish Vote,* who document the influence on Truman of his domestic political advisors, especially Clifford, and discount the argument that the president was personally deeply sympathetic to Zionism.

40. Byrnes was deeply concerned with matters of war and peace, however, according to his own record of his government war duties and his role in postwar peace negotiations: *Speaking Frankly* (New York: Harper, 1947). There is only one brief mention of Palestine in this book, p. 22, although more attention is devoted to the topic in Byrnes's memoir, *All in One Lifetime* (New York: Harper, 1958).

41. This is amply shown in Davidson, "Truman the Politician"; see also Snetsinger, *Truman, the Jewish Vote;* Gendzier, "U.S. Policy in Israel/Palestine"; and Fred Lawson, "The Truman Administration and the Palestinians," in *US Policy on Palestine,* ed. Suleiman, pp. 59–80, and Cohen, *Truman and Israel,* pp. 149ff.

42. For details see Gendzier, "U.S. Policy in Israel/Palestine," p. 43.

43. Secretary of State to Legation, Jedda, August 17, 1948, *FRUS, 1948,* vol. 2, pt. 2, *The Near East, South Asia, and Africa,* p. 1318.

44. For more on the American-Saudi relationship, see Robert Vitalis, *America's Kingdom: Mythmaking on the Saudi Oil Frontier* (Palo Alto, CA: Stanford University Press, 2006), and Toby Jones, *Desert Kingdom: How Oil and Water Forged Modern Saudi Arabia* (Cambridge, MA: Harvard University Press, 2010).

45. Henry Kissinger, *Years of Renewal* (New York: Simon and Schuster, 1999), p. 373. This third volume of Kissinger's memoirs provides eloquent testimony to the fact that for all the pain the embargo inflicted on the American consumer, Nixon and his secretary of state never allowed it to affect the close relationship between the United States and Saudi Arabia: pp. 372–74. For further evidence, see the preceding volume of his memoirs, *Years of Upheaval* (Boston: Little, Brown,

1982), pp. 974–76, where Kissinger notes that Crown Prince Fahd assured him that "the bilateral relationship with the United States had the top priority of the Saudis," p. 975.

46. While he does not put it so bluntly, this is also how veteran establishment analyst John Campbell describes the Truman administration's treatment of episodes from the 1947 partition resolution, through the 1948 Bernadotte Plan (which would have returned most Palestinian refugees to their homes and obliged Israel to give up some of the territory it seized during the 1948 war), and the abortive 1949 UN Conciliation Commission for Palestine, and afterwards, in "American Efforts for Peace," in *The Elusive Peace in the Middle East,* edited by Malcolm Kerr (Albany: State University of New York Press, 1975), pp. 255–61. For a contrasting view, which underplays the weight of these domestic and electoral considerations, see Steven L. Spiegel, *The Other Arab-Israeli Conflict: Making America's Middle East Policy, from Truman to Reagan* (Chicago: University of Chicago Press, 1985).

47. There is a large literature on this topic. For an excellent assessment, see Roger Louis and Roger Owen, eds., *Suez 1956: The Crisis and Its Consequences* (Oxford, UK: Oxford University Press, 1989).

48. For the background to this shift, see Abraham Ben Zvi, *Decade of Transition: Eisenhower, Kennedy, and the Origins of the American-Israeli Alliance* (New York: Columbia University Press, 1998), and Warren Bass, *Support Any Friend: Kennedy's Middle East and the Making of the U.S.-Israel Alliance* (New York: Oxford University Press, 2003).

49. Malcolm Kerr, *The Arab Cold War: 'Abd al-Nasir and His Rivals, 1958–1970,* 3rd ed. (London: Oxford University Press, 1971). On the crucial role of the Yemen war in the run-up to the 1967 war, see Eugene Rogan and Tewfik Aclimandos, "The Yemen War and Egypt's War Preparedness," in *The 1967 Arab-Israeli War,* edited by Roger Louis and Avi Shlaim (Cambridge, UK: Cambridge University Press, 2012), pp. 149–64.

50. For analysis of why the Johnson administration took this position, and why it acquiesced in Israel's 1967 attack, see Charles Smith, "The United States and the 1967 War," in *The 1967 Arab-Israeli War,* ed. Louis and Shlaim, pp. 165–92, as well as Quandt, *Peace Process,* pp. 23–52.

51. For details, see Khalidi, *Sowing Crisis,* pp. 114–49, and Craig Daigle, *The Limits of Détente: The United States, the Soviet Union, and the Arab-Israeli Conflict, 1969–1973* (New Haven, CT: Yale University Press, 2012), a meticulous study based on a broad familiarity with the newly declassified US documents on the period, stemming from Daigle having served as coeditor of the relevant volume of *FRUS.*

52. This episode is discussed further in chapter I. Declassified Documents Reference System (hereafter, DDRS), "Summary of a meeting in Jerusalem between Secretary of State William Rogers, Israeli prime minister Golda Meir, and other US and Israeli government officials regarding plans for a Middle East peace agreement. Memo. Department of State. OMITTED. Issue Date: May 6, 1971. Date Declassified: April 21, 2004. Complete. 56 page(s)." Document CK3100548322.

53. See DDRS, "Summary of Henry Kissinger's noon telephone call to Assistant Secretary of State Joseph Sisco . . . White House. OMITTED. Issue Date: Feb 28, 1971. Date Declassified, Nov. 01, 2004. Complete. 3 pages(s)."

54. Kissinger, *Years of Renewal*, p. 353.

55. Another element was involved: Kissinger often seemed more interested in turf battles with the State Department than in pursuing Middle East peace, as is visible in his handling of a 1973 Egyptian attempt to draw the United States into an active peacemaking role: Doc. 24, "Conversation between President Nixon and his National Security Advisor (Kissinger)," Washington, February 23, 1973, Nina Howland and Craig Daigle, eds., *FRUS, 1969–1976*, vol. 25, *Arab-Israeli Crisis and War, 1973* (Washington, DC: US Government Printing Office, 2011), pp. 67–68, where Nixon insists that Israel has to be less intransigent and Kissinger complains, "But the thing that kills us always in the Middle East is when State goes running like crazy without knowing where it is going." Nixon was aware of this tendency and disapproved: "I don't want any of this feeling of State fighting the White House" he told a State Department official in Kissinger's presence: Doc. 49, "Conversation among President Nixon, his Advisor for National Security Affairs (Kissinger), and the Assistant Secretary for Near Eastern and South Asian Affairs (Sisco)," Washington, April 13, 1973, ibid., p. 147. Nixon's assessments of the Middle Eastern situation were often more acute than Kissinger's: eight months before the start of the October War of 1973, a memo from Kissinger said that "it is difficult to argue that another few months delay in moving towards a negotiation would be disastrous for US interests." Nixon accurately minuted: "I totally disagree. This thing is getting ready to blow." Doc. 25, "Memorandum from the President's Assistant for National Security Affairs to President Nixon," February 27, 1973, ibid., p. 70.

56. The most comprehensive study of superpower involvement in the 1973 war and the lead-up to it is Daigle, *The Limits of Détente*. See also Salim Yaqub, "The Politics of Stalemate: The Nixon Administration and the Arab-Israeli Conflict, 1969–1973," in *The Cold War in the Middle East: Regional Conflict and the Superpowers, 1967–1973*, edited by Nigel J. Ashton (London: Routledge, 2007), pp. 35–58.

57. Robert Dallek, *Nixon and Kissinger: Partners in Power* (New York: HarperCollins, 2007), p. 520. Kissinger, cited in Daigle, *The Limits of Détente*, p. 3, called Leonid Brezhnev's threat to intervene "one of the most serious challenges" to a US president by a Soviet leader.

58. See National Security Archive, George Washington University, "The October War and US Policy," ed. William Burr, in particular Document 54: "Memcon between Meir and Kissinger, 22 October 1973, 1:35–2:15 p.m.," http://www.gwu.edu/fflnsarchiv/NSAEBB/NSAEBB98/, cited in Khalidi, *Sowing Crisis*, p. 130.

59. Nixon considered that Kissinger overdid this favoritism, as is shown by a 1973 remark (transcribed from the White House tapes) that he made to Alexander Haig in characteristically borderline anti-Semitic fashion: "Henry's totally filibustered the Mideast for almost four years, too, because he is totally attacking what the Jew-

ish agenda wants. Now, he really is. He really is. . . . I'm just saying, too, though, Henry has somewhat of a blind spot here, because he doesn't want to do anything with the Israelis except reassure them and get them more arms. Well, now, the Israelis need a little restraint here, too, Al." Doc. 6, "Conversation between President Nixon and Army Vice Chief of Staff (Haig)," Washington, January 23, 1973, *FRUS, 1969–1976*, vol. 25, *Arab-Israeli Crisis and War, 1973*, p. 8. Nixon's bigotry was evenhanded. He told Kissinger: "They're probably just, you know, the damned Arabs just talk." Doc. 22, "Conversation between President Nixon and his Assistant for National Security Affairs (Kissinger)," Washington, February 21, 1973, ibid., p. 55.

60. Kissinger, and other American policymakers, saw this clearly from the very beginning of the process. Speaking of the first Sinai disengagement accord, he said, "The disengagement agreement, above all, would mark Egypt's passage from reliance on the Soviet Union to partnership (in Sadat's phrase) with the United States." Kissinger, *Years of Upheaval*, p. 825.

61. See Khalidi, *Sowing Crisis,* especially pp. 114–40.

62. For details, see Avi Shlaim, *Collusion across the Jordan: King Abdullah, the Zionist Movement, and the Partition of Palestine* (New York: Columbia University Press, 1988); Mary Wilson, *King Abdullah, Britain and the Making of Jordan* (Cambridge, UK: Cambridge University Press, 1988). The reasons no Palestinian state was created in 1948 also included, importantly, the incapacities of the Palestinian leadership and its inability to mount a serious state-building project during the Mandate period, as well as the weaknesses of, and divisions among, the Arab states, many of which had just obtained an often-still-nominal independence.

63. For details see Irene Gendzier, "September 2011 and May 1948: The Great Fear Now and Then; An Essay on US Policy towards Recognition and Refugees," ZNet, July 23, 2011, http://www.zcommunications.org/.

64. Kerr, introduction to *The Elusive Peace in the Middle East,* p. 11.

65. Meron Benvenisti, former deputy mayor of Jerusalem, in the early 1980s established the West Bank Database Project, which showed that Israeli colonization in the West Bank had ineluctably closed off the option of a two-state solution, creating a situation of "quasi-permanence," precisely as intended: *The West Bank Data Project: A Survey of Israel's Policies* (Washington, DC: American Enterprise Institute, 1984). Benvenisti emphatically restated these conclusions in a recent interview in *Haaretz* with Ari Shavit: "Jerusalem-Born Thinker Has a Message for Israelis: Stop Whining," October 11, 2012, http://www.haaretz.com/weekend/magazine/.

66. A perfect example of how the situation in the occupied territories is concealed can be found in the Israeli government's failed attempt to prevent CBS from screening a *60 Minutes* special on Palestinian Christians, which showed that their emigration was the result of hardships resulting from the occupation rather than Islamist persecution. This attempted censorship was admitted on-screen by Israeli ambassador Michael Oren. CBS was prevented from televising

the segment during the Christmas season, however. See M. J. Rosenberg, "Suppression: The Israeli Government and *60 Minutes*," *Huffington Post*, April 26, 2012, http://www.huffingtonpost.com/. The dialogue between Oren and Bob Simon, the CBS presenter, excerpted in Rosenberg's piece, is telling:

*Simon:*  And it was a reason to call the president of—chairman of CBS News?

*Oren:*  Bob, I'm the ambassador of the State of Israel. I do that very, very infrequently as ambassador. It's just—that's an extraordinary move for me to complain about something. When I heard that you were going to do a story about Christians in the Holy Land and my assumption—and—and had, I believe, information about the nature of it, and it's been confirmed by this interview today.

*Simon:*  Nothing's been confirmed by the interview, Mr. Ambassador, because you don't know what's going to be put on air.

*Oren:*  Okay. I don't. True.

*Simon:*  Mr. Ambassador, I've been doing this a long time. And I've received lots of reactions from just about everyone I've done stories about. But I've never gotten a reaction before from a story that hasn't been broadcast yet.

*Oren:*  Well, there's a first time for everything, Bob.

67. Miller has used the term repeatedly, notably in a May 23, 2005, opinion piece of the same title in the *Washington Post* and, two years later, in his book *The Much Too Promised Land: America's Elusive Search for Middle East Peace* (New York: Random House, 2008), p. 75. Miller notes that the phrase was first mentioned in volume 2 of Kissinger's memoirs, *Years of Upheaval*, p. 620, which states that to meet Israel's expectations of unconditional American support of its negotiating position, the United States "would have to act in effect as Israel's lawyer," even while trying to achieve the contradictory aim of gaining Arab confidence.

I

## The First Moment:
## Begin and Palestinian Autonomy in 1982

1. Jimmy Carter was perhaps the most sympathetic of all US presidents toward Palestinian rights, but as we shall see he failed to make any significant progress in this regard while in office. He thereafter underwent a further evolution, writing *Palestine: Peace Not Apartheid* (New York: Simon and Schuster, 2006), which showed his understanding of the need for a just resolution of the Palestine problem. The book aroused the ire of fervent supporters of Israel and the criticism of partisans of existing US policies on Palestine, but sold very well.

2. Until 1992 the United States voted in the General Assembly in favor of annual resolutions on the Palestinian refugees "recalling" GA 194. In subsequent years,

under the Clinton administration, it abstained, until 1998, when it joined Israel as the only state voting against the resolution, which it has continued to do since.

3. See Charles Smith, "The United States and the 1967 War," in *The 1967 Arab-Israeli War,* edited by Roger Louis and Avi Shlaim (Cambridge, UK: Cambridge University Press, 2012), pp. 185–88, and William Quandt, *Peace Process: American Diplomacy and the Arab-Israeli Conflict since 1967,* 3rd ed. (Washington, DC: Brookings Institution, 2005), pp. 44–47.

4. The commitment made in the Israel–United States Memorandum of Understanding dated September 1, 1975, was replete with generous and costly promises to Israel: see Meron Medzini, *Israel's Foreign Relations: Selected Documents, 1974–1977,* vol. 3 (Jerusalem: Ministry of Foreign Affairs, 1982), pp. 281–90, available at the website of the Israeli Ministry of Foreign Affairs, "Foreign Relations: Historical Documents, 1974–77," http://www.mfa.gov.il/MFA/.

5. As Yasser 'Arafat pointed out in a 1978 interview with David Hirst of the *Guardian* ("The PLO Position," *Journal of Palestine Studies* 7, no. 3 [Spring 1978]: 171–74), "242 deals with refugees. We are not refugees. We are a people, the core of the whole problem." http://www.jstor.org/stable/2536214.

6. Quandt, *Peace Process,* pp. 182–84. William Quant served on the National Security Council [NSC] during this period, and offers an illuminating analysis of Carter's initiatives (pp. 177–91). See also the Brookings Institution Middle East Study Group's 1975 report, *Towards Peace in the Middle East* (Washington, DC: Brookings Institution, 1975), which called for Palestinian self-determination either in the form of a Palestinian state or "a Palestinian entity voluntarily federated with Jordan." Two members of the study group, Zbigniew Brzezinski and Quandt himself, were later to play key roles in the Middle East policymaking of the Carter administration, in which other members of the Study Group served, including Sol Linowitz, Robert Bowie, Henry Owens, and Philip Klutznick.

7. The linkages between advocates of an extreme anti-Soviet line and fervent supporters of Israel have yet to be fully explored. See John Mearsheimer and Stephen Walt, *The Israel Lobby and US Foreign Policy* (New York: Farrar, Straus and Giroux, 2007), for a discussion of aspects of this matter, and Anne Norton, *Leo Strauss and the Politics of American Empire* (New Haven, CT: Yale University Press, 2004), for an elegant analysis of some of the roots of neoconservatism and its fixation on Israel. See also Jacob Heilbrunn, *They Knew They Were Right: The Rise of the Neocons* (New York: Doubleday, 2008).

8. The Geneva conference had convened briefly in 1974 under American-Soviet joint sponsorship with the participation of a few of the parties to the Arab-Israeli conflict, but had quickly recessed and never reconvened. Quandt, *Peace Process,* pp. 187–89; the text of the American-Soviet joint communiqué is available on the website of the Brookings Institution; see Appendix D, http://www.brookings.edu/research/books/2005/peaceprocess3.

9. The Brookings Report is discussed in note 6, above.

10. Craig Daigle, *The Limits of Détente: The United States, the Soviet Union, and the Arab-Israeli Conflict, 1969–1973* (New Haven, CT: Yale University Press, 2012),

pp. 23ff., shows that at the outset of his presidency, Nixon had the same incli-
nation to involve the USSR in a settlement of the Arab-Israeli conflict, initially
via two-party US-Soviet talks, an effort that in the end was as fruitless as that of
Carter, for some of the same reasons.

11. William Quandt, who was present during the negotiations, makes it clear in *Peace
Process*, pp. 200–201, that it was the Egyptians, supported by the Americans, who
pushed the hardest at Camp David for a better deal on the Palestinian track, although their stand was undermined by Sadat's willingness to make concessions on
this issue in order to secure what concerned him the most: land and sovereignty in
the Sinai Peninsula.

12. The text of the accords and accompanying letters can be found in Quandt, *Peace Process*, Appendix E, http://www.brookings.edu/research/books/2005/peaceprocess3.

13. Nor were the Palestinians mentioned per se in the Mandate for Palestine that the
League of Nations granted to Great Britain. See Rashid Khalidi, *The Iron Cage: The
Story of the Palestinian Struggle for Statehood* (Boston: Beacon, 2006), pp. 32ff.

14. These ties began as liaison meetings with PLO security officials in Beirut for protection of the US Embassy, the American University of Beirut, and other US interests
there, but expanded to include political contacts with midranking PLO officials, or
prominent Palestinians close to the organization. Meant to be secret, they became
known to the Israeli intelligence services. Andrew and Leslie Cockburn, *Dangerous
Liaison: The Inside Story of the US-Israeli Covert Relationship* (New York: Harper
Collins, 1991), p. 334, suggest that Israel's disapproval of even such a minimal
American relationship with the PLO was a factor in its 1979 assassination of 'Ali
Hassan Salameh, also known as Abu Hassan. Salemeh was the senior PLO security
officer involved in these contacts, whom the Cockburns call "a vital and indepen-
dent CIA intelligence source." This is also suggested by the then–US ambassador to
Lebanon John Gunther Dean, in an oral history at the Carter Library: http://www
.jimmycarterlibrary.gov/library/oralhistory/clohproject/Lebanon.pdf.

15. Kissinger's commitment to Israel not to "recognize or negotiate" with the PLO
is mentioned in *Years of Renewal* (New York: Simon and Schuster, 1999), p.
456. He notes (pp. 1041–42) that he had instructed the US ambassador to Lebanon, Dean Brown: "We want to get in some contact with the PLO." Kissinger
defensively insists that "we considered Lebanon a special case," and that he
had told President Ford, "We have no commitment to Israel not to talk to
the PLO exclusively about the situation in Lebanon." He disingenuously added
that "lower-level security personnel may have had contacts with PLO func-
tionaries . . . But there were no substantive exchanges." This line is maintained
by a later US ambassador to Lebanon, John Gunther Dean: "I had received
authorization to meet with the PLO. I was given this authorization to take care
of security matters and in defense of American interests." Dean nonetheless
later noted that the PLO helped him negotiate the release of American hostages
in Tehran in 1979, clearly a matter unrelated to the security situation in Lebanon. Carter Library oral history, http://www.jimmycarterlibrary.gov/library/
oralhistory/clohproject/Lebanon.pdf.

16. The full text of the secret letter, dated September 1, 1975, can be found in Quandt, *Peace Process*, Appendix C, http://www.brookings.edu/research/books/2005/peaceprocess3.

17. Frank Giles, "Golda Meir: 'Who Can Blame Israel?'," *Sunday Times*, June 15, 1969, p. 12.

18. In fact, Vladimir Jabotinsky's Revisionist movement, the ideological cradle of the Likud Party, which has dominated Israeli politics since 1977, had always claimed *both* banks of the Jordan, including Transjordan, as constituting the "Land of Israel," based on the usual biblical ledgermain, and on a quaint construal of the League of Nations Mandate for Palestine. That this ideological plank had not been entirely abandoned as late as 1977 can be seen from the reference to the "Western Land of Israel" (i.e., Palestine) in the Likud party platform of that year, cited in the epigraph to this chapter.

19. See Meron Benvenisti, *Sacred Landscape: The Buried History of the Holy Land since 1948* (Berkeley: University of California Press, 2000). Benvenisti, a former deputy mayor of Jerusalem, was the son of one of the select group of geographers tasked by the new Israeli state with finding Hebrew substitutes for over nine thousand Palestinian place names after 1948.

20. Under Article 1(4) of the First Additional Protocol to the Geneva Conventions, relating to the Protection of Victims of International Armed Conflicts, June 8, 1977, international humanitarian law applies to "armed conflicts in which peoples are fighting against colonial domination and alien occupation and against racist regimes in the exercise of their right of self-determination."

21. Examples of attacks that claimed hundreds of Arab civilian victims from 1937–39 are enumerated by Yossi Sarid, previously a cabinet minister and for thirty-two years a member of the Knesset, who refers to a Hebrew-language work, *The History of the War of Liberation*, produced by members of groups led by the two men, in "Are Begin and Shamir Also Considered Terrorists?" *Haaretz*, June 24, 2011, http://www.haaretz.com/.

22. DDRS, "Summary of a meeting in Jerusalem between Secretary of State William Rogers, Israeli prime minister Golda Meir, and other US and Israeli government officials regarding plans for a Middle East peace agreement. Memo, Department of State. OMITTED. Issue Date: May 6, 1971. Date Declassified: April 21, 2004. Complete. 56 page(s)." Document CK3100548322.

23. See DDRS, "Summary of Henry Kissinger's telephone call to Assistant Secretary of State Joseph Sisco regarding President Richard M. Nixon's request that the State Department soften its dialogue with Israel over that country's decision to violate its cease-fire. Memo, White House, Feb. 28, 1971." Document CK3100573382. Kissinger told Sisco: "Why shouldn't we have done this with the Soviets and gotten something from the Soviets? . . . Why couldn't we tell the Soviets to get their bases the hell out of there?" to which Sisco responded: "Assuming we get a peace settlement, there will be a general disinvolvement [*sic*] by the Soviets in the Middle East . . . Russian influence will go down with the Arabs as they become disenchanted—this is assuming we get a settlement."

24. DDRS, "Summary of a meeting in Jerusalem between Secretary of State William Rogers, Israeli Prime Minister Golda Meir . . ." May 6, 1971, Document CK3100548322. Nixon repeatedly expressed frustration with the intransigence of the Israelis, noting, e.g., on a memo by Kissinger: "We are now Israel's *only* major friend in the world. I have yet to see *one iota* of give on their part—conceding that Jordan and Egypt have not given enough on their side. This is the time to get moving—and they must be told that *firmly*." Doc. 25, Memorandum from the President's Assistant for National Security Affairs (Kissinger) to President Nixon," February 23, 1973, FRUS, 1969–1976, vol. 25, *Arab-Israeli Crisis and War, 1973*, p. 71. For more details on this 1971 episode and its sequels see Daigle, *The Limits of Détente*, pp. 168ff.

25. One of these efforts, in 1973, is well covered in a series of documents in *FRUS, 1969–1976*, vol. 25, *Arab-Israeli Crisis and War, 1973* (notably nos. 22–29), which also show that the Egyptians were still smarting two years later from the failure of their 1971 effort.

26. Gen. Saad El-Shazli, *The Crossing of the Suez: The October War, 1973* (London: Third World Centre, 1980), pp. 30–31. I was present at a meeting in Beirut in the spring of 1975 when Yasser 'Arafat and Salah Khalaf (Abu Iyyad) told a visiting foreign delegation that Sadat had told them before the war that he had misinformed the Syrians, saying: "The Syrians deceived us in 1967. Why should I not deceive them now?" This is confirmed in part by Abu Iyyad's autobiography, with Eric Rouleau, *My Home, My Land: A Narrative of the Palestinian Struggle* (New York: Times Books, 1981), pp. 121–26.

27. The shift of most of Israel's airpower to the Golan front on October 9, 1973, the fourth day of the war, is confirmed by the memoir of one of the Israeli division commanders in Sinai, Maj. Gen. Avraham Adan, *On the Banks of the Suez: An Israeli General's Personal Account* (London: Arms and Armour Press, 1980), p. 172.

28. See Quandt, *Peace Process*, pp. 237–40, for a sense of how unimportant the issue of Palestinian representation was to all three parties to the Palestinian autonomy talks, as will be shown further in the pages that follow.

29. "Secret: Record of a Meeting held on Tuesday 11th September 1979 between Dr. Burg and Mr. Robert Strauss," Israel State Archives/A/4316/7, cited in Seth Anziska, conference paper, "Autonomy as National Disenfranchisement: The Palestinian Question from Camp David to the Lebanon War, 1978–1982," London School of Economics, April 20, 2012 (hereafter: Anziska, "Autonomy").

30. The convening of the Geneva conference and later proposals for a multilateral comprehensive forum for a resolution of the conflict were based on SC 338 of October 22, 1973, which called for implementation of 242 in all of its parts and for immediate negotiations "between the parties concerned *under appropriate auspices* [author's emphasis] aimed at establishing a just and durable peace in the Middle East." This wording was universally taken to mean a multilateral forum.

31. For further details, see Rashid Khalidi, "The Soviet Union's Arab Policy in 1975," in *Yearbook of the Palestine Question: 1975* (Arabic), edited by Camille Mansour

(Beirut: Institute for Palestine Studies, 1977), pp. 314–53, and Khalidi, "Soviet Policy in the Arab World in 1976: A Year of Setbacks," in *Yearbook of the Palestine Question: 1976*, (Arabic), edited by Camille Mansour (Beirut: Institute for Palestine Studies), 1979, pp. 397–420; and Khalidi, *Soviet Middle East Policy in the Wake of Camp David*, IPS Papers, no. 3 (Beirut: Institute for Palestine Studies, 1979).

32. These difficulties are well analyzed in Quandt, *Peace Process*, pp. 237–40.

33. "Proposals for the introduction of full autonomy for the Palestinian Arabs, inhabitants of Judea Samaria and the Gaza District, and for the preservation of the rights of the Jewish People and Israel's security in these areas of Eretz Israel (Palestine)." This is an undated 1978 document in Begin's handwriting from the donation of Nadav Aner, who was deputy director of the Prime Minister's Office, held at the Menachem Begin Heritage Center Archives, Jerusalem [hereafter: "Proposals," Begin 1978 document], cited in Anziska, "Autonomy."

34. Eugene Rostow was a prototypical neoconservative. Named by his socialist parents for Eugene Debs (his brothers were Walt Whitman Rostow and Ralph Waldo Emerson Rostow), he served under Lyndon Johnson as undersecretary of state for political affairs (in which capacity he was instrumental in the drafting of SC 242), and ended his official career as the most senior Democrat in the Reagan administration by heading the Arms Control and Disarmament Agency from 1981–83.

35. For details see the interviews on aspects of the 1982 war with three American participants: Ambassador to Israel Samuel Lewis, Ambassador Morris Draper, and Assistant Secretary Nicholas A. Veliotes. Library of Congress, Foreign Affairs Oral History Collection of the Association for Diplomatic Studies and Training, http://memory.loc.gov/ammem/collections/diplomacy/.

36. A reliable account can be found in Quandt, *Peace Process,* pp. 251–53. Haig's version in his memoirs is far less trustworthy: *Caveat: Realism, Reagan, and Foreign Policy* (New York: Macmillan, 1984).

37. For the text of the plan, see Laura Eisenberg and Neil Caplan, *Negotiating Arab-Israeli Peace: Patterns, Problems, Possibilities,* 2nd ed. (Bloomington: Indiana University Press, 2010), http://naip-documents.blogspot.fr/2009/09/document-41.html.

38. Redacted author, National Intelligence Council, to Director of Central Intelligence, Deputy Director of Central Intelligence, "Memorandum on US-Israeli Differences over the Camp David Peace Process, August 24, 1982," Secret, September 24, 2010. CIA-RDP 84B00049R00160401004–1, CIA Records Search Tool (CREST), National Archives and Records Administration, College Park, MD. My thanks go to Seth Anziska, who found this document via the CREST system in the National Archives, Washington, DC.

39. The memo was probably the work of the national intelligence officer for the Middle East, the intelligence community's top regional analyst. Knowledgeable sources have suggested to me that the author was Robert Ames, the CIA's senior Middle East analyst, who was killed in the bombing of the US Embassy in Beirut a few months later, on April 18, 1983.

40. "Proposals," Begin 1978 document, cited in Anziska, "Autonomy."

41. For details, see Quandt, *Peace Process*, pp. 344–45.

42. On August 3, 1982, Habib responded to repeated PLO requests for such assurances: "Regarding US Government guarantees as regards security for the departing Palestinian forces along with the security of the camps . . . : We will provide these guarantees." They were embodied in letters between the US and Lebanese governments: *Department of State Bulletin* 82, no. 2066 (September 1982), pp. 2–5. Details are in Rashid Khalidi, *Under Siege: PLO Decisionmaking during the 1982 War* (New York: Columbia University Press, 1986), pp. 168–71 and 177. None of the US communications was on letterhead paper, or addressed to the PLO.

43. In the early stages of the invasion, the largest Palestinian refugee camp in Lebanon, 'Ayn al-Hilwa, near Sidon, had been largely destroyed during a ferocious ten-day assault by Israeli forces including aerial and artillery bombardment: see Khalidi, *Under Siege*, pp. 51–52.

44. I witnessed this nighttime illumination, which at the time seemed inexplicable: I asked myself why the Israelis were firing star shells, used to illuminate a battlefield, when there was no fighting going on. This occurred after the Israeli cabinet had justified the occupation of the western part of the city, and the subsequent massacre, by falsely claiming that "about 2000 terrorists equipped with modern weapons remained in West Beirut, thus blatantly violating the departure agreement." The cabinet statement was read by Foreign Minister Yitzhak Shamir to US envoy Morris Draper at a Jerusalem meeting attended by Sharon and other Israeli officials on September 17, 1982, at the height of the massacre. Seth Anziska cited this and other documents that he found in the Israel State Archives in a *New York Times* op-ed article, "A Preventable Massacre," September 16, 2012, http://www.nytimes.com, which includes a link to the transcript of the cabinet meeting. The most comprehensive analysis of the massacre was undertaken by Bayan Nuwayhid al-Hout, *Sabra wa Shatila, Aylul 1982* [Sabra and Shatila, September 1982] (Beirut: Institute for Palestine Studies, 2003), English translation, *Sabra and Shatila, 1982*, London: Pluto, 2004.

45. Asked later whether the United States had failed to keep its word to the PLO, and whether Israel had violated commitments it had made to him, US mediator Philip Habib responded forthrightly: "Of course." Khalidi, *Under Siege*, p. 176.

46. In a January 28, 1982, meeting with Haig, Begin said of the legality of the settlements: "Mr. Ronald Reagan put an end to that debate. He said the settlements are not illegal. A double negative gives a positive result. In other words they are legal or legitimate. . . . Therefore the question of legality is finished so far as the United State and Israel is concerned. The President, Mr. Reagan, stated it clearly, for all times. The question whether it is an obstacle to peace, I think that we can prove it is not, by experience." "Meeting between Committee on Autonomy, Chairman Dr. J. Burg, Minister of Interior and USA Secretary of State, Mr. Alexander Haig, Jan, 28, 1982, 8:10 AM, Cabinet Room, Government Secretariat, Prime Minister's Office, Jerusalem," Israel State Archives/Ministry of Foreign Affairs/6898/8, cited in Seth Anziska, "Autonomy."

47. Reagan's speech and the "talking points" he sent to Begin can be found in Quandt, *Peace Process*, Appendix H, http://www.brookings.edu/research/books/ 2005/peaceprocess3.

48. Among other features of the Reagan Plan that were objectionable to Begin's government were the assertion that the withdrawal provisions of SC 242 applied to the West Bank and Gaza Strip, and a call for the Palestinians to have authority over land and responsibility for internal security under a five-year autonomy regime.

49. Cited in Ronald Reagan, *An American Life* (New York: Simon and Schuster, 1990), pp. 433–34.

## II

## The Second Moment:
## The Madrid-Washington Negotiations, 1991–93

1. For the full text of this document, see William Quandt, *Peace Process: American Diplomacy and the Arab-Israeli Conflict since 1967*, 3rd ed. (Washington, DC: Brookings Institution, 2005), Appendix M, http://www.brookings.edu/research/ books/2005/peaceprocess3.

2. This was SC 678 of November 29, 1991.

3. Abu Iyyad, the PLO's number two leader and chief of intelligence, for these and other reasons bitterly opposed the PLO's support for Iraq's invasion of Kuwait. On January 14, 1991, just before the allied air war on Iraq began, he and two other PLO leaders were assassinated in Tunis by an agent of the Iraqi-backed Abu Nidal terrorist group, which his operatives had recently helped to cripple by sowing lethal dissension in its ranks: Patrick Seale, *Abu Nidal: A Gun for Hire* (London: Hutcheson, 1992).

4. Britain convened a conference on Palestine at St. James Palace in London in 1939 that was attended by representatives of several Arab countries, the Palestinians, and the Jewish Agency, but the two sides met separately with the British rather than with each other. The Geneva conference convened by Kissinger in December 1973 included only Israel, Egypt, and Jordan, under nominal American-Soviet cosponsorship.

5. As mentioned in the previous chapter, President Nixon had contemplated such an approach involving the USSR at the outset of his presidency, leading to lengthy and fruitless two-party US-Soviet talks.

6. For the text of the US-Soviet invitation, dated October 18, 1991, see Quandt, *Peace Process*, Appendix N, http://www.brookings.edu/research/books/2005/peaceprocess3.

7. The Letter of Assurances to the Palestinians, whence the epigraph to this chapter is taken, is cited in note 1, above.

8. At the St. James Palace conference representatives of the Palestinians and the Jewish Agency were not on an equal footing, but in any case the two sides never negotiated with one another.

9. I served as one of these advisors, as will be discussed below.

10. Indeed, in a letter setting out the conditions for the bilateral negotiations that were to begin in December 1991 in Washington, DC, Baker noted that "since the negotiations are likely to be held in US government buildings, access to these buildings will be available only to those declared as delegates. Other advisors and staff will not be permitted at the site of the negotiation." Papers of the Palestinian delegation to the Palestinian-Israeli negotiations (hereafter: PPD www.palestine-studies.org/ppd .aspx), Baker to all parties, November 22, 1991. The Americans only relaxed these rules after the Israeli attitude softened following the election of Rabin in 1992.

11. Palestine Papers, Legal Unit of the PLO Negotiations Affairs Department, "Draft Minutes, Permanent Status Negotiations, Meeting: US and Palestinian Teams, Jerusalem, 26 June, 2000. Confidential," http://transparency.aljazeera.net/files/ 11.PDF.

12. Clyde Haberman, "Shamir Is Said to Admit Plan to Stall Talks 'for 10 Years,'" *New York Times,* June 27, 1992, http://www.nytimes.com/.

13. Palestine Papers, Legal Unit of the PLO Negotiations Affairs Department, "Draft Minutes, Permanent Status Negotiations, Meeting: US and Palestinian Teams, Jerusalem, 26 June, 2000. Confidential," http://transparency.aljazeera.net/files/ 11.PDF.

14. Ibid.

15. For details, see Rashid Khalidi, *The Iron Cage: The Story of the Palestinian Struggle for Statehood* (Boston: Beacon, 2006), pp. 197–206.

16. Benjamin Disraeli, *Tancred,* cited in Edward Said, *Orientalism* (New York: Pantheon, 1978), p. xiii.

17. Aaron David Miller, *The Much Too Promised Land: America's Elusive Search for Middle East Peace* (New York: Random House, 2008), p. 212.

18. Comprehensive works involving judicious and balanced analysis include Quandt, *Peace Process*; Clayton Swisher, *The Truth about Camp David: The Untold Story about the Collapse of the Middle East Peace Process* (New York: Nation Books, 2004); and Laura Eisenberg and Neil Caplan, *Negotiating Arab-Israeli Peace: Patterns, Problems, Possibilities,* 2nd ed. (Bloomington: Indiana University Press, 2010).

19. Mahmoud Abbas, *Tariq Oslo* [The road to Oslo] (Beirut: al-Matbu at Publishing, 1994); Haydar 'Abd al-Shafi, "Looking Backwards, Looking Forward," *Journal of Palestine Studies* 31, no. 1 (Autumn 2002), pp. 28–35; Hanan Ashrawi, *This Side of Peace: A Personal Account* (New York: Simon & Schuster, 1995); Shlomo Ben Ami, *Scars of War, Wounds of Peace: The Israeli-Arab Tragedy* (New York: Oxford University Press, 2006); Ghassan Khatib, *Palestinian Politics and the Middle East Peace Process* (London: Routledge, 2011); Daniel Kurtzer and Scott Lasensky, *Negotiating Arab-Israeli Peace: American Leadership in the Middle East* (Washington DC: US Institute of Peace Press, 2008); Camille Mansour, "The Palestinian-Israel Peace Negotiations: An Overview and Assessment," *Journal of Palestine Studies* 22, no. 3 (Spring 1993), pp. 5–31, and *The Palestinian-Israeli Peace Negotiations: An Overview and Assessment, October 1991–January 1993* (Washington, DC: Institute

for Palestine Studies IPS Paper, 1993); Miller, *The Much Too Promised Land*; Mamduh Nawfal, *Qissat Ittifaq Oslo* [The story of the Oslo agreement] (Amman: Dar al-Shuruq, 1996); Shimon Peres, *Battling for Peace* (London: Orion, 1995); Ahmad Quray' (Abu al-'Ala), *al-Riwaya al-filistiniyya al-kamila lil-mufawadat: Min Oslo ila kharitat al-tariq* [The complete Palestinian story of the negotiations: From Oslo to the Roadmap], vol. 1, *Mufawadat Oslo, 1993* [The Oslo negotiations]; vol. 2, *Mufawadat Camp David (Taba wa Stockholm) 1995–2000* [The Camp David negotiations, Taba and Stockholm, 1995–2000]; vol. 3, *al-Tariq ila kharitat al-tariq 2000–2006* [The path to the Roadmap 2000–2006] (Beirut: Institute for Palestine Studies, 2005, 2006, 2011); Dennis Ross, *The Missing Peace: The Inside Story of the Fight for Middle East Peace* (New York: Farrar, Straus and Giroux, 2004); Uri Savir, *The Process: 1,100 Days That Changed the Middle East* (New York: Random House, 1998); Nabil Shaath, "The Oslo Agreement: An Interview with Nabil Shaath," *Journal of Palestine Studies* 23, no. 1 (Autumn 1993): 5–13; Raja Shehadeh, *From Occupation to Interim Accords: Israel and the Palestinian Territories* (London: Kluwer, 1997); Gilead Sher, *The Israeli-Palestinian Peace Negotiations, 1999–2001: Within Reach* (London: Routledge, 2006).

20. The book was *Palestinian Identity,* which was originally published in 1997.

21. Documents from this collection are identified throughout as: Papers of the Palestinian delegation to the Palestinian-Israeli negotiations (PPD). All the documents from this collection cited in this book are available in online form at www.palestine-studies.org/ppd.aspx

22. These participants include Ashrawi, *This Side of Peace*, and Miller, *The Much Too Promised Land*; the analysts Quandt, *Peace Process*, Eisenberg and Caplan, *Negotiating Arab-Israeli Peace*, and Kathleen Christison, "Splitting the Difference: The Palestinian-Israeli Policy of James Baker," *Journal of Palestine Studies* 24, no. 1 (Autumn 1994): 39–50.

23. This was certainly the impression obtained by Hanan Ashrawi, *This Side of Peace*.

24. PPD, Baker to Husseini, February 10, 1992, transmitted via the US Consulate General in Jerusalem, www.palestine-studies.org/ppd.aspx.

25. PPD, "Minutes of meeting at the United States State Department with Secretary of State James Baker, Feb. 20, 1992," www.palestine-studies.org/ppd.aspx.

26. Thus Senator John McCain, while in Israel in February 2012, said that "there should be no daylight between America and Israel" over Iran: Herb Keinon, "McCain Decries Daylight between Israel, US on Iran," *Jerusalem Post*, February 21, 2012, http://www.jpost.com/.

27. Miller, *The Much Too Promised Land*, p. 75. Miller is far more frank about his own biases in his memoir than are some of his colleagues, notably Dennis Ross.

28. Ibid., p. 205.

29. "Excerpts from President Bush's News Session on Israeli Loan Guarantees," *New York Times*, September 13, 1991, http://www.nytimes.com/.

30. For more details on the loan guarantee issue, see Quandt, *Peace Process*, pp. 309–10 and 314.

31. PPD, "Minutes of Meeting at the State Department, Wednesday, February 26, 1992," www.palestine-studies.org/ppd.aspx. Kurtzer was then deputy assistant secretary of state, and was addressing Faysal Husayni, Hanan Ashrawi, and other Palestinian negotiators. In a similar vein, Assistant Secretary of State Edward Djerejian stated during the same meeting: "We're taking a concrete approach for the first time in US history to adhere to the 1967 principles. What more can you ask the US to do?"

32. Idith Zertal and Akiva Eldar, *Lords of the Land: The War over Israel's Settlements in the Occupied Territories, 1967–2007* (New York: Nation Books, 2007), pp. 121–29, describe Rabin's paralyzing inability to act against the settlement movement, in spite of his "loathing of the settlers." This emotion was fully reciprocated by the settlers, one of whose fervent supporters, Yigal Amir, assassinated him in 1995.

33. Baker publicly criticized Israeli settlement activity, noting in congressional testimony on May 22, 1991, that "every time I have gone to Israel in connection with the peace process, on each of my four trips, I have been met with the announcement of new settlement activity," and adding: "I don't think that there is any bigger obstacle to peace than the settlement activity that continues not only unabated but at an enhanced pace." *Journal of Palestine Studies* 20, no. 4 (Summer 1991): 181–85. Baker took a harsher line with Israel than any American policymaker since, reaffirming that East Jerusalem was occupied territory, and chiding the Shamir government for its obstructionism, reciting the White House phone number before Congress on June 13, 1990, and telling the Israeli government, "When you are serious about peace, call us."

34. PPD, "Memo on meeting with A. Kreczko and T. Feifer, Washington, DC, December 8, 1991," www.palestine-studies.org/ppd.aspx. The speaker was Alan J. Kreczko, then deputy legal advisor at the State Department.

35. "Looking Back, Looking Forward: An Interview with Haydar 'Abd al-Shafi," *Journal of Palestine Studies* 32, no. 1 (Autumn 2002): 31.

36. 'Abd al-Shafi made this point himself in the interview: ibid.

37. For details, see Khalidi, *The Iron Cage*, new preface to 2010 paperback edition, pp. ix–xiv, and pp. 198–206. It is worth noting that the GDP per capita of Palestinians has been nearly halved since the beginning of the Oslo process.

38. PPD, "Outline of the Model of the Palestinian Interim Self-government Authority (PISGA)" undated, marginal notation: "FINAL: Delivered on 14/1/1992," www.palestine-studies.org/ppd.aspx.

39. PPD, Israeli proposal, "Ideas for Peaceful coexistence in the territories during the interim period," February 20, 1992, www.palestine-studies.org/ppd.aspx.

40. In the banal form of the song from the enormously influential pro-Israel 1960 film *Exodus*: "This land is mine, God gave this land to me."

41. PPD, Israeli cover letter, Rubenstein to 'Abd al-Shafi, February 21, 1992 [marginal notation: "Rec'd. Feb. 24, 92"], www.palestine-studies.org/ppd.aspx.

42. PPD, "Palestinian Interim Self-Government Arrangements, Expanded Outline of Model of Palestinian Interim Self-Government Authority: Preliminary Measures and Modalities for Elections," March 1, 1992, www.palestine-studies.org/ppd.aspx.

43. PPD, "Minutes, Land Working Group, Session 1, Round 10, 17 June 1993," www
.palestine-studies.org/ppd.aspx. I was the speaker.
44. PPD, "Memo on Joint Concept/Land Working Group Meeting 24/6/93," with
marginal notation: "Highly Confidential," www.palestine-studies.org/ppd.aspx.
45. These negotiators were surprised by how far-reaching the PLO-Israeli understandings were: they were told by the PLO that the Rabin government had in essence agreed to allow PLO forces into the occupied territories to serve as the core
of the "strong police force" envisaged in the Declaration of Principles [DOP] that
was drawn up soon afterwards in Oslo, and of whose details these negotiators were
kept in the dark.
46. The Israeli representatives in these secret contacts with the PLO had been headed
by retired Maj. Gen. Shlomo Gazit, a confidant of Rabin's who had held a range of
top security posts, about whom more below.
47. PPD, "Draft Minutes, Meeting with the Americans," June 23, 1993, www.palestine-
studies.org/ppd.aspx. The US officials present were Daniel Kurtzer and Aaron David Miller. I was present, and my memory differs slightly regarding minor details
of the meeting, but all quotes are from the minutes produced by the Palestinian
delegation.
48. This comment was overheard by a Palestinian delegate while Ross and others were
waiting for PLO leaders Yasser 'Arafat and Abu Mazin (Mahmoud 'Abbas) to ar-
rive at Dulles Airport in Washington, DC, before the signing of the Oslo Accords
in September 1993: Interview, Su'ad al-'Amiry, New York, February 23, 2012.
49. This frustration with the Americans was expressed privately by some of the Israeli
negotiators to their Palestinian counterparts: confidential conversation, Washington, DC, May 15, 1993.
50. PPD, "Minutes. Meeting with US State Department Officials, 13 May 1993," www
.palestine-studies.org/ppd.aspx.
51. Eisenberg and Caplan, *Negotiating Arab-Israeli Peace*, p. 174
52. For the text of the Oslo DOP, see Quandt, *Peace Process*: Appendix Q, http://www
.brookings.edu/research/books/2005/peaceprocess3.
53. It was included in an Israeli draft DOP dated May 6, 1993, presented to the Palestinians in Washington.
54. Shehadeh, *From Occupation to Interim Accords,* p. 116.
55. See ibid., and also Mansour, "The Palestinian-Israel Peace Negotiations," Ashrawi,
*This Side of Peace,* and 'Abd al-Shafi, "Looking Back, Looking Forward," and especially Ghassan Khatib, *Palestinian Politics and the Middle East Peace Process*, pp.
84–98, as well as Rashid Khalidi and Camille Mansour, "Reflections on the Peace
Process and a Durable Settlement," *Journal of Palestine Studies* 26, no. 1 (Autumn
1996): 7–9 and 12–14. For an assessment published the day after the Oslo Accords
were signed, see Rashid Khalidi, "Blind Curves and Detours on the Road to Self-
Rule," *New York Times*, September 14, 1993.
56. For PLO-Israel exchange of letters and the Declaration of Principles see Quandt,
*Peace Process*: Appendixes P and Q, http://www.brookings.edu/research/books/
2005/peaceprocess3.

57. See his three-volume memoir, *al-Riwaya al-filistiniyya,* cited in note 19.
58. E.g., Mahmoud 'Abbas [Abu Mazin], *Tariq Oslo* [The road to Oslo] (Beirut: al-Matbu'at Publishing, 1994).
59. The 1947–49 war and the 1969–70 Egyptian-Israeli War of Attrition both lasted considerably longer than the ten-week 1982 war.
60. In Camille Mansour's words, "in Oslo they did not negotiate on the details." Another involved participant, Hassan Abu Libdeh, stated that they were "never concerned with the details, including [those] of the Oslo agreement." Interviews cited in Khatib, *Palestinian Politics,* p. 89.
61. Several other Fateh leaders closely involved with the occupied territories had earlier met the same fate, including Kamal 'Adwan in Beirut in 1973 and Majid Abu Sharar in Rome in 1981.
62. One of the shrewdest and most perceptive members of the historic core leadership of Fateh, Abu Iyyad had strongly opposed the fatal decision to align the PLO with Iraq after its 1990 invasion of Kuwait. His death was a heavy blow to the PLO.
63. Ashrawi, *This Side of Peace,* p. 259.
64. See Hilde Henriksen Waage, "Norway's Role in the Middle East Peace Talks: Between a Strong State and a Weak Belligerent," *Journal of Palestine Studies* 34, no. 4 (Summer 2005): 6–24, and "Postscript to Oslo: The Mystery of Norway's Missing Files," *Journal of Palestine Studies* 38, no. 1 (Autumn 2008): 54–65. Based on Norwegian diplomatic documents, they reveal these mediators' striking partiality to Israel.
65. This event was a panel at Amherst College on March 4, 1994, and I was present when Gazit spoke.
66. PPD, Israeli cover letter, Rubenstein to 'Abd al-Shafi, February 21, 1992, www.palestine-studies.org/ppd.aspx.
67. Rabin certainly knew better, or should have: his deputy and advisor, Yossi Beilin, told members of the Palestinian Washington delegation eight days before the June 15, 1992, Israeli elections "that Labor, including Rabin, understand that a real self-governing authority will lead to a Palestinian state, and have no problem with that." Beilin added: "if Labor formed coalition with Meretz [which in the end it did] . . . there would be a unilateral freeze on settlements." PPD, "Memo of Meeting. . . . Herziliyya, June 15, 1992," www.palestine-studies.org/ppd.aspx.
68. Palestine Papers. PLO Negotiations Support Unit, NSU to Dr. Seab Erekat, "Talking Points for Dayton Meeting," August 15, 2006, http://transparency.aljazeera.net/en/projects/thepalestinepapers/201218224248265394.html.
69. This conversation took place in my presence in 1992.
70. I have examined carefully the minutes of twenty-two meetings between American officials and Palestinian negotiators between October 1991 and June 1993, in many of which I participated, and a large number of other minutes from subsequent negotiations during the Clinton and Bush administrations, most of which are discussed in the following chapter. The pattern could not be clearer.
71. Speaking of Israeli-Egyptian negotiations, Nixon went on to say: "Now, we all know the Israelis are just impossible. I mean—we have two impossibles . . . and the

Israelis have not given a goddamn inch." The point was that the Israelis would not be budged, the United States had to accommodate them, and therefore the Arabs had to be deceived into thinking something was happening. Doc. 49, "Conversation among President Nixon, his Advisor for National Security Affairs (Kissinger), and the Assistant Secretary for Near Eastern and South Asian Affairs (Sisco)," Washington, April 13, 1973, *FRUS, 1969–1976*, vol. 25, *Arab-Israeli Crisis and War, 1973*, p. 146.

## III
## The Third Moment:
## Barack Obama and Palestine, 2009–12

1. White House, "Remarks by President Obama in Address to the United Nations General Assembly," press release, http://www.whitehouse.gov/the-press-office/2011/09/21/remarks-president-obama-address-united-nations-general-assembly.

2. It was apparently individuals like Sidney Blumenthal linked to the campaign of Hillary Clinton, to whom he was a "senior advisor," who first injected some of these names into public discourse in an attempt to smear Obama. See Jacob Berezin, "Sidney Blumenthal Joins Hillary Campaign," *Huffington Post*, November 19, 2007, http://www.huffingtonpost.com/. Such dirty tricks reportedly led White House Chief of Staff Rahm Emanuel to deny him a job in the Obama administration: Peter Baker, "Emanuel Wields Power Freely, and Faces the Risks," *New York Times*, August 15, 2009, http://www.nytimes.com/.

3. For example, the endlessly repeated claims that I "founded" or was a member of the board of a local Arab American 501(c)3 (to which the Woods Foundation, on whose board Obama sat, made grants) could easily have been shown false, had any of the many journalists who repeated this fabrication checked the group's publicly available records. They would have seen that I never had anything to do with the group; but then a prime "incriminating" link between me and the later-president would have gone up in smoke.

4. "An 'Idiot Wind,'" *Washington Post*, editorial, October 31, 2008, http://www.washingtonpost.com/.

5. These accusations are seemingly endless: even the insertion of an Israel-friendly plank on Jerusalem in the Democratic platform at the national convention in Charlotte, North Carolina, in September 2012, supposedly at the personal instigation of the president, was not enough for some, such as David Frum, a former speechwriter for George W. Bush: David Frum, "Obama Committed on Jerusalem? Riiiiight," *Daily Beast*, September 6, 2012, http://www.thedailybeast.com/.

6. To the eight years when George W. Bush was in office, one might add the first year and a half of the Reagan administration, when Alexander Haig was in charge of foreign policy. With the important exception of the 1982 Lebanon war, Reagan's main policy impact on the Middle East was to consecrate and reinforce trends in dealing with the Palestinian issue that had been set down by his predecessors.

7. Like those of previous presidents and their senior foreign policy aides, these materials are freely available via the White House and State Department websites and the press and other media.

8. "Remarks of Illinois State Sen. Barack Obama Against Going to War with Iraq," October 2, 2002, http://web.archive.org/web/20080130204029/http://www.barackobama.com/2002/10/02/remarks_of_illinois_state_sen.php. In this speech, Obama stated that he did not oppose all wars: "What I am opposed to is a dumb war. What I am opposed to is a rash war." He noted correctly that "even a successful war against Iraq will require a US occupation of undetermined length, at undetermined cost, with undetermined consequences," warning that it would strengthen recruitment for al-Qa'ida.

9. Indeed, one of his rare public comments on Middle East problems aside from the Iraq war came in the same October 2002 antiwar speech, in which he criticized the oppression, suppression of dissent, corruption, inequality, and economic mismanagement fostered by "our so-called allies in the Middle East, the Saudis and the Egyptians."

10. One can deduce a very limited amount regarding Obama's private views on these subjects from articles based on interviews with people who knew him, such as the comprehensive reportage of Pauline Dubkin Yearwood in "Obama and the Jews," *Chicago Jewish News*, October 24, 2008, http://www.chicagojewishnews.com/. She reports, accurately, that his views were not always apparent, even to those who knew him fairly well, adding that someone who was close to Obama, the outspoken and distinguished Chicago rabbi Arnold Wolf, noted: "He listened a lot but said very little. He'll listen and listen and you don't always know what he thinks." Wolf found that on the Middle East Obama was "very cautious. Whenever we talked about issues, I would always be more radical than he."

11. There are of course numerous exceptions even in the twentieth century, such as Theodore Roosevelt, Dwight Eisenhower, Richard Nixon, and George H. W. Bush.

12. For some, suspicious of Obama's origins, his public statements will never be enough: they doubt his very place of birth and must look into his soul to ascertain his "real" views. They do so in remarkably inventive ways on the web and in the troglodyte precincts of the American right wing. However, this kind of conspiracy theorizing can only be taken seriously as a pathology to be studied.

13. Among the first such efforts are Fawaz Gerges, *Obama and the Middle East: The End of America's Moment?* (New York: Palgrave Macmillan, 2012), and Zaki Laidi, *Limited Achievements: Obama's Foreign Policy* (New York: Palgrave Macmillan, 2012).

14. Although I knew Obama for a number of years when we both lived in the Hyde Park neighborhood and taught at the University of Chicago, I moved to Columbia University in New York in mid-2003, and such contact as we had had was thereafter interrupted. When I left Chicago, Obama had not yet announced his candidacy for the US Senate, and thus *none* of what follows draws on observations based on

personal contact with him from that date onwards. Much has been written—most of it of little value—about Obama's private views on Israel and Palestine, with the strong implication that these were his "real" views. However, it was already crystal clear by this point to anyone who knew him at all well that the man was an ambitious and savvy politician, not some sort of idealistic radical. Moreover, it should have been glaringly obvious to anyone who understood anything about American politics that if Obama had any hopes of being elected to higher office, the heavily stacked contours of the political terrain on the American national scene where Israel was concerned would play the major role in shaping his positions on these topics. That is precisely what has happened.

15. The Cairo and Istanbul speeches can be found at: http://www.whitehouse .gov/the-press-office/remarks-president-cairo-university-6-04-09 and http://www .whitehouse.gov/the_press_office/Remarks-Of-President-Barack-Obama-At-Student-Roundtable-In-Istanbul, respectively.

16. Peter Beinart argues in *The Crisis of Zionism* (New York: Times Books, 2012), pp. 78–92, that Obama's opinions on Middle East issues are rooted in a liberal Jewish outlook derived from figures who influenced him, like the late Rabbi Arnold Wolf. This may be true. However, this is still very much an Israel-centric vision (which in Rabbi Wolf's case involved a deep and abiding commitment to justice). Yearwood, "Obama and the Jews," quotes Wolf a few months before he died in late 2008 as expressing regret and a degree of fatalism about the Obama campaign's embrace of political orthodoxy over Israel: "He knows more than most people do about the (Middle East) situation, but he's going to go very cautiously and not do anything that shakes up the Jewish community. I'm not sure I agree with that, but that's what's going to happen."

17. David Remnick wrote of Netanyahu's outlook as it pertains to Iran in "The Vegetarian: A Notorious Spymaster Becomes a Dissident," *New Yorker*, September 3, 2012, p. 26: "Netanyahu also provides a historical dimension to his reluctance to rely on American promises. At a speech to AIPAC, in Washington, last March, he recounted how, in 1944, the US War Department spurned a plea from the World Jewish Congress to bomb the death camps at Auschwitz. 'Never again will we not be masters of the fate of our very survival,' he said. 'We deeply appreciate the great alliance between our two countries. But when it comes to Israel's survival we must always remain the masters of our fate.'" Andrew Sullivan links Netanyahu's worldview to his hero worship of his father, the scholar and extremist Ben-Zion Netanyahu, who was a close associate of Vladimir Jabotinsky, spiritual father of the radical right-wing Revisionist Zionism of which Begin, Shamir, and now the younger Netanyahu are the heirs: Andrew Sullivan, "Why Continue to Build the Settlements?" *Daily Beast*, March 30, 2012, http:// andrewsullivan.thedailybeast.com/.

18. Obama's earliest political mentors in Chicago included Abner Mikva, Newton Minow, Marilyn Katz, Bettylu Saltzman (the daughter of Philip Klutznick, who was a leading figure in the American Jewish community), and Rabbi Arnold Wolf, all of

whom were broadly liberal or progressive in their views, and generally moderate in their outlook on Israel. Thereafter, as he became more involved in electoral politics, his financial backers included Chicagoans Lester Crown, former president and chair of General Dynamics, several members of the Pritzker family, owners of the Hyatt hotel chain, and another neighbor, Alan Solow, later head of the Conference of Presidents of Major American Jewish Organizations. All were major financial backers of Israel. Once launched on the national stage, Obama developed a far broader base of donors and backers, but many of them were as committed to vigorous support of Israel as was the latter group.

19. Eric Lichtblau and Jodi Rudoren, "Skinny-Dipping in Israel Casts Unwanted Spotlight on Congressional Travel," *New York Times*, August 22, 2012, http://www.nytimes.com/.

20. For a forceful assessment of the power and influence of the Israeli military over its country's policies, see Patrick Tyler, *Fortress Israel: The Inside Story of the Military Elite Who Run the Country—And Why They Can't Make Peace* (New York: Farrar, Straus and Giroux, 2012). Indeed, the author notes (p. 10), "As an American, it was impossible to miss the breathtaking ambition of the Israeli officer corps to lead, instead of follow, US policy in the Middle East."

21. It was not some wild-eyed conspiracy theorist, but rather Ehud Barak, former Israeli chief of staff and prime minister and current defense minister, who in an interview with the Israeli newspaper *Yediot Aharonot* on May 2, 2008, said: "We entered into Lebanon . . . [and] Hizballah was created as a result of our stay there." Israeli scholars and journalists have amply documented the encouragement that the Israeli domestic intelligence service, the General Security Service, or Shabak, gave to Hamas at its inception: see Shaul Mishal and Avraham Sela, *The Palestinian Hamas: Vision, Violence, and Coexistence* (New York: Columbia University Press, 1990). See also Richard Sale, "Israel Gave Major Aid to Hamas," UPI, February 24, 2001.

22. A critique of this Holocaust-centric worldview is succinctly and forcefully put forth by Avraham Burg, former Speaker of the Israeli Knesset (and son of Dr. Yosef Burg, a minister in every government from 1951 until 1986), in *The Holocaust Is Over: We Must Rise from Its Ashes* (New York: Palgrave Macmillan, 2008).

23. As those who have visited Masada can attest, this scene of mass suicide in the face of a foe bent on extermination has become a crucial site for transmitting these values: Nachman Ben Yehuda, *The Masada Myth: Collective Memory and Mythmaking in Israel* (Madison: University of Wisconsin Press, 1995).

24. Obama speech to AIPAC, March 4, 2012: http://www.guardian.co.uk/world/2012/mar/04/obama-aipac-speech-read-text.

25. The speech was given on June 4, 2008: "Transcript: Obama's Speech at AIPAC," http://www.npr.org/.

26. "Remarks by the President on a New Beginning," Cairo University, Cairo, Egypt, June 4, 2009, http://www.whitehouse.gov/the-press-office/remarks-president-cairo-university-6-04-09.

27. In a video message of less than a minute and a half that Obama sent to the June 2012 national conference of the American-Arab Anti-Discrimination Committee, the president never even mentioned Palestine. The ADC is perhaps the largest Arab American group. "President Barack Obama's Address at the 2012 ADC National Convention," http://www.youtube.com/.

28. In his brief time as a US senator, Obama cosponsored S. 2370, the "Palestinian Anti-Terrorism Act of 2006," threatening a cutoff of US aid if Hamas were included in the PA, S. 534 of 2006, "Condemning Hezbollah and Hamas and their state sponsors and supporting Israel's right to self-defense," and S. 522 of 2008, "Recognizing the 60th anniversary of the founding of the modern state of Israel and reaffirming the close bonds between the United States and Israel."

29. Months before the 1973 war, Nixon noted that CIA director Richard Helms had assured him that Israel "could lick any and all of their enemies, provided the Soviet stays out, for five years without any more planes, because their, he says [sic], the advantage is enormous." Doc. 32, "Conversation between President Nixon and his National Security Advisor (Kissinger)" Washington, February 28, 1973. *FRUS, 1969–1976*, vol. 25, *Arab-Israeli Crisis and War, 1973*, pp. 100–101. A later CIA director, James Schlesinger, put it in this understated way: "It has never been characteristic of Israeli officials to understate the dangers facing Israel." Doc. 50, "Memorandum from Director of Central Intelligence Schlesinger to the President's Assistant for National Security Affairs," Washington, April 16, 1973, *FRUS, 1969–1976*, vol. 25, *Arab-Israeli Crisis and War, 1973*, p. 150. For a recent study that discusses American estimations of the situation before the 1967 war see Charles Smith, "The United States and the 1967 War," in *The 1967 Arab-Israeli War*, edited by Roger Louis and Avi Shlaim (Cambridge, UK: Cambridge University Press, 2012). In an address to the National Defense College on August 8, 1982, then prime minister Begin reviewed all of Israel's wars, concluding correctly that several were "wars of choice" (for which one might substitute "wars of aggression") and made it clear that in 1967 Israel was in no danger of extermination: "In June 1967 we again had a choice. The Egyptian army concentrations in the Sinai approaches do not prove that Nasser was really about to attack us. We must be honest with ourselves. We decided to attack him." Begin was of course trying to justify the 1982 "war of choice" he had just launched against Lebanon. "Address to Prime Minister Begin at the National Defense College, 8 August 1982," available at the website of Israel Ministry of Foreign Affairs, "Foreign Relations: Historical Documents, 1982–84," http://www.mfa.gov.il/MFA/.

30. In response to yet another round of saber-rattling by Israeli prime minister Binyamin Netanyahu about the imminence of Iran obtaining nuclear weapons in August 2012, American officials calmly reiterated that "the U.S. intelligence assessment remains that the Islamic Republic is undecided on whether to build a bomb and is years away from any such nuclear capability." Dan Williams, "All Threats 'Dwarfed' by Iran Nuclear Work: Israel PM," Reuters, August 12, 2012 http://www.reuters.com/.

31. In the words of perhaps the most astute American expert on these matters, Gary Sick, senior NSC specialist on Iran in two administrations: "Over the past two years, as the veiled threats of an attack became ever more shrill, virtually the entire Israeli security establishment came out in opposition to such an operation." In "Please Exhale, Israel Is Not Going to Attack Iran," *Gary's Choices,* blog entry by Gary Sick, August 14, 2012, http://garysick.tumblr.com/. See also Stuart Winer, "Former Army Chief Speaks Out against Iran Strike," *Times of Israel,* August 14, 2012, http://www.timesofisrael.com/; and Remnick, "The Vegetarian."

32. Goldberg wrote about his experience in the Israeli Defense Forces in his book, *Prisoners: A Story of Friendship and Terror* (New York: Knopf, 2006). In the estimation of *New York Magazine* writer Jason Zengerle, "When it comes to the topic of Israel, Goldberg is currently the most important Jewish journalist in the United States. He is the favored interlocutor for both Barack Obama and Benjamin Netanyahu; the leaders, as well as their advisers, seem to do much of their talking to one another through interviews with him. One White House aide likes to describe Goldberg as the 'official therapist' of the US-Israel relationship. And among Jewish journalists who write and think about Israel, he's become something of a referee." "The Israeli Desert," *New York Magazine,* June 3, 2012, http://nymag.com/.

33. Jeffrey Goldberg, "Obama to Iran and Israel: 'As President of the United States, I Don't Bluff,'" *Atlantic,* March 2, 2012, http://www.theatlantic.com/.

34. Obama speech to AIPAC, March 4, 2012, http://www.guardian.co.uk/world/2012/mar/04/obama-aipac-speech-read-text.

35. *The Writings and Speeches of Edmund Burke,* vol. 9, *The Revolutionary War 1794–97; Ireland,* edited by R. B. McDowell (Oxford, UK: Clarendon, 1991), p. 616.

36. Obama speech to AIPAC, March 4, 2012.

37. Goldberg, "Obama to Iran and Israel." The Goldstone Report was issued by the UN Human Rights Council in the wake of the Israeli attack on Gaza in December 2008–January 2009. The *Mavi Marmara* was part of a humanitarian flotilla attempting to break the Israeli blockade of the Gaza Strip; the ship was boarded by Israeli commandos with the loss of the lives of nine passengers.

38. John McCain, for example, employed the "no daylight" rhetoric, as cited in note 26 in chapter II. For the bus metaphor, see Niv Ellis, "Romney: Obama 'Threw Israel under the Bus,'" *Jerusalem Post,* January 27, 2012, http://www.jpost.com/, and Mackenzie Weinger, "Mitt Romney: Democrats Threw Israel under Bus," *Politico,* September 5, 2012, http://www.politico.com/. Romney stated that the controversy at the Democratic National Convention over a plank in the party platform affirming Jerusalem as Israel's capital was "one more example of Israel being thrown under the bus by the president."

39. American casino mogul Sheldon Adelson was the main supporter of Newt Gingrich's failed bid for the Republican presidential nomination and was the largest single funder of the Romney campaign and other efforts to unseat Obama in 2012. A *New York Times* editorial, "What Sheldon Adelson Wants," June 23, 2012,

indicates Adelson's primary interest in both: "The first answer is clearly his disgust for a two-state solution to the Israeli-Palestinian conflict, supported by President Obama and most Israelis. He considers a Palestinian state 'a steppingstone for the destruction of Israel and the Jewish people,' and has called the Palestinian prime minister a terrorist. He is even further to the right than the main pro-Israeli lobbying group, the American Israel Public Affairs Committee, which he broke with in 2007 when it supported economic aid to the Palestinians." For a profile of another big political donor with an Israel-centric agenda, see Chemi Shalev, "Jack Rosen: Turning US Presidents from Friends in Need to Friends Indeed," *Haaretz*, October 18, 2012, http://www.haaretz.com/.

40. The most striking example is the Saban Center for Middle East Policy at the Brookings Institution, set up and funded by the Israeli American billionaire TV and entertainment proprietor Haim Saban, who is profiled by Connie Bruck in "The Influencer: An Entertainment Mogul Sets His Sights on Foreign Policy," *New Yorker*, May 10, 2010, http://www.newyorker.com. Saban is a powerful advocate for Israel within the Democratic Party, albeit apparently not a party donor on the same scale as Sheldon Adelson is to the Republicans, according to his own words in his op-ed "The Truth about Obama and Israel," *New York Times*, September 5, 2012. In that article he asserts, "As a sign of its support, the Obama administration even vetoed a Security Council resolution on Israeli settlements, a resolution that mirrored the president's position and that of every American administration since the 1967 Arab-Israeli war."

41. A case in point is Sheldon Adelson's financial backing for *Ysrael ha-Yom*, a free newspaper and Israel's largest-circulation daily, which was established to support Netanyahu and Likud. Another is the Murdoch-controlled News International multinational empire (in which Saudi Prince Walid ibn Talal ibn 'Abd al-'Aziz Al Sa'ud is a major investor), whose media properties, including Fox News, the *Wall Street Journal*, the *New York Post*, and many other US, British, and Australian outlets, are all fiercely pro-Netanyahu and anti-Palestinian.

42. "Speech of PM Netanyahu to a Joint Meeting of US Congress," May 24, 2011. The text of the speech can be found at the website of Israel Ministry of Foreign Affairs, Government: Policy Statements, 2011, http://www.mfa.gov.il/MFA/.

43. Beinart, *The Crisis of Zionism*, p. 154.

44. Peter Beinart argues convincingly in his article "The Failure of the American Jewish Establishment," *New York Review of Books*, June 10, 2010, and more fully in his book *The Crisis of Zionism* that there has been a significant rightward shift of an aging leadership of the institutions of the American Jewish community that are most supportive of a hard line on Israel, like the Conference of Presidents of Major Jewish Organizations, AIPAC, the American Jewish Congress, the ADL, and others, which have thus distanced themselves from the more liberal and younger strata of that community.

45. According to a 2012 Congressional Research Service report, "US Foreign Aid to Israel," http://www.fas.org/sgp/crs/mideast/RL33222.pdf, Israel is the largest

recipient of US aid since World War II, receiving a total thus far of $115 billion. Military aid to Israel (economic aid to one of the richest countries in the world was finally phased out in 2007) has gone from $2.55 billion in FY 2009 to over $3.1 billion requested by the Obama administration in FY 2013, plus almost another $100 million in the defense budget for development of an Israeli missile shield. This is only one case where US assistance is not part of the foreign aid budget, but rather part of the massive and opaque defense and intelligence budgets.

46. Misha Glenny op-ed, "A Weapon We Can't Control," *New York Times*, June 25, 2012, http://www.nytimes.com/.

47. The conclusions of the UN report were largely borne out by the findings of inquiries by Amnesty International, Human Rights Watch, and the Israeli human rights NGO B'Tselem. For the text of the report see UN Human Rights Council, "United Nations Fact Finding Mission on the Gaza Conflict," http://www2.ohchr .org/english/bodies/hrcouncil/specialsession/9/factfindingmission.htm.

48. Shurat HaDin Israel Law Center, an aggressive right-wing Israeli NGO, is a primary opponent of the use of legal means against Israel, while itself being a leading practitioner of the use of such means against critics of Israel: http://www.israel-lawcenter.org/. Several other right-wing Israeli NGOs follow the same approach, including NGO Monitor, http://www.ngo-monitor.org/article/ngo_lawfare. An American group with the same aims and ideological orientation is the Lawfare Project, http://www.thelawfareproject.org/.

49. It was pointed out in response at the same May 2010 meeting that when Palestinians abstain from "terrorism" in response to the urgings of the United States (as in the president's 2009 Cairo speech), and instead use nonviolent legal and diplomatic means to press their case, they are accused of "delegitimizing" Israel, presumably meaning that they are supposed to roll over and do nothing, except rely on biased and misguided American sponsorship of further endless and fruitless negotiations: private communication to the author, May 21, 2010.

50. The Cairo speech is at http://www.whitehouse.gov/the-press-office/remarks-president-cairo-university-6-04-09, and that given in Istanbul at http://www .whitehouse.gov/the_press_office/Remarks-Of-President-Barack-Obama-At-Student-Roundtable-In-Istanbul.

51. In Istanbul, Obama said on this subject only that a solution to the Israeli-Palestinian conflict "will be based on two states, side by side: a Palestinian state and a Jewish state," and that "in the Muslim world this notion that somehow everything is the fault of the Israelis lacks balance."

52. A good summary of these grievances can be found in Dov Waxman, "The Real Problem in US-Israel Relations," *Washington Quarterly* 35, no. 2 (Spring 2012): 71–87.

53. Jodi Rudoren, "Israeli Leaders Could Be Dissuaded from Striking Iran," *New York Times*, August 15, 2012. There was tail-wagging-the-dog-type pressure aplenty as well: a former Israeli national security advisor and deputy chief of staff is quoted in the same article: "But '[the Israelis] have to make the decision whether to strike

or not before November' . . . so they need to hear from Mr. Obama 'in the coming two weeks, in the coming month.'"

54. The relevant section of Bush's letter reads: "In light of new realities on the ground, including already existing major Israeli populations [*sic*] centers, it is unrealistic to expect that the outcome of final status negotiations will be a full and complete return to the armistice lines of 1949, and all previous efforts to negotiate a two-state solution have reached the same conclusion. It is realistic to expect that any final status agreement will only be achieved on the basis of mutually agreed changes that reflect these realities." http://georgewbush-whitehouse.archives.gov/news/releases/2004/04/20040414–3.html.

55. This was the burden of the argument put forward by Salam Fayyad, prime minister of the PA, to Stephen Hadley, Bush's national security advisor. Hadley brushed off Fayyad, saying, "Our position on settlements is consistent and has not changed. But let us focus on the now. There is an opportunity in the Gaza Disengagement." Palestine Papers, "Meeting, National Security Council," April 16, 2005. http://transparency.aljazeera.net/en/projects/thepalestinepapers/201218233655812228.html.

56. As mentioned in chapter I, the United States voted in favor of GA 194 of 1948, which mandated that Palestinians had these rights, and until 1992 voted annually in the General Assembly for resolutions that reaffirmed this resolution. It joined Israel in abstaining on such a resolution in 1993, and by 1998 both countries were voting against it, as they have done since.

57. The relevant passage states: "The Occupying Power shall not deport or transfer parts of its own civilian population into the territory it occupies." http://www.icrc.org/ihl.nsf/full/380.

58. Abrams had the added distinction of having been convicted in October 1991 of two misdemeanors for lying to Congress. He was pardoned by George H. W. Bush just before he left office. Abrams was also publicly censured in 1997 by the DC Court of Appeals for three times giving false testimony to Congress. http://www.fas.org/irp/offdocs/walsh/summpros.htm.

59. Thus in 1996 a group including Perle and Feith had presented incoming Likud prime minister Netanyahu with a policy paper entitled "A Clean Break: A New Strategy for Securing the Realm," which recommended various extreme and aggressive options to the Israeli government, including opposing the Oslo Accords and the idea of comprehensive peace with the Arabs, and the "rollback" of hostile entities and states, meaning forcible regime change, policies they later propagated for adoption by the United States during the George W. Bush administration. http://www.iasps.org/strat1.htm.

60. The transcript of Rice's July 21, 2006, news conference where she made these comments can be found at http://www.washingtonpost.com/wp-dyn/content/article/2006/07/21/AR2006072100889.html.

61. These were posted by the British *Guardian* newspaper in association with the Qatari al-Jazeera satellite TV network on their respective websites under the rubric

"The Palestine Papers." These documents, which I have cited several times, show every possible indication of being genuine, and greatly extend our knowledge base through the late Clinton and especially Bush II administrations, for which solid documentation is relatively scarce.

62. Of course, in another sense, Israel itself is the metropole of the colonial endeavor in the occupied territories. In yet another sense, however, one that would have instantly been recognized by the generation of the founder of modern political Zionism, Theodor Herzl, the Western world as a whole is the metropole for the entire Zionist enterprise insofar as it was and is a colonial phenomenon, something of which Herzl and his generation were not in the least ashamed.

63. Among the numerous American "charitable" organizations (all of which have 501c3 tax-deductible status) engaged in financial support of the Israeli settlement, colonization, and occupation enterprise is the Irving Moskowitz Foundation, named for and run by the Florida bingo and gambling magnate of the same name, which has been at work in Jerusalem and elsewhere in the occupied territories since 1969 supporting extreme religious nationalist groups like Ateret Cohanim with several million dollars in subventions annually. http://www.rightweb.irc-online.org/profile/Moskowitz_Irving.

64. Palestine Papers, "Minutes from Bilateral US-Palestinian Session, Post-Annapolis," July 16, 2008, http://www.guardian.co.uk/world/palestine-papers-documents/2942.

65. This was a trilateral meeting with Palestinian and Israeli delegations headed by Abu Ala and Israeli foreign minister Tzipi Livni. Palestine Papers, Trilateral Meeting Minutes, Jerusalem, June 15, 2008, http://transparency.aljazeera.net/en/projects/thepalestinepapers/201218233143171169.html.

66. Palestine Papers, Rice-Abu Ala Meeting, March 31, 2008. Similarly, David Welch, the assistant secretary for Near Eastern affairs, brushed aside the domestic constraints on the Palestinians and warned them: "Do not interrupt the negotiations for other reasons, such as the announcement of [Israel] constructing new residential units in settlements." http://transparency.aljazeera.net/en/projects/thepalestinepapers/20121823221962189.html.

67. Palestine Papers, Fayyad-Hadley Meeting, April 16, 2005. Lewis Libby and Eliott Abrams attended this meeting, which took place in Washington, but Hadley did most of the talking on the American side. http://transparency.aljazeera.net/en/projects/thepalestinepapers/201218233655812228.html.

68. Mitchell had been obliged to abandon any hope of changing the policy toward Hamas less than eighteen months after he took up his position, as can be seen from his answer to a question about Hamas in an August 2010 press conference in which he argued strenuously that the situation in Northern Ireland with the IRA was quite different from that in Palestine with Hamas. http://www.whitehouse.gov/the-press-office/2010/08/31/press-briefing-special-envoy-middle-east-peace-senator-george-mitchell.

69. The degree of American support for Fateh-dominated PA leadership against Hamas is a constant theme in the documents revealed in the Palestine Papers.

Thus in 2008, Condoleezza Rice and the Palestinian delegation headed by Abu al-'Ala devoted most of one meeting to discussing how to meet the challenge posed by Hamas, which was also part of the discussion the same day between the Palestinians and an Israeli delegation headed by Tzipi Livni: Palestine Papers, "Minutes from Berlin Meetings Post Annapolis," June 24, 2008, http://transparency.aljazeera.net/en/projects/thepalestinepapers/201218233057343352.html.

70. It was formally titled the "Sharm El-Sheikh Fact-Finding Committee Report," and was delivered to President Bush on April 30, 2001. It reads today as a remarkably evenhanded document, another reason Mitchell may have been regarded with suspicion by Israeli decision-makers, used to far less than evenhanded American mediation. http://eeas.europa.eu/mepp/docs/mitchell_report_2001_en.pdf.

71. This information is based on the account of a participant in these meetings who asked for anonymity. Interview, February 1, 2010.

72. Private interview with unnamed interlocutor with Mitchell, February 1, 2012.

73. See Miller, *The Much Too Promised Land*, and Kurtzer and Lasensky, *Negotiating Arab-Israeli Peace.*

74. Ross, *The Missing Peace*, which is described in a lengthy, carefully researched, and scathing review by Jerome Slater in *Tikkun* as "tendentious, biased, and misleading." "The Missing Pieces in The Missing Piece," http://www.tikkun.org/.

75. For details see Peter Beinart, "Obama Betrayed Ideals on Israel," *Daily Beast,* March 12, 2012, http://www.thedailybeast.com/, and Max Blumenthal, "Dennis Ross: The Undiplomatic History," al-Akhbar English, November 14, 2011, http://english.al-akhbar.com/content/dennis-ross-undiplomatic-history.

76. In their press release on his appointment, the Washington Institute for Near East Policy noted that Ross's portfolio included a "wide range of Middle East issues, from the Arab-Israeli peace process to Iran." Beinart, "Obama Betrayed Ideals."

77. In a 2001 interview for the record with Philip Zelikow, Ross said of Baker in 1989: "So what we did is, he let me set up a private channel with the Israelis right away. Zelikow: Who was on the Israeli end of the channel? Ross: Ely [Elyakim] Rubinstein was the initial [contact]." This illuminates the role played by Ross in the Palestinian-Israeli negotiations, during which Rubinstein, with whom this interview shows Ross had been in close contact for two years, was head of the Israeli delegation. http://millercenter.org/president/bush/oralhistory/dennis-ross.

78. He served in that capacity from June 25, 2009, until November 10, 2011.

79. Beinert, "Obama Betrayed Ideals."

80. Laura Rozen, "Benjamin Netanyahu takes US Offer to His Cabinet," *Politico*, November 14, 2010, http://www.politico.com/.

81. Daniel Kurtzer, "With Settlement Deal, United States Will Be Rewarding Israel's Bad Behavior," *Washington Post*, November 21, 2010, http://www.washingtonpost.com/.

82. For my contemporary take on Ross's exit (it began with the words: "Dennis Ross has left the building . . ."), see Rashid Khalidi, "Ross's Departure," *Hill*, November 11, 2011, http://thehill.com/.

83. Natasha Mozgovaya, "Lieberman Praises Obama's UN General Assemby Speech," *Haaretz*, September 21, 2011, http://www.haaretz.com/.

84. In the president's speech to AIPAC a few days before, he devoted four exceedingly mild paragraphs to Israeli-Palestinian peace efforts and seventeen muscular ones to the Iranian nuclear issue. http://www.guardian.co.uk/world/2012/mar/04/obama-aipac-speech-read-text.

85. As eminent Iran expert Gary Sick, in "What If Israel Bombs Iran?," CNN, http://www.cnn.com, and others have shown, "Most of the top security officials in the Pentagon have warned against such a war." Thus Obama was supported in his position by all the key segments of the bureaucracy: the military, the intelligence community, and the diplomats.

86. "Excerpts from President Bush's News Session on Israeli Loan Guarantees," *New York Times*, September 13, 1991, http://www.nytimes.com/.

## CONCLUSION

1. PPD, Minutes of "Concept Working Group," June 23, 1993, www.palestine-studies.org/ppd.aspx.

2. Among the best books on the topic are Saree Makdisi, *Palestine Inside Out: An Everyday Occupation* (New York: Norton, 2008), Raja Shehadeh, *Palestinian Walks: Notes on a Vanishing Landscape* (London: Profile, 2007), Eyal Weizman, *Hollow Land: Israel's Architecture of Occupation* (New York: Verso, 2007), and Idith Zertal and Akiva Eldar, *Lords of the Land: The War over Israel's Settlements in the Occupied Territories, 1967–2007* (New York: Nation Books, 2007).

3. This was Peter Beinert, "Obama Betrayed Ideals on Israel," *Daily Beast*, March 12, 2012, http://www.thedailybeast.com/.

4. See Clayton Swisher, *The Truth about Camp David: The Untold Story about the Collapse of the Middle East Peace Process* (New York: Nation Books, 2004), pp. 133–405, for an exhaustive analysis based on comprehensive interviews with almost all the participants, which shows how poorly prepared the Camp David Summit was. Aaron David Miller, *The Much Too Promised Land: America's Elusive Search for Middle East Peace* (New York: Random House, 2008), p. 280, cites Madeleine Albright as saying about Ehud Barak, "We went to Camp David on his word." See also Charles Enderlin, *Shattered Dreams: The Failure of the Peace Process in the Middle East, 1995–2002*, translated by Susan Fairfield (New York: Other Press, 2003), pp. 165ff., for a scrupulously reported, well sourced, and very detailed account of the Camp David fiasco.

5. See Robert Kaplan, *Arabists: The Romance of an American Elite* (New York: Free Press, 1993), one of many salvos in the lengthy barrage by the likes of right-wing pro-Israel polemicists Martin Kramer and Daniel Pipes that in time helped to dislodge from positions of responsibility in the US government officials who had some knowledge and understanding of the peoples, history, and societies of the

Arab countries. See Stephen Glain, "Freeze-Out of the Arabists," *Nation*, November 1, 2004, http://www.thenation.com/.

6. This process can be followed in Rashid Khalidi, *Sowing Crisis: The Cold War and American Dominance in the Middle East* (Boston: Beacon, 2009).

7. "Washington's Farewell Address 1796," Avalon Project, http://avalon.law.yale.edu/18th_century/washing.asp.

8. PPD, Israeli cover letter, Rubinstein to 'Abd al-Shafi, February 21, 1992 [marginal notation: "Rec'd. Feb. 24, 92"], www.palestine-studies.org/ppd.aspx.

9. See Rory McCartney, "Barak: Make Peace with Palestinians or face Apartheid," *Guardian*, February 3, 20120, http://www.guardian.co.uk/; Barak Ravid, David Landau, Aluf Benn, and Shmuel Rosner, "Olmert to Haaretz: Two-State Solution or Israel Is Done For," *Haaretz*, November 29, 2007, http://www.haaretz.com/.

10. This problem goes back even before the period discussed in this book. See Rashid Khalidi, "The 1967 War and the Demise of Arab Nationalism: Chronicle of a Death Foretold," in *The June 1967 War: Origins and Consequences*, edited by William Roger Louis and Avid Shlaim (Cambridge, UK: Cambridge University Press, 2012), pp. 264–84, for a discussion of how, as early as the 1960s, Egypt and Syria placed nation-state interests and regime survival ahead of pan-Arab concerns, including the question of Palestine.

11. See the scathing final report of Alvaro de Soto, the United Nations' envoy to the Quartet, after his resignation in 2007. It shows the powerlessness of the Quartet and the UN in the face of the American-Israeli alliance, and should be required reading by all concerned with a balanced view of the situation at that time. http://image.guardian.co.uk/sys-files/Guardian/documents/2007/06/12/DeSotoReport.pdf.

## ACKNOWLEDGMENTS

1. See Walter Fischel, *Ibn Khaldun and Tamerlane* (Berkeley: University of California Press, 1952).

# INDEX